RECRUITMENT AND TRAINING OF PRIMARY TEACHERS

RECRUITMENT AND TRAINING OF PRIMARY TEACHERS

Edited by

B.V. VERGHESE

ANMOL PUBLICATIONS PVT. LTD.

NEW DELHI - 110 002 (INDIA)

ANMOL PUBLICATIONS PVT. LTD.
4374/4B, Ansari Road, Daryaganj
New Delhi - 110 002
Ph.: 23261597, 23278000
Visit us at: www.anmolpublications.com

Recruitment and Training of Primary Teachers

ISBN 81-261-1049-X

PRINTED IN INDIA

Published by J.L. Kumar for Anmol Publications Pvt. Ltd., New Delhi - 110 002 and Printed at Mehra Offset Press, Delhi.

Contents

Preface

Teaching young children to read and write, to understand the world around them, to grasp and be able to apply fundamental mathematical and scientific principles, to use their developing intelligence and imagination, to live and work, harmoniously with others, all these require that an effective teacher should possess knowledge and understanding of the content of the subjects and topics being taught, as well as the ability to manage a class, explain clearly, ask intelligent and appropriate questions, and monitor and assess learning.

This book presents the authoritative and rich information on a number of crucial issues like—skilful teaching, management of teaching, first encounters with a class, systematic studies of class management, managing children's behaviour and work, supply of teachers, public views of management, explaining and explanations, teachers' questions, teachers' subject knowledge, educational problems, right teaching position, helping beginners to grow etc.

I am grateful to all the scholars whose writings and fruits of painstaking research are cited or substantially made use of in this book. I am also thankful to all my friends and colleagues who have assisted me while preparing the manuscript. Last but not the least, I am grateful to Mr. J.L. Kumar, Managing Director, Anmol Publications Pvt. Ltd., New Delhi for undertaking the publication of this work.

—B.V. Verghese

1

Skilful Teaching

The Need for Skilful Teaching

Primary teachers have always needed a wide range of subject knowledge and a large repertoire of professional skills. Teaching young children to read and write, to understand the world around them, to grasp and be able to apply fundamental mathematical and scientific principles, to use their developing intelligence and imagination, to live and work harmoniously with others, all these require that an effective teacher should possess knowledge and understanding of the content of the subjects and topics being taught, as well as the ability to manage a class, explain clearly, ask intelligent and appropriate questions, and monitor and assess learning.

There are many factors which have combined, during the last few years of the twentieth century, to demand from teachers even higher levels of professional competence. They include the rapid growth in the acquisition of knowledge, the changing nature not only of adult employment, but also of recreation and leisure, the increased public pressure for accountability, the development of new forms of educational and information technology, and the broadening role of the primary teacher. Any single one of these individual issues would require a radical review of the teacher's professional role, and of the nature of professional competence required to accommodate change and improve practice. In combination they represent an overwhelming pressure for improvement by all practitioners, even the many who already manifest a high degree of skill in the classroom.

In the nineteenth century teacher training institutions were known as normal schools', on the grounds that there was some single 'norm' endorsed by society. The function of a training establishment was to perpetuate this stereotype, and a 'Master of Method' was employed in the model school to ensure that each new generation of teachers was poured into the same approved mould (Rich 1933). Today the factors mentioned above combine to require levels of skill, understanding, imagination, and resilience from teachers which go infinitely beyond the rudimentary common sense and mechanical competence fostered by the normal schools of the last century.

The massive explosion of knowledge gathering during the last fifty years has produced banks of data in such profusion that no human being is now capable of grasping more than the tiniest fraction of their contents. There are examples of computer-stored research data, such as the Lockheed Dialog system, which contain research report-in in hundreds of fields, and the largest files in subjects like chemistry and biology can disgorge millions of abstracts.

It is not only in the pure and applied sciences that knowledge has burgeoned, but also in several other areas of human endeavour, including the humanities, with thousands of new books and articles in many fields being , published each year. In addition to this formidable advance in the discovery of new information there has been a considerable development of new skills. Transplant and bypass surgery, for example, unknown only a few years ago, have become a standard part of many surgeons' professional armoury.

The implications for teachers of this knowledge explosion are clear. If you cannot know everything, you must know something. Hence the many efforts made either at regional or national level to determine the *content* of education what children of a particular age or level of ability ought to learn, or by teachers themselves at local level to shape and implement a coherent curriculum. Secondly, if you cannot know or learn everything, you must be able to find out for yourself, and this is why the *process* of learning has become important, as well as, though not instead of, the content. Thirdly, since their pupils can acquire only a tiny fraction of the knowledge and skills currently available to humanity, teachers must develop teaching strategies which not only transmit information, but also encourage children to learn independently and as a member of a group. Although no committee would ever have composed Beethoven's Fifth Symphony, it is also unlikely that any individual could have sent a rocket to the moon. A great deal of human achievement will in future be the result of *teamwork.*

Alongside the demands placed on teachers by the expansion of knowledge and skills are those caused by the significant social changes in recent years which are taking place on a scale unparalleled in any period other than wartime. During the 1970s one million jobs disappeared from manufacturing industry in Britain, and millions more were obliterated during the following two decades. Most were unskilled and semi-skilled forms of employment which will probably never return.

Faced with youth unemployment on a large scale, many teachers, especially in inner-city schools, found during the 1980s and 1990s that traditional forms of motivation, such as urging pupils to work hard at school so that they would obtain a good job, no longer had the appeal they once enjoyed. Disaffection over the apparent futility of learning can even be experienced by quite young primary pupils. It offers another formidable challenge to the professional ingenuity of the teacher.

Employers, meanwhile, able to erect artificial barriers when applicants for jobs vastly exceed the actual vacancies, may require high GCSE grades for posts previously taken by the less well qualified. A levels where GCSE was once sufficient, and a degree in what was formerly a non-graduate profession. This spiralling demand for qualifications puts yet more pressure on teachers to use their skills effectively during the compulsory years of schooling, especially in the early years when firm foundations should be laid. In our increasingly technological and bureaucratic society those who leave school under-educated, for whatever reason, are at risk, likely to be unemployed or fall victim to loan sharks and the other predators in society.

The more optimistic scenario, that labour will shift out of the factory and into the leisure industry, that people will have more free time in future and be relieved of the tedium of monotonous jobs, that early retirement will give a boost to community and lifelong education, is no less demanding on teachers' skills. To enjoy leisure, adults must have learned how to use it fruitfully. Citizens in the twenty-first century are more likely to be willing to learn throughout their lives if they have been fired and enthused, rather than rebuffed and demoralised, in school. The quality of personal relationships between teacher and taught, therefore, is a direct result of the interpersonal skill of the teacher, who usually sets the tone in a class, or has to take the initiative to improve relationships should they go away.

A notion of teaching skill that embraced only the transmission of knowledge would be a poor one in such a context.

Furthermore in the twenty-first century many people will work in service industries, and others will run small businesses. This shift out of the factory and into closer contact with people, rather than machinery, requires a high degree of imagination, inventiveness, drive and interpersonal skills. Again a sound basis for those qualities can be established in good primary schools, and teachers who nurture them should be greatly valued.

Public pressure for accountability has increased throughout the 1980s and 1990s, and it is an international phenomenon. Uncertainty overemployment, scarcity of resources and demands for proper scrutiny of any enterprise receiving funding, public or private, have combined to provide a widespread call for a high degree of competence in the teaching profession, with particular focus on the primary phase, from parents, politicians, and the press. This has been mirrored in Britain in the various Acts of Parliament which have introduced requirements on schools to publish information about themselves, carry out the appraisal of teachers and heads, teach a national curriculum, and apply national tests to children aged 7 and 11, the scores from which can then be published and compared with those of other schools. This is not the place to go into the pros and cons of the measures taken by British governments during the 1980s and 1990s, as I have done that elsewhere (Wragg 1988. 1990, 1991). It is cited here as an example of a further external pressure on schools for highly skilled teaching.

The development of new technology such as the micro-computer, forms of teletext, the interactive video disc, direct broadcasting by satellite and cable television offer a further challenge to primary teachers. One important feature of some of the more recent forms of technological development is that the micro-computer and the interactive video disc in particular, offer an interactive facility on a scale not previously available, changing the position of the teacher as the single authoritative initiator of, or respondent to, enquiry. In 1985 and 1986 the BBC Domesday Project involved 14,000 schools using modern technology to survey the whole of the United Kingdom, in celebration of the 900th anniversary of the original Domesday book. Pupils who took part were mainly aged 9 to 13, and two significant interactive video discs were produced as a result.

Such developments test the flexibility and adaptability of teachers, who need to be able to modify their teaching styles to accommodate some at least of the many new developments which have a potential to improve learning. Indeed, broadcasting technology itself has made teachers more vulnerable than ever before. The teacher attempting to teach the topic 'Insects' to a primary class fifty years ago would not have been compared with anyone other than another teacher. Today she will be compared with the finest television presenters in the world, whose programmes on insects enjoy multi-million-pound budgets and access to the very best of wildlife film available.

Even if primary teachers were able to concentrate entirely on their classroom role as transmitters of knowledge, skills and values to the next generation, the assignment would be a formidable one. However, the role of the teacher has broadened during the last decades of the century. The real or imagined ills of society are often attributed, rightly or wrongly, to schooling. Teachers can find themselves playing many roles, such as social worker (dealing with children whose families experience economic and social deprivation), jailer (coping with children reluctant to come to school), administrator (handling the increasing bureaucracy surrounding curriculum and assessment), public relations officer (meeting parents, members of the community, dealing with local meetings), and numerous others. Teaching is certainly not a job for the faint-hearted.

In many countries changes in birth rates have led to concomitant changes in school size and in the age distribution of the teaching profession. The roller-coaster graph of annual birth cohorts is followed by a related graph of teacher recruitment. In Britain and other industrialised countries like Germany, the birth rate fell dramatically for over a decade and then rose again. A British peak of nearly a million births in 1964 was followed by a thirteen-year decline of a third. The consequence of this was that primary school populations fell by over a quarter during the first few years of the 1980s, leading lo numerous primary school closures and mergers.

A rapid expansion in the recruitment of teachers during the 1960s and early 1970s was followed by a decline in the 1980s, when many primary trained teachers failed to find a job at all until the later years of the decade as schools expanded once again. By 1990 three out of every rive primary teachers were aged over 40, leading to reduced promotion prospects and falling morale. On the positive side, there was a great deal of professional experience available, which certainly helped considerably when the. national curriculum was introduced in 1989. The negative aspect, however, is that after years of repeats repeats of favoured teaching strategies, it is not always easy to make changes when they become necessary.

One way to reduce, if not avoid, falling morale when promotion prospects are less in evidence than they were formerly is for teachers to take pride in honing their professional skills, and a number of in-service courses, especially certain school-based ones, have attempted to facilitate professional development and self-appraisal for experienced teachers.

It was not possible in the Leverhulme Primary Project at Exeter University to investigate and analyse all the vast complexity of skills mentioned above as necessary for teaching the present and future generations of young children. It was decided, therefore, in the strand of the project which I directed, to concentrate in particular on class management, but also to investigate such key skills as explaining and questioning, as well as teachers' subject knowledge and the strategies teachers employ when they are on new or unfamiliar ground. The matters of subject knowledge and student teachers are also taken up in more detail in the other major strand of the Leverhulme Primary Project, directed by Professor Neville Bennett, and reported in the companion volume to this one, *Learning to Teach* (Bennett and Carre 1993).

Identifying and Defining Teaching Skills

The Leverhulme Primary Project took place at Exeter University during a period from the 1988 Education Act to the General Election of 1992 when debates about educational standards were commonplace and sometimes acrimonious. For the reasons cited earlier in this chapter there is understandable concern that the levels of attainment of children should rise to help them meet the increasing demands of life in the late twentieth and early twenty-first centuries. Even if the quality of teaching improves, it may not improve far or fast enough to match the escalating demands on teachers.

Unfortunately the accompanying debate about teaching

competence has too often been oversimplified and caricatured as 'traditional' versus 'progressive', 'formal' versus 'informal', 'phonics' versus 'real books', when the reality of classroom life is that many teachers prefer to use a mixture of methods rather than fill out a single stereotype. The Leverhulme Primary Project was based on the premise that all teachers have to manage a class of children, however differently conceived their styles of class management may be. and that such professional communication skills as questioning and explaining are witnessed in every primary classroom.

There was, therefore, no conscious favouring of any single style of teaching. Individual researchers do, of course, have personal preferences and prejudices like other people, but wherever possible we tried to push these to the periphery and concentrate on interpretations of what we saw and then both report these as research findings as well as develop teaching materials and ideas, an empirical approach in the main. Our intention, however, was that teachers should be able to read, in the books on research findings, about what we had discovered, and that, in the accompanying workbooks on professional skills, such as *Class Management* (Wragg 1993), *Questioning* (Brown and Wragg 1993) and *Explaining* (Wragg and Brown 1993), trainee and experienced teachers would be encouraged to analyse and determine their own teaching strategies, rather than merely copy someone else's preferences. In the various strands of the project we observed over a thousand lessons, conducted more than a thousand interviews with teachers, students and pupils, gave tests to over a thousand teachers and pupils, and analysed over two thousand questionnaire responses. Some of the samples were carefully selected national ones with balanced numbers of teachers from large and small, urban and rural, northern and southern schools, others were more rough-and-ready, opportunity samples of teachers willing to be observed, or agreeable to being interviewed at length.

There is less dissent about what constitutes effective teaching in discussion between people outside the profession than there is in the research and evaluation literature. Good teachers, it is commonly held, are keen and enthusiastic, well organised, firm but fair, stimulating, know their stuff, and are interested in the welfare of their pupils. Few would attempt to defend the converse: that good teachers are unenthusiastic, boring, unfair, ignorant, and do not care about their pupils.

Once the scrutiny of teaching is translated into the more precise terms demanded by the tenets of rigorous systematic enquiry, the easy agreement of casual conversation evaporates. Biddle and Ellena (1964), reporting the Kansas City role studies, found that there was not even clear agreement amongst teachers, parents and administrators about the role teachers should play.

In the 1970s and 1980s some of the attempts to see consensus in the research literature were criticised. For example, Gage (1978), summarising research studies which had attempted to relate teaching style to children's learning, concluded that in the early years of schooling certain kinds of teacher behaviour did show some consistent relationship to children learning reading and arithmetic. From this he derived a set of prescriptive 'Teacher should statements like 'Teachers should call on a child by name before asking the question.' 'Teachers should keep to a minimum such activities as giving directions and organising the class for instruction' or 'During reading-group instruction, teachers should give a maximal amount of brief feedback and provide fast-paced activities of the "drill" type'.

Among the criticism of prescriptions based on summaries of recentfindings is the proposition that much American work in particular is based on short-term tests of memory; that formal didactic styles of teaching often show up better on short-term measures and could, therefore, easily be perpetuated; that the 'gains' of method A compared with method B are often slight. This last argument is skilfully countered by Gage (1985) in his book *Hard Gains in the Soft Sciences.* He shows how significant policy decisions, in fields such as medicine and public health, are often made on a degree of statistical 'superiority' that would receive little attention in educational research. He quotes examples of trials of beta blockers and low-cholesterol diets to reduce the incidence of heart attacks, which showed only 2.5 and 1.7 per cent differences respectively between experimental and control groups' mortality rates, but which nonetheless led to significant changes in public health policy and practice.

Doyle (1978) observed that reviewers of research into teacher effectiveness 'have concluded, with remarkable regularity, that few consistent relationships between teacher variables and effectiveness can be established'. Even reviewers of the same studies have sometimes reached different conclusions about them (Giaconia and Hedges 1985). Some investigations have used meta-analysis (Glass 1978) to aggregate studies and identify trends and effects, but the conclusions are often mixed, and sometimes, especially when pioneers of some new approach conduct research into their own practice, a noticeable Hawthorne Effect occurs. That Kulik *el al.* (1979) found consistently higher learning gains in classes using the Keller Plan (a form of teaching which involves pupils completing individual assignments) compared with control groups is not an argument for saying that all teachers should copy the approach. Teachers often aspire to achieve a mixture of shorter-term (complete a worksheet, learn a principle) and longer-term (develop a sustained interest in music, lead a healthy lifestyle) objectives.

The difficulty of identifying and evaluating teaching skills and their effectiveness is neatly illustrated by an interesting experiment at the University of Michigan. Guetzkow *et al.* (1954) divided first-year students on a general psychology course into three groups. The first group was given a formal lecture course with regular tests, the second and third groups took part in tutorials and discussions. At the end of the course the lecture group not only outperformed the tutorial discussion groups on the final examination, hut was also more favourably rated by the students. So far this represents a victory for lecturing and testing on two commonly used criteria: test performance and student appraisal.

The investigators discovered, however, that the students in the discussion groups scored significantly higher than the lecture groups on a measure of interest in psychology, the subject being studied. They hypothesised that though the lecture-group students gave a favourable rating of the teaching they had received, this may have been because they had less anxiety about grades for the course through their weekly feedback from test scores. It was decided to monitor the subsequent progress of all the groups. Three years later not one student in the lecture group had opted to study the subject further, but fourteen members of the two discussion and tutorial groups had chosen to major in psychology. Thus on short term criteria the lecture method was superior, but taking a longer perspective the discussion method appeared to motivate students more powerfully, and ultimately some must have learned a great deal more (McKeachie 1963).

Defining teaching skill in such a way that all would agree, therefore, is not a simple matter. If we were to say that teaching skills are whatever strategies teachers use to enable children to learn, then most people would want to rule out intimidation, humiliation, the use of corporal punishment or other forms of teacher behaviour of which they personally happen to disapprove. It is perhaps easier when seeking a definition of teaching skill to describe some of the characteristics of skilful teaching which might win some degree of consensus though not universal agreement.

The first might be that the behaviour concerned 'facilitates pupils' learning of something worthwhile', such as facts, skills, values, concepts, how to live harmoniously with one's fellows, attitudes, or some other outcome thought to be desirable. The notion of something being 'worthwhile' brings together both content and values in teaching. Skill is not a uni-dimensional concept. Teaching someone to steal might in one sense be skilfully done but it would attract professional odium rather than admiration. A second quality therefore could be that it is acknowledged to be a skill by those competent to judge, and these might include teachers, teacher trainers, inspectors, advisers and learners themselves. We shall see in previous chapters that pupils can be shrewd in their appraisal of the teacher's craft, and that the ability to explain is often highly rated by them.

For it to be a recognised part of a teacher's professional competence the skill should also be capable of being repeated, not perhaps in exactly the same form, but as a fairly frequent rather than a single chance occurrence. A chimpanzee might randomly produce an attractive colourful shape once in a while, given a brush and some paint, but an artist would produce a skilfully conceived painting on a more regular basis. Teachers who possess professional skills, therefore, should be capable of manifesting these consistently, not on a hit-or-miss basis.

One frequently cited observation on skills is that of the philosopher Gilbert Ryle (1949), who distinguished, in his book *The Concept of Mind*, between being able to state a factual proposition and being able to perform a skilful operation. The difference between 'knowing that' and 'knowing how' is the difference between inert knowledge and intelligent action. Unfortunately, some competent teachers are not especially articulate about their skill, and it would be wrong to assert that skill may only be recognised as such if the person manifesting it is capable of explaining and analysing it in textbook language. The intelligence of an action may perfectly well be explained by another, and the behaviour is not necessarily unintelligent or shallow if its perpetrator is tongue-tied about it.

One problem encountered in defining teaching skills is that though in some contexts the term 'skill' has good connotations, attracts adulation, is a gift of the few.'the result of years of practice or the mark of an expert, in other circumstances it is looked down upon, regarded as mechanical, the sign of a rude technician rather than an artist. We tend, for instance, to admire a surgeon's skill or that of a tennis player. Both may have had the same years of dedicated practice, but the intellectual nature of the knowledge and understanding required by the surgeon is vastly more exacting than that required by a sportsman.

Where the imagination is involved, even more fine distinctions exist. A sculptor would probably be disappointed to read a report that described his latest masterpiece as an example of skill. He would expect eulogies to contain words like 'artistic' and 'creative'. For those who liken teachers more to expressive artists than to surgeons, the very term 'skill' may be seen as belittling, reducing creative endeavour to mechanical crudity. It is difficult to dry-clean the term of these emotional associations with other kinds of human enterprise.

This uncertainty about the proper standing of the notion of skill when applied to teaching is partly explained by the varied nature of the teacher's job. Pressing the right button on a tape recorder, or writing legibly on the blackboard, require but modest competence, and are things most people could learn with only a little practice. Responding to a disruptive 10 year old, or knowing how to explain a difficult concept to children of different ages and abilities by choosing the right language register, appropriate examples and analogies, and reading the many cues which signal understanding or bewilderment, require years of practice as well as considerable intelligence and insight. Although the term 'interpersonal skills' is now quite widespread, there is still some reluctance to classify human relationships in this way.

When children learn something there is often a magical quality about the excitement of discovery, the warmth of regard between teacher and taught, or the novelty to the learner of what is taking place, and the romanticism seems to be destroyed if teaching is seen as too deliberate, calculated, manipulated or over-analysed. Hence the debate, to which I shall return in previous chapters, about learning to teach and whether the act of teaching should be seen as a whole, or is at all capable of being separated into discrete, if interrelated, sub-skills.

My own view is that the extreme optimism of the supporters of the so-called Performance- or Competency-based Teacher Education programmes fashionable in the United States during the 1970s was misplaced. It was assumed that teaching could be broken down into hundreds and indeed thousand of particles, that trainees could learn each of these, and that they could be certificated on the basis of their proven ability to manifest whatever set of competencies had been prescribed. Lists of approved competencies were produced such as the 1,276 compiled by Dodl (1973) under the heading *The Florida Catalog of Teacher Competencies* and hierarchies were assembled with the skills required given a level. Thus an operation by the teacher like 'form reading groups and give a good rationale for the grouping' was seen as being at a lower level than, 'implement managerial procedures for efficient group operation'. There was an arbitrary quality to some of these hierarchies, and competency-based teacher education was criticised by writers such as Heath and Nielson (1974) for not being founded on any sound empirical evidence. The survey of teaching competence in initial training courses in parts of Britain by Her Majesty's Inspectorate (DES 1991) rejected the notion of such narrowly conceived notions of competency. Houston (1985) concluded his survey of competency-based teacher education by observing:

> Amid the worldwide actions in competency-based teacher education, it must be remembered that while the concept is sound and fundamental, the implementation is still primitive in terms of its inherent promise.

In the Leverhulme Primary Project we decided to concentrate on more general broadly based skills, with particular emphasis on class management. We also decided to focus on crucial skills, such as questioning and explaining, and to study aspects of teachers' subject knowledge, a particular problem for generalist class teachers, who, in a world where knowledge is being gathered at a phenomenal rate, are expected to grasp several academic disciplines. These areas of skill tend, according to the tenets described above, to represent activities which require professional competence, intelligent action and sensitivity from teachers. They were not so vague as to defy analysis, nor so minute and piddling (like 'smiling' or 'ability to hold chalk') as to attract ridicule, nor were they likely to be dismissed by practitioners as unimportant. They were all valuable aspects of teaching for beginners and experienced teachers alike. They do not, however, represent a complete list of teaching skills, as we inevitably left unstudied many other areas of professional competence. Even though we have observed and analysed large numbers of lessons in many primary classrooms, we recognised that we could hope to make only a modest contribution to the understanding and nurturing of the teachers' professional art and craft.

Classroom Observation

Up to the late 1950s there were very few examples of research on teaching which had used direct observation of lessons. Many inferences about classroom life were drawn from interviews, questionnaires or from folklore, anecdotes and hearsay. During the 1960s and 1970s this situation changed rapidly, and hundreds of reports were published ranging from case studies of a single classroom to large-scale observations of practice in hundreds of lessons. Throughout the 1980s and 1990s classroom observation became a regular feature of evaluation projects and research into classroom competency of various kinds. The legal requirement for teacher appraisal in many countries often includes an obligation for teachers to be seen at work in their own classroom, so evidence from classroom observation is used not only in research projects but in formal assessments of competence.

There is not the space here to document the many forms of enquiry which have been undertaken nor the thousands of 'findings' reported in the literature around the world. These are in any case to be found in several standard reference books such as those by Dunkin and Biddle (1974), Delamont (1976), Wragg (1976), Cohen and Manion (1981), Stallings and Mohlman (1985), and many others.

There are considerable advantages and a few disadvantages to studying classrooms by observing what happens at first hand. The major disadvantage is that the presence of an observer invariably has an effect on what takes place, however slight, and there is no foolproof way of knowing what might have transpired had no outsider been there. Samph (1976) planted microphones in classrooms and then sent observers either announced or unexpected some weeks later. He found that teachers made more use of questions and of praise and were more likely to accept pupils' ideas when someone was present. Teachers and indeed pupils may attempt to provide what they think the visitor expects, and this will vary according to the impression or stereotype they form of the observer concerned. Teachers may be irritated by a visitor and behave indifferently from normal, hence the need for observers, where possible, to study a series of lessons rather than a single one.

Several traditions of observing classrooms have developed. In the United States the great majority of published classroom studies have been based on a degree of quantification, often using some kind of category system. This tradition dates back to the attention studies of the 1920s and 1930s reported by Jackson (1968), and even earlier. It gained in popularity during the 1950s and 1960s, especially after the seminal article by Medley and Mitzel (1963) describing how to construct category systems. Some of the work is closely related to behaviourist learning theory; other studies attempt to relate measurements of the frequency of certain kinds of behaviour to tests of pupil learning or other estimates of outcome.

Since the hope of this kind of research was to establish a body of knowledge which would show some consistency about what successful teachers do, several writers have attempted to establish theories of teaching and learning based on systematic empirical enquiry. Techniques such as meta-analysis (Glass 1978) have been developed which aggregate quantitative studies based on correlation coefficients, chi-squares, or analysis of variance, and determine an overall effect size. Thus, it is possible to calculate from several studies the average relationship between, say, the teacher's use of praise and pupils' learning. Although the apparent neatness of such an aggregation may appeal to some administrators looking for guidance from research, the proposition that fairly exact relationships can be discovered between what teachers do or are and what pupils learn has been criticised by several writers. Jackson (1962) described the findings of half a century of study on the relationship between teachers' personalities and pupil learning as 'so low in intellectual food value that it is almost embarrassing to discuss them'. Typically, small but significant correlations of around 0.2 or 0.3 have been commonplace, leaving a great deal still unexplained.

The more carefully conducted quantitative analyses of teaching have nevertheless yielded some useful and interesting information, even though much less has been delivered than was once hoped. For example, the extremely busy nature of the teacher's job is now well documented. Teachers may have up to 200 days a year with their classes, and an early survey by Jackson showed over 1,000 interpersonal exchanges in a day (Jackson 1962); teachers' use of praise seemed relatively infrequent and haphazard (Brophy 1981); some teachers in inner-city schools spent up to 75 per cent of their time trying to keep order (Deutsch 1960); or teachers allowed on average one second between a pupil's answer and their own statement (Rowe 1972). It is quite clear that in the course of the millions of exchanges in which teachers may engage during a quite short phase of their career they can find little time for a leisurely scrutiny of classroom processes. Kerry (1984) found that the classroom transactions of teachers in his sample consisted of 54 per cent to do with management, 42 per cent informing and only 4 per cent which he labelled as 'stimulating', that is, provoking higher levels of thought.

Many teachers develop fairly fixed patterns of teaching which may well be laid down at the training stage. When new curricula, school reorganisation or other changes in circumstances come along, it is difficult to unlearn habits and strategies which have been rehearsed millions of times, even if they are no longer appropriate. Hence the criticism in some of Her Majesty's Inspectors' reports of teachers who have not looked critically at their own teaching styles, or the difficulties experienced by teachers trying to use a fresh curriculum with old teaching methods. Alexander *et at.* (1992) repeated the assertion that proper scrutiny of classroom processes was necessary, in a report on primary teaching commissioned by the Secretary of State.

Alongside these many quantitative studies has been a different style of enquiry based more on the pencil and notebook tradition used by anthropologists seeking to analyse human behaviour by recording phenomena in detail, and then inviting participants to explain them. Sometimes the investigator is also a participant, as in the case study by Hamilton (1975) of the introduction of integrated science teaching in two Scottish schools, sometimes a non-participant, like King (1978), who documented practice in three infant schools and deliberately avoided becoming enmeshed in the life of the classrooms in which he spent many hours.

Incisive ethnographic accounts of classrooms often give intimate case details and interpretations which some of the quantitative accounts might have missed. The observations made in lessons by Ball (1981), who recorded how a ten-form-entry comprehensive school changed from a system of broad banding to one of mixed-ability classes, are quite close in tenor to those reported in the 1978 HMI paper on the same topic, which was based on evidence from the classrooms of several schools. The strategies employed by teachers of different subjects, the arguments underlying their behaviour and the reaction of pupils, however, are all described in much greater detail through the single case study.

Lacey (1970) taught twelve lessons a week himself, and spent another twelve lessons a week observing teachers and their classes in his study of Hightown Grammar. The result is an analysis of teaching and a description of individual pupils and teachers that set classroom processes in the wider context of the school in its social environment. A similar depth and breadth of insight was offered by Hargreaves (1967) in his study of Lumley Secondary Modern School.

In addition to the two major styles of enquiry there has been other research into teaching based on different procedures and traditions. Blurton Jones (1972) brought together a collection of research reports based on the ethological techniques used by students of the behaviour of animals, and Barnes (1971), Stubbs (1976), Edwards and Furlong (1978), and Feagans and Farran (1981), are among several investigators who have reported linguistic analysis of classroom transactions. Though verbal aspects of teaching and learning have commanded attention from researchers, increasing interest has been shown in non-verbal aspects of classroom communication by, among others. Argyle (1967), Knapp (1980), and Wilkinson (1975), the last of whom combined a variety of techniques for the analysis of both verbal and non-verbal behaviour.

Studying teachers and pupils by direct observation of what they do and say provides valuable information on which to base judgements about skilful teaching and intelligent action. There are many observation procedures from which to choose, each with its supporters and practitioners. It is a pity that the debate between proponents of various schools has occasionally been acrimonious. Attempting to decide whether, for example, quantitative studies are better than qualitative ones is about as fruitful as trying to determine whether a black-and-white photo of the front of the building gives a truer representation of reality than a painting of the rear, a scale drawing or an aerial photograph, or whether bacon and eggs are tastier than fish and chips. I have written a fuller account of classroom observation in the book *An Introduction to Classroom Observation* (Wragg 1993), also published by Routledge.

The Leverhulme Primary Project

We decided in the Leverhulme Primary Project to use a variety of methods. but to put classroom observation right at the centre of our research. The research was conceived as two major linked strands. This book describes the classroom management strand which the present writer directed. The other major strand concentrated on the development aspect of teacher competence by exploring the relationship of subject matter and pedagogical knowledge to the emergence of teaching competence during an initial training programme. That strand was directed by Professor

Neville Bennett and its findings are reported in the parallel book to this one, *Learning to Teach* (Bennett and Carre 1993).

Our intention was to study classroom management across a broad front, looking at the management of pupil behaviour, of knowledge, the teachers' management of very first encounters, when roles and relationships are established, and of professional skills such as questioning and explaining. During the period of the project from 1988 to 1992 there was a great deal of debate about and scrutiny of teachers' professional competence. The Elton Report (1989) looked specifically at class management; numerous reports, some official, some quasi-official, some based on research, others on polemic or political beliefs, gave accounts of different aspects of classroom practice in the primary school. The discussion paper by Alexander *et al.* (1992), which was produced in response to an enquiry set up by the then Secretary of State, Kenneth Clarke, concluded that amongst the most pressing needs were:

> — extending teachers' skills in the main organisational strategies we have discussed, giving particular attention to whole class teaching and properly focused on organised group work;
>
> — extending teachers' skills in the key classroom techniques of explaining and questioning
>
> (Alexander *et al.*, 1992, paragraph 178)

Several other reports addressed matters such as reading standards, whether teacher training should be more school-based, the place of the specialist teacher in primary schools, teacher appraisal, and teachers' subject knowledge. In most of these there was an explicit or implicit reference to teachers' classroom skills and new ability to adapt and develop them.

In order to study this range of class management demands on primary teachers, we embarked on nine sub-projects. These were:

1. *Effective/ineffective classroom management* - a study of how student and experienced teachers handle disruptive incidents.
2. *Intervention programme* - experiments with training materials during teacher training programmes.
3. *Pupils' views of class management* - the perceptions of primary school children of different ages of what constitutes effective class management.
4. *First encounters* - what happens when beginners and experienced teachers meet a new class for the first time.
5. *Attitude change* - how student teachers' attitudes to class management change during teaching practice.
6. *Explaining*--how primary teachers explain concepts to children.
7. *Questioning*—the use of different kinds of questions by teachers.
8. *Teachers' knowledge* - particularly of unfamiliar subject matter and what strategies they use to cope with teaching a fresh topic,
9. *Supply teachers* - how they manage classes, given that they must meet new groups on a far more regular basis than teachers in permanent posts.

Having identified important topics for scrutiny, we decided on the following strategies:

Involve the Profession

Some teacher training procedures have excluded classroom practitioners. We decided it was most important to involve heads and teachers: to solicit their views in interviews and questionnaires, to obtain descriptions of practice, to research into classroom behaviour, to use teachers to field-test training procedures with students on teaching practice, and to ask them to give a professional evaluation of our materials. It was equally important to involve he teacher training profession, and we decided that all the above should apply to them too.

Teachers Should Seek Their Own Styles

Although one can learn a great deal from intelligent current practice, any raining materials based purely on what teachers are seen to do would be ultra-conservative. Had such a procedure prevailed in the medical profession, doctors would still be using leeches. Teachers exercise skill and make their decisions in different contexts. In the absence of any single consensus about effective teaching, therefore, practitioners need to learn to use their senses to appraise situations and their intelligence and imagination to respond. The notion of teachers being researchers in their own classrooms, or engaging in regular reflection in order to improve practice, has been developed by, among others. Stenhouse (1975) and Schoen (1983). In order to reflect, however, teachers need information about their own and others' classrooms on which they can then exercise judgement. Practitioners can learn a great deal from their fellow human beings, and so the training materials we produced were devised in such a way that teachers could work either alone or together to analyse each other's teaching. Historically, teaching has been a far more isolated job than it needed to be. In previous chapters there will be a further consideration of learning from and with a professional partner.

Research and Development

Some curriculum development projects have no research

base at all. and may be none the worse for it depending more on the professional and creative wisdom of team members than on some kind of systematic enquiry. We decided to combine research and development in the Leverhulme Primary Project.

There are a number of difficulties involved in a research and development project. The first is that it is rarely possible to complete a thorough enquiry first and then produce the programme afterwards. A research project takes about three years, by the time the design has been worked out, the fieldwork has been completed and analysed, and the implications have been identified. If one starts development only at that stage, then circumstances may already have changed compared with when the research phase was first undertaken. On the other hand, if one starts with development, then research can consist only *of post hoc* evaluations, and it may be difficult to incorporate findings once well tested materials are already in existence.

Within these limitations different lines of research were necessary. Some were relatively short-lived, others ran for a full three years. Different kinds of methodology were used, including classroom observation, interviews, tests of learning or attitude, photographs (to elicit the reaction of pupils and teachers to classroom events) and diaries. The advantage of a research and development project, if it works well, is that it both provides research data for teachers, teacher trainers and fellow researchers in the same field, and also offers directly training materials and ideas based on the research. It would be foolish to try to base a curriculum development project entirely on one's own or even other people's research. Perhaps the best example of the slavish application of research findings was programmed learning, which dwindled in popularity after the 1960s, partly because of the tedium experienced by those working through endless sequences of mind-corroding frames containing the classic ingredients of active responding, small steps, immediate confirmation and high correct response rates. We decided that our own and other researchers' findings would inform training materials, not dominate them.

The research in this project adopted a variety of standard research practices and one or two less common ones, like the use of photographs. Whenever quantitative methods were used, two or more observers were trained in classrooms or by using videotapes, until a high level of agreement was achieved in the use of whatever category or sign system was being employed. In qualitative research two or more members of the team analysed data, such as transcripts or interviews, until there was agreement about the salient features or the selection of illustrative quotations or examples.

In writing an account of research findings which we hope will be read by experienced heads and teachers, student teachers, researchers, lay people interested in primary education, administrators, and policy workers, we are caught in the usual dilemma facing those addressing different audiences. Sometimes the text does contain tables based on one of the commonly used statistical techniques, like correlations, chi-squares, t tests, analysis of variance, or multivariate analysis such as factor or cluster analysis. I have tried to use natural language wherever possible, and readers who are not interested in the detail of the research findings should not feel guilty if they skip over some of the statistical tables and concentrate more on the case material and summaries of research results.

2

The Management of Teaching

In his classic text *The Theory of Social and Economic Organisation* (1964) Max Weber observed that power in any social relationship is reflected in the probability that one person will be in a position to carry out his own will despite resistance. In theory, teachers have the power to control the behaviour of children in their charge. Since society has given them the 'duty of care,' as it is known in legal parlance, because they are acting as a parent substitute, *in loco parentis,* they must be given power to administer fair punishments, for example, so that they can carry out their duties.

This neat view of life in the classroom does not always translate easily into actuality. A major survey of over 500 primary schools by Her Majesty's Inspectorate (DES 1978) concluded that'a quiet working atmosphere was established in nine out of ten of the classes wherever it was needed.' But behind his general orderliness lies an intricate complexity which involves far more than just the socially acceptable behaviour of pupils. Teachers have to manage the learning of their pupils as well as their classroom behaviour. They must constantly make selections from their repertoire of personal and professional skills, deciding what children shall study and by what means; the extent to which pupils should themselves be encouraged to make decisions; when, to whom, and what sort of questions to ask and what explanations to give; whether pupils shall work in groups, as individuals, as a whole class or in some other combination;how time and space should be deployed—where, for example, to place tables and chairs, and where to stand when addressing individuals or groups: how best to husband and deploy resources—like books, materials, equipment or cash; what rules will operate in their classroom; what sort of relationships they would like with children, fellow teachers and the wider community, parents, ancillary staff, governors; how to manage tensions and crises, of individuals or groups; what range of professional roles to play, when, for example, to act as a substitute parent or social worker to a despairing child from an unhappy home, or to stand back from this; how to manage the monitoring and assessment of children's progress.

Within school, teachers are, inescapably, members of a social and management structure, and, in their study of inner London schools, Rutter *et al.*, (1979) concluded that, in those schools judged to be 'better' on various criteria, such as test scores and attendance rates, teachers felt more involved in decision-making. They were also part of a wider community with, in turn, is values and practices. Managing children is usually thought to be harder in schools located in areas with high crime rates. Johnson and Brooks (1979) have produced a useful model (see figure 2.1) of this intricate nexus of relationships between tasks which society expects teachers to perform, such as planning and organising lessons, the many kinds of setting in which teaching and learning may take place, the values that teachers and learners may hold, and the tensions between people and amongst roles.

Class management is a topic which is frequently mentioned in professional debate about primary schools.

The Plowden Report (1967) posited a non-authoritarian but nevertheless planned regime based on consideration for others and industry.

> For all the appearances of free-and-easiness, for all the absence of the traditional forms of discipline, there is, behind it all, not only a deep understanding of children, but careful planning. The two basic assumptions are that children respond in kind to courteous and considerate treatment by adults, and that the will work with concentration and diligence at tasks which are suited to their abilities. Neither assumption is true for all children, or for any child all the time, but both are true enough to make them a workable basis for many primary schools.

The large-scale survey of over 500 primary schools by Her Majesty's Inspectorate (DES 1978) spoke of two general approaches to teaching and the styles of management that went with them, one 'mainly didactic,' he other mainly exploratory.' The report warned, however, of the misleading nature of such oversimplification, and stated:

> It is clear from the evidence that a variety of types of organisation was used in arranging the work of the classes. Generally, the organisation was designed to provide satisfactorily for children of different attainments and abilities, to accommodate various types of work, including practical work, and to take advantage of the resources and teaching strengths available within a particular school.

The queštion of class management was referred to in the survey by HMI (DES 1987) of new teachers in schools.

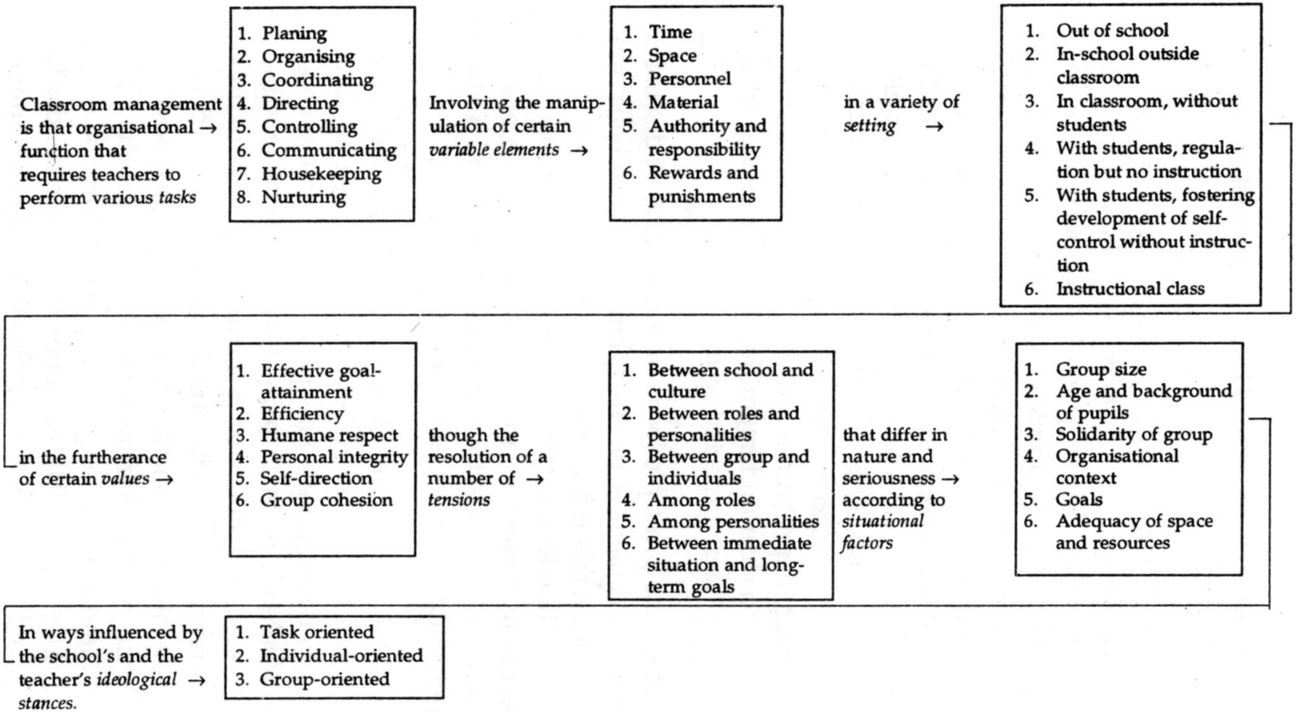

Fig. 2.1. A conceptual model of classroom management (from Johnson and Brooks 1979).

Here the precepts informing HMI's judgement were spelled out explicitly:

> Good management of classes containing children up to the age of seven was characterised by planning which provided opportunities for groups and individuals to work on tasks of intrinsic interest, allied to the ability to maintain an overview of the activities of all the children and to intervene as necessary. Good management of junior age classes was typified by detailed planning, effective organisation of resources, the provision of interesting learning-experiences, high expectations on the part of the teacher, and a clear understanding by the pupils of what they were expected to do.

Often the principle focus in considering or discussing class management is on discipline and pupil behaviour, even though this is but one, albeit very important, aspect of it. The Elton Report (1989) emphasises the 'whole school' aspect of management: that it should be seen as planned, not accidental, conscious and not *ad hoc*, and a shared responsibility, not an isolated one:

> We recommend that head teachers and their senior management teams should take the lead in developing school plans for promoting good behaviour. Such plans should ensure that the school's code of conduct and the values represented in is formal and informal curricula reinforce one another promote the highest possible degree of consensus about standards of behaviour among staff, pupils and parents; provide clear guidance to all three groups about these standards and their practical application; and encourage

> staff to recognise and praise good behaviour as well as dealing with bad behaviour.

Another report commissioned by the Secretary of State on primary classroom practice (Alexander *et al.* 1992) also considered such organisational aspects as the use of whole class, group and individual teaching, concluding that many teachers used all three, as the were not mutually exclusive. It cautioned that doctrine should not override educational judgements on such organisational matters:

> Teachers need the skills and judgment to be able to select and apply whichever organisational strategy—class, group or individual—is appropriate for the task at hand. The judgment, it must be stressed, should be educational and organisational, rather than, as it so often is, doctrinal.

Class management is a central notion in classroom research, in teacher education, both at initial and post-experience level, in teacher appraisal, and in the public mind. It is neither simple nor uni-dimensional. There are numerous views about its nature, and the research literature, which cannot be fully covered in the limited confines of this book, abounds with studies of class management using a variety of approaches, interpretations and data-gathering strategies. It not only contains an important set of interrelated skills in its own right, but is also intricately bound up with other professional skills, for without competence in class management teachers cannot display to full advantage the other skills they may possess. In this context, it can be reported as a 'threshold variable,' as teachers need to have sufficient skills in organisation, control and co-ordination to allow the rest of their professional competence flourish.

It is not possible to describe at this point more than a small amount of the research done in class management, and more references to research are included in later chapters, but the field has been surveyed by several writers such as Dunkin and Biddle (1974), Docking (1980) and Emmer (1985). There is no shortage of 'how to handle classes' books for student teachers, often written by practitioners such as Francis (1975) and Marland (1975), or teacher trainers (Robertson 1981). Some of the books and pamphlets on class management for teachers try to incorporate research findings, like *Maintaining Discipline in Classroom Instruction* (Gnagey 1975), the work book *Class Management and Control*, which was field-tested as part of the Teacher Education Project by Wragg (1981), and the workbook on primary class management (Wragg 1993) which grew out of the Leverhulme primary Project. Others concentrate on a particular set of research findings and precepts, such as the 'behavioural interactionist' perspective (Wheldall and Glynn 1989), which combines the analysis of behaviour and behaviourist learning theory with the view that learning is interactive and children need to initiate as well as respond.

Although a great deal of the research in the field has been undertaken in the last twenty-five years, American studies by Wickman (1928), who enquired into teachers' definitions of behaviour problems, and the so-called 'attention studies' of the 1920s and 1930s, when an observer sat at the front of the class scanning faces to assemble a simple measure of attentiveness (Jackson 1968), show that interest in the topic is not entirely recent.

In Britain, Highfield and Pinsent (1952) obtained estimates of what were perceived as pupil misdemeanours from a sample of 724 teachers. Restlessness and fidgeting, laziness and boisterous, noisy behaviour were seen as the most common forms of misconduct. Several surveys, some by local authorities or teacher associations, have addressed the problem of more serious misbehaviour. Lowenstein (1975) intended to show trends in 'violent and obstrusive behaviour,' but failed to do so because, he claimed, there was a lack of objectivity and accuacy on the part of teachers filling in report forms and describing incidents.

A number of investigators, some through scrutiny of several teachers, others by in-depth case studies of individual classrooms or schools, have tried to map out the strategies which teachers use to control the behaviour of groups or individual pupils. One of the best-known and most influential series of research programmes was undertaken by Jacob Kounin and his associates from the late 1950s to the early 1970s. Kounin concentrated on, among other events, the teacher's reaction to pupil deviance, and studied the clarity, firmness and roughness of what he called 'desists,' that is, teachers' attempts to terminate behaviour of which the disapproved.

In a study of forty-nine teachers of children aged 5 to 8, of grades 1 and 2, Kounin (1970) observe each for one whole day, and concentrated in his analysis of videotapes and transcripts on the techniques of group management teachers employed. He coined a set of some what off beat terms to describe various kinds of teacher behaviour that seemed to be positively related to the involvement of pupils in their work or to freedom from deviance in the classroom. These included the following:

1. *With-itness* Having eyes in the back of your head and thus picking up misbehaviour early.
2. *Overlapping* Being able to do more than one thing at once—for example, deal with someone misbehaving whilst at the same time keeping the children you are with occupied.

3. *Smoothness* Keeping children at work by not:
   (a) Intruding suddenly when they are busy (thrusts).
   (b) Starting one activity and then leaving it abruptly to engage in another (dangles).
   (c) Ending an activity and then returning to it unexpectedly (flip-flops).
4. *Overldwelling* Avoiding staying on an issue for longer than necessary.
5. *Momentum* Freedom from slow-downs.

Kounin found strongest relationships between 'withitness,' the ability to scan the class, and pupil involvement and lack of deviance, with correlations of from 0.307 to 0.615, depending whether children were working individually at their desks or engaged in whole-class activity, when the correlations were higher.

In an earlier set of studies Kounin and Gump (1958), looking at twenty-six kindergarten teachers, identified the 'ripple effect,' that is, the impact of something the teacher does on pupils other than the target child, for example, when a teacher say, 'Haven't you started yet, John?' and other pupils to have commenced work. The findings were not entirely conclusive, though a later study suggested that the ripple effect made most impact on the highly motivated pupils, and that liking or disliking the teacher also influenced the degree of effect. Reviewing Kounin's work, Dunkin and Biddle (1974) concluded that it held considerable promise for the eventual improvement of classroom teaching, and it has certainly been influential on much that followed it.

Emmer (1985), in his overview of class management research, divided the field up into a number of domains. Criteria for effective management included in such matters as pupil engagement, absence of conflict and deviant behaviour, time management fulfilment of goals and pupil learning. He also highlighted theoretical perspectives, such as a behaviour modification or a humanist-interactionist orientation; Specific management tasks, like beginning the school day, whole-class and group teaching, end-of-day routines and transitions from one activity to another; the early part of the school year, maintaining the classroom management system, and the place of rewards and punishments; and contextual features, such as the organisation of the school and pupil achievement level.

Whereas some investigators have concentrated, on studies of several classrooms, other researchers have conducted intensive case studies of a smaller number. Woods (1979) described what he called 'mortification techniques' used by some teachers which strip the personality of certain pupils, as well as forms of fraternisation and negotiation which are often employed when first-line approaches fail. Other investigators have catalogued various 'coping strategies' witnessed during observation, including D. Hargreaves (1975), A. Hargreaves (1978), and Stebbins (1981). These include not only those described by Woods (1979), but also the use of promises, and keeping pupils busy so there is little time for deviance.

Freiberg (1983), writing about the notion of consistency in classroom management, cites a number of models of class management, including those that focus on psychological roles, methods of communication, the behaviour of the individual, pupil responsibility or rule-based models. A comprehensive summary of these has been produced by Charles (1981). Several of the models, notably those based on Skinnerian behaviourist theory using behaviour modification techniques, have sizeable and, in some cases, controversial research literature attached to them. Others, like Roger's (1970) (1969) for what he calls 'reality therapy,' that is, the involvement of pupils in decisions about rules and procedures, have produced some empirical research but tend to be less positivistic in style.

The Management of Time on the Task

Some investigators have chosen to study one particular dimension of class management, like the time pupils appear to spend on the task they are supposed to be doing, on the grounds that the more time pupils on academic activities the more they may learn. Brophy and Evertson (1976) in a correlational study of 7-9 year-olds, found that Kounin's categories of with-itness, overlapping and smoothness were related not only to good behaviour, but also to greater pupil learning. Their conclusion was that the amount of time the pupil was engaged on the task was 'the key to successful classroom time the pupil was engaged on the task was 'the key to successful classroom management.' The notion of 'time on the task' or 'academic engaged time' attracted considerable research interest, and the California Beginning Teacher Evaluation Study (Denham and Lieberman 1980) devoted much of its enquiry to the nature and amount of time spent by pupils on the task in hand.

This issue was taken up by Gage (1978), who summarised several studies of academic learning time, and concluded that time was in itself 'a psychologically empty quantitative concept.' What was needed, he argued, was a more refined analysis of the notion of time. In the California Beginning Teacher Evaluation Study, such factors as allocated time and success rate were taken into account, but more value—and problem-laden concepts such as the degree to which the tasks set were worthwhile, were not fully scrutinised.

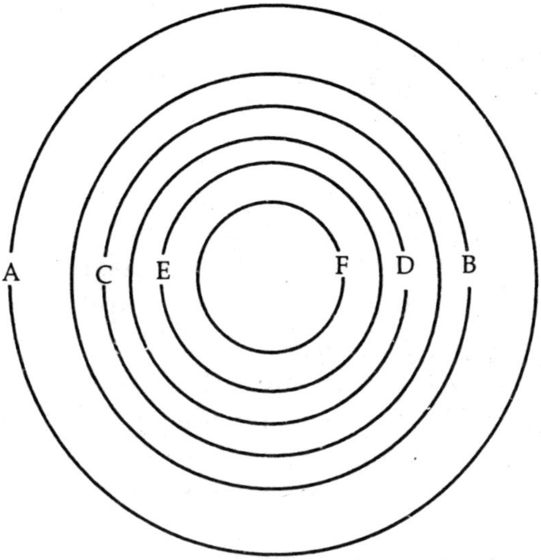

Fig. 2.2. Time Circles: a model of time management (not to scale)

Circle A, all time	Circle B, time spent in school
Circle C, time assigned to a subject	Circle D, time actually spent on the task
Circle E, time on a worthwhile task	Circle F, with some degree of success

One way of conceptualising effective time management would be to see it as a 'bull's eye' model (Wragg 1984), that is, a set of concentric circles (Figure 2.2 not to scale): the largest, circle A, would be 168 hours per week, that is, the total time available during seven days and nights. Inscribed within it, he next circle, B, would be quite small by comparison, only some twenty-four hours, being roughly the amount of time spent in school averaged over the year. This ranks in scale with some studies of children watching television which have shown an average of twenty-five hours per week (Balding 1990). Circle C would show the amount of time assigned to the area under security, for example, number work in the infant school or science for 10 year-olds. This would vary from school to school. It could be two hours in one school and four hours in another.

So far, none of the circles is a direct reflection of the class management skill of the individual teacher, since allocations are usually fixed by governors, heads and teachers. The size of the smaller circle, however is indeed affected by the individual teachers' skill. Circle D would be the amount of time pupils actually spend on the tasks in hand. If the school had assigned three hours to science, then teachers with ineffective class management, or very adverse circumstances, might find pupils engaged in learning for less than an hour. Other classes might spend over two hours. Totals for individual pupils, rather than class means, will show an even wider spread. Some of the studies in the Leverhulme Primary Project considered this aspect, and they are reported in later chapters of this book.

Circle E brings in the domain of 'worthwhile tasks.' Engaged time in a certain classroom might be high, but the task set might involve the equivalent of copying out telephone directories, so the concept of what is worthwhile, a major philosophical issue discussed by, among others, Peters (1966), is important but highly subjective and contentious. It must, however, logically be a subset of engage time. Again, it will be a function of the skill of the teacher how much time is spent on worthwhile activities.

Finally, the concept of success at the task must be incorporated. If children spend time learning erroneous concepts in science, their experience is less profitable than it would have been if they had learned correct ones. Thus, the final circle F encompasses that portion of circle E which is done with some degree of success. This circle is closely related to the matter of primary teachers' subject knowledge, which we also investigated in the present project. One operational definition of skilful classroom management, therefore, would be the extent to which teachers are capable of maximising circle F for each child, that is, the amount of time spent on something worthwhile with some degree of success, in other words, 'hitting the bullseye. The model is certainly not the only way of conceptualising time management: one could add such important aspects as enjoyment, but it is offered as a way of depicting some of the factors frequently mentioned when the matter is discussed.

Mc Namara (1981) has criticised the emphasis on time management, in some studies, arguing that, taken too far, it can become an end in itself. It can also become a recipe for over-directive teaching. In the Leverhulme Primary Project research described in the following chapters, time on task does constitute one aspect of some of our studies, but we concentrated also on other constituents, such as rules and relationships, the handling of disruption, the management of pupil behaviour and of the teachers' own professional skills.

Schools of Thought

It has already been stated above that, in a pluralist society, there will be more than one perspective on a subject like class management. Sometimes public debate is reduced right down to two contending factions, 'traditional' and progressive,' though evidence from surveys cited above shows that this is an oversimplification of a much more complex situation. Below are but seven conceptions out of a potentially much larger set of viewpoints. They are neither rigid nor permanent classifications in that teachers may, for example, behave in an authoritarian manner in one context, but in a different way in another. Similarly the use of behaviour modification can be handled in an authoritarian way, with the teacher specifying all the conditions, or be negotiated by teacher and pupil. Thus some of these notions can be laid over others in a two or three-dimensional model of class management, but, equally, some can be seen as mutually exclusive. They are, therefore, general orientations and beliefs, not permanent conditions. Teachers have to react rapidly to, perhaps, 1, 000 or more interpersonal transactions in a single day Jackson (1968), so their responses may be varied and subject to more than one single influence.

Authoritarian

The principal belief here is that teachers are paid to establish and maintain order within a school. They probably, therefore, know best, and should expect to be obeyed. Authoritarianism is sometimes stereotyped as 'had' or 'unkind,' but this need not be the case at all. There are many teachers who are firmly in charge, and exercise authority, whom one could not describe as lacking kindliness, understanding or concern for the child as an individual. In Victorian times great stress was laid on the authority of the teacher, and classes frequently chanted in unison learned answers to standard questions. Teachers were expected to exercise firm social control over behaviour and also over the knowledge children acquired, and corporal punishment was used extensively. In more recent times, corporal punishment has been abandoned and the role of the teacher has come under close scrutiny, with vigorous debate about whether what is taught should be determined by the class teacher, fashioned by children themselves or laid down centrally in a national curriculum by statute.

Geoffrey Bantock assert what for him is the inescapable 'authority' of the teacher in his book *Freedom and Authority in Education* (1965):

> The teacher, however much he may attempt to disguise the fact, must, if only because he is not appointed or dismissed by pupils, represent an authority. He must do so, also, because he is inescapably 'other' than the children. For one

> thing, he is older: he has inevitably undergone experiences which given him a different background of assumption from that of his charges. He is, that is to say, psychically different. He has, too, certain legal responsibilities and is answerable to the community at large for aspects of his behaviour. There is therefore unavoidable, 'mechanically,' as it were, a gulf which no attempt at disguise can hide, because it is endemic in the situation, 'given.' Nor do I think that it should be disguised. Power is an inescapable element in adult life, with which we all at some time or other have to come to terms and I deprecate a great deal of the current insincerity which strives to hide the true situation and thus prepares the child for a fictious world, not one of reality, even when the circumstance is blanketed under some such grandiose title as 'training in the self-responsibilities of citizenship. It is to be deprecated for a number of reasons, not least of which is the need to learn respect for the idea of authority as such, as a necessary element in the proper functioning of the community.

Teachers operating in an authoritarian mode would expect to make many of the decisions about content and procedure, with perhaps fewer explanations or justification of the reasons for such decisions. There might be less permitted movement or talking to other pupils. More directions would be given with the intention that they should be carried out. Hand raising before speaking would probably be insisted upon. Supporters of this mode of management argue that chaos ensues unless a teacher is clearly 'in charge,' that children themselves welcome teachers to be strict, that teachers have the experience to know what children should be doing. Critics argue that authoritarian teaching can easily become repressive, that children need to learn to manage and determine their own behaviour if our rapidly changing society is to be truly democratic.

Early work in classroom interaction, occurring as it did before and after the Second World War, took a negative view of authoritarian teaching. Anderson (1939) observed the contacts between nursery children and teachers who were categorised as either 'dominative' or 'integrative' and found more dominative contacts (snatching toys striking playmates, giving commands to others) between children in the classes of teacher classified as 'integrative' there were reported to be more integrative acts (sharing toys, offering help playing harmoniously). Lewin *et al.* (1939) carried out their well known study of the effects of adults role playing 'authoritarian,' 'democratic' and 'laissez-faire' styles of leadership on small groups of boys in boys' clubs. They reported more acts of aggression during the absence of the 'authoritarian' style leader, whereas the 'democratic' group appeared to work equally well whether the leader was present or not. This research was not only based on very small samples, however, but was also undertaken at a time when, because of the rise of fascism, there was a strong belief that authoritarian fathers and teachers had produced a complaint citizenry, easily taken over by a dictator. It was this concern that, for many years, gave authoritarian teaching a largely negative association.

Permissive

This is usually regarded as the polar opposite of authoritarian teaching Children's freedom to develop autonomy, it is argued, will be inhibited by undue interference from the teacher. The following extract from A.S. Neill's *Summerhill* (1961) illustrated this concept in a form which has been influential on some schools, but rarely copied in its original form.

> Summerhill is a self-governing school, democratic in form. Everything connected with social, or group life, including punishment for social offences, is settled by vote at the Saturday night General School Meeting.
>
> Each member of the teaching staff and each child, regardless of his age, has one vote. My vote carries the same weight as that of a seven-year-old.
>
> One may smile and say. 'But your voice has more value, hasn't it? Well, let's see. Once I got up at a meeting and proposed that no child under sixteen should be allowed to smoke. I argued my case: a drug, poisonous, not a real appetite in children, but mostly an attempt to be grown up. Counter-arguments were thrown across the floor. The vote was taken. I was beaten by a large majority.
>
> The sequel is worth recording. After my defeat, a boy of sixteen proposed that no one under twelve should be allowed to smoke. He carried his motion. However, at the following weekly meeting a a boy of twelve proposed the repeal of the new smoking rule, saying, 'We are all siting in the toilets smoking on the sly just like kids do in a strict school, and I say it is against the whole idea of Summerhill.' His speech was cheered, and that meeting repealed the law. I hope I have made it clear that my voice is not always more powerful than that of a child.

'Permissive' is but one term which may be used here.

Others include 'informal', 'progressive' and 'democratic.' Each of these terms carries with it associations, either of approval or of opprobrium, and there is no real clarity about distinctions between them, though some writers would prefer 'democratic' on the grounds that it is a term more likely to gain approval than 'permissive,' with its 'anything goes' associations, or 'progressive,' which may bring on an attack from the political right. Teachers operating in this less didactic mode are not so likely to issue commands, use reprimands or punishment. Freedom of movement is more likely to be permitted and the buzz of conversation amongst pupils may be louder. Emphasis will be more on pupils taking responsibility for their own behaviour. Supporters argue that management in Victorian times was repressive, producing too many uninventive and complaint adults, that children are capable of sensible behaviour, provided they are trusted. Critics claim that permissiveness too frequently degenerates into a laissez-faire *ad hoc* classroom where too little time is spent on learning, where social chit-chat can consume much of the time in school, at the expense of what the children are supposed to be studying.

Whereas the work of those who investigated authoritarianism induced a creative association in the years following the Second World War, a set of research studies in the 1960s and 1970s, summarised by Gage (1978), tended to establish a similar image for less directive approaches. Bringing together studies by several investigators, as well as comparing syntheses of research findings by Rosenshine (1976), Medley (1977), Crawford and Gage (1977) and Glass *et al.* (1977), he contrasted what he called 'direct' and 'open' teaching. 'Direct' is largely didactic, information-giving teaching, the term often derived from studies using the Flanders (1960) ten-category system of interaction analysis. This codes 'direct' teaching as lecture, command or criticism, as opposed to questioning, praise and acceptance of ideas and feelings, which are deemed to be more 'indirect' or 'open.' Gaze concluded that, so far as teaching basic skills in the early years of primary education was concerned, there might be a slight superiority of 'direct' over 'open' approaches, but that this difference would need to be tested experimentally before it could be said to constitute a causal relationship.

Behaviour Modification

This approach is based on the learning theories developed by B.F. Skinner (1954) and his associates. We learn our best, it is believed, when positive behaviour is *reinforced,* often by reward or recognition. Thus children who seek attention and are 'told off' are actually being encouraged to misbehave further to attract more attention. The role of the teacher is to help children learn socially desirable behaviour. The role of the teacher is to help children to learn socially desirable behaviour. The conventions of behaviour modification require teachers to ignore anti-social behaviour, on the grounds that failure to reinforce it by giving it attention will lead to is extinction, and reward or publicly recognise approved behaviour, sometimes by giving out tokens, in the belief hat this reinforces and it makes it more likely to occur.

This form of class management has been criticised, partly because in early work in the United Sates drugs were used on hyperactive children. Critics argue that the treatment is mechanistic, seeing people as machines, not humans, that formal reward systems are merely a from of bribery, and that it is too overt a manipulation of young people. They also say that ignoring misbehaviour does not necessarily improve it and that, in the case of children who use swear words, for example, 'reinforcement' may come from other pupils. Supporters counter this by saying that most teachers, and indeed most human beings in their relationships generally, use reinforcement techniques, and it is dishonest to pretend otherwise, that many children have learnt to behave badly and want to behave well if only someone will show them how, and that 'contract' systems, whereby children specify what they themselves would like to achieve, have removed the 'teacher manipulation' objection.

Certainly the early use of behaviour modification in the 1950s and 1960s was often undertaken in a mechanical way. Reinforcers were seen as consisting of two kinds, *primary,* that is, basic life-sustaining, non-learned item on conditions like nourishment, warmth, and *conditioned* reinforcers, rewards we learn to understand and appreciate, like money or praise. Children who behaved in a manner of which the teacher approved were given tokens or praise on a consistent basis. More recently behavioural approaches to class management have become the subject of negotiation rather than imposition. Nowadays it is more likely that proponents will begin with the observable, and assemble baseline data on whether a child appears to pay attention to the task in hand, for example, and there will usually be a deliberate attempts to change behaviour. However, it is also likely that a much more determined attempt will be made to involve the child in independent learning and autonomy, rather than dependence (wheldall and Glynn, 1989).

Interpersonal Relationships

The belief here is that learning takes place where positive relationships exist between the teacher and the class and amongst pupils. The teacher's role is to develop a healthy classroom climate within which learning will automatically thrive. Often much influenced by the views of Carl Rogers (1970) and his followers. Teachers put a premium on personal relationships both between themselves and pupils, and amongst pupils. There may, therefore, be more involvement of pupils in, say, the negotiation of rules, with discussion and suggestions about why these make sense. When problems occur, the teacher may employ what Glasser (1969) called 'reality therapy,' whereby an interview takes place between the pupil and the teacher with whom he has the strongest rapport, to establish why things are going wrong, what are the consequences of the pupil's attitudes and actions, and how he might proceed in future. Supporters of this point of view regard personal relationships as of crucial importance to all human beings and argue that children must learn how to establish positive relationships with their peers and with adults from an early age. They point out that frequently, in schools, situations which would be difficult in other contexts are easily managed in classrooms where relationships are good. Critics counter that this can easily be overstated, that the pursuit of good relationships can begin to override the acquisition of skills and knowledge, and that there are classrooms where relationships are sound but where little is learnt.

Whereas the research literature on a topic like behaviour modification is huge, there is far less systematic enquiry, though a great deal of analytical writing, on such matters as the precepts of Carl Rogers or 'reality therapy. Some studies have been conducted into the nature of classroom relationships (Hargreaves *et al.* 1975), the kinds of people who enjoy good relationships with others, some of it inspired by Maslow's theory of self-actualisation Maslow, 1970) and the field has been summarised by Brammer (1985). Those who work in this mode, however, are often averse to and suspicious of he 'findings' of research conducted in the sort of quantitative tradition which arms citations in the literature.

Scientific

Professor Nate Gage, of Stanford University, in his book *The Scientific Basis of the Art of Teaching* (1978) and *Hard Gains in the Soft Sciences* (1985) has put forward the proposition that teaching is a science as well as an art, and that teaching can be systematically studied and analysed. Once we know enough, behaviour can be predicted and 'successful' strategies identified. An example of this approach would be the work by Jacob Kounin (1970), described earlier in this chapter, who, in his book *Discipline and Group Management in Classrooms,* used systematic observation of videotapes of primary classrooms to identify what he called 'desist' techniques, that is, action by teachers which seemed to be particularly effective when children misbehaved. He did not identify one single 'desist' as supremely effective, but rather described a series of strategies which were used by teachers who appeared to be successful in dealing with misbehaviour.

Gage argues that careful analysis of the relationships between classroom process data and various measures of outcome, whether these change in behaviour, knowledge or attitude, is an important first step in the establishment of a scientific basis for the art of teaching. Rosenshine and Furst (1973) described this as a *descriptive-correlational-experimental loop.* For example, suppose an investigator decided to study class management in the primary school and to consider in particular which pupils were called upon by the teacher to answer questions during whole-class teaching. Watching lessons and noting which pupils answered questions would be the first stage of this loop, the *descriptive* phase. Let us assume that, when the researcher gave tests of what the pupils had learned, he found a significant correlation between answering questions in class and learning the subject matter of the lesson. This would constitute the second, or *correlational* phase of the loop. It may be the case, however, that quicker learners answer more questions in class, so there might be a correlation but no causal link between process and outcome. In the third phase of the loop, therefore, the teacher would deliberately call on some pupils who had not volunteered to answer to see if, under *experimental* conditions, frequency of answering was related to actual learning.

The difficulty of this approach is, of course, that many 'findings' are based on short-term tests of memory, and that true experiments are notoriously difficult to conduct. It is not possible to 'script' a lesson. One may be able to script the teacher's questions, but then not be able to control the nature and direction of pupils' answers. Nor are curriculum materials, even self-instructional ones, entirely teacher-proof. Nonetheless it is worth teachers experimenting in their own classrooms, and research findings can be a stimulus for further enquiry at individual classrooms, and research findings can be a stimulus for further enquiry at individual classroom level. An infant teacher who had read about Kounin's notion of 'with-itness,' for example, might try splitting her attention between the pupil she was hearing read and the rest of the class from time to time, to see if she felt intuitively that this improved her class management. Or she might make a quick tour of the class, once children had begun work, making comments publicly on the work of one or two children, to see if the 'ripple effect' seemed to have a positive influence on others.

Critics argue that teaching is an art and cannot be analysed or taught in any systematic way, that there is not, as yet, sufficient research evidence to constitute a science of teaching, and that teachers are more influenced by their own personal experience than by what they read in research reports. Supporters point out that medieval doctors defended the use of leeches on similar grounds, that research evidence is necessary if teaching is to move forward, and that rather than replace a teacher's artistry, carefully collected evidence forms what Gage called a 'scientific basis' to enhance it.

Social System

Some researchers and writers have considered aspects of management that extend beyond the walls of a single classroom. People in school are believed to belong to a sub-system of a wider social organisation in which many influences are at work on the group's behaviour. These may be academic, political, social, financial or emotional. Failure to understand these processes, it is said, will inhibit the teacher's ability to work effectively in a school, although learning itself is seen as an individual process. It is difficult to translate this belief into behavioural terms, but the teacher would probably be interested in the wider aspects of education, be knowledge able about the schools' catchment area, the family background, religious beliefs and community traditions and values.

Many school problems, argue adherents of this viewpoint, cannot be dealt with in isolation. Poor housing, financial hardship, family circumstances, parents' employment or lack of it, their education, aspirations and attitudes, all these may exert more powerful influences over pupils' behaviour than anything that happens in school. Teachers need to know about the religious beliefs of the children in their classes, for instance, so that they understand why a child might be away from school celebrating a particular festival, or why the pupil might hold a certain view of diet, physical education and dance, or family life. Critics counter by saying that teachers have little or no control over these external factors, and, whilst able to be understanding, must or necessity heard from teachers at conferences. 'I am a teacher, not a social worker.'

Numerous writers have analysed and described these wider background issues. Such matters as the effects of home background on children's learning were considered in the research undertaken for the Plowden Report (1967) which underlined the importance of parental attitudes, Rutter *et al.* (1979) and Mortimore (1988) have studied different primary and secondary schools to understand the relationship between such factors as leadership and management within the school and pupil achievement and attitudes. Schools in similar social environments were found to have different levels of achievement, and the authors attributed this to such matters as management style within the school, leading to the argument that 'schools can make a difference,' a matter of some dispute amongst researchers (King 1980). Duke (1979) established a link between good pupil behaviour and a consistent school policy on discipline.

Folklore

There is belief amongst many practitioners that experienced teachers already possess intuitive professional expertise which may often be articulated in unpretentious terms, and I am not here disparaging that view. It is held by some that most teachers, over the years, have built up a stock of 'tricks of the trade.' These can be learned, it is said, and the young teacher will be equipped with an omni-purpose set of recipes which will be useful in most situations. Among the most common tips reported by teachers and students we interviewed during the Leverhulme Project were: 'Prepare and plan carefully,' 'Be well organised and anticipate problems,' 'Develop different strategies for different ages of children,' 'Establish good personal relationships.' 'Be firm in your guidelines, and let children know the limits,' 'Keep children busy.' How this manifests itself in the classroom depends on the kind of folklore which has been purveyed, but someone offered the common tip 'Start strict and ease off later' may well attempt to be more severe than she might otherwise have been in the early stages of teaching practice or when starting a new post in a primary school.

Those who believe in tips claim that considerable accumulated professional wisdom lies behind them, that such tips are fairly universal in many schools and cultures, and that generations of trainees have gratefully acknowledged their value. Critics argue that tips are lacking in any theoretical basis, are random and unrelated to each other, and may suit the person who proffers them but not the recipient.

The Present Study of Management Issues

It was not possible during the Leverhulme Primary Project to investigate every aspect of this vast field, and so we had to select certain key aspects for special study, as described in Chapter 1. The remaining chapters of this book describe some of our findings. It seemed logical to begin with a study of the genesis of class management at the beginning of the school year, and chapter 3 describes our interviews with and observations of, a sample of experienced teachers starting their new school year in September, as well as to student teachers commencing teaching practice. The literature suggests that these first few days are an important phase, when ground rules and personal relationships are established, and there are few studies of this establishing period, so we gave it a high priority.

One significant focus in the project was on teaching styles, and chapter 4 brings together observations of several hundred lessons given by student and experienced teachers to see what principal strategies of class management they employed. Chapter 5 focuses specifically on the handling of disruptive and deviant behaviour. The data here come from the analysis of hundreds of 'critical events' observed in classrooms, as well as from teachers comments on a set of photographs showing children misbehaving. Chapter 6 describes a special set of twenty case studies of supply teachers. These teachers have to manage a variety of classes, often at short notice, so we felt a great deal could be learned from them. Interviews and photographs of disruptive classroom scenes were used to elicit responses.

One of the most consistent areas of educational research is that of pupil perceptions of teaching. No study of class management would be complete without the pupil perspective, and chapter 7 describes the findings from several hundred interviews with primary pupils, in which we used the same chapter 8 and 9, on the other hand, focus specifically on teachers' management of two important professional classroom skills: explaining, often reported as the one most valued by children, and questioning. Chapter 8 reports a study of 128 explanations to children aged 8 and 9, and chapter 9 describes an analysis of over 1, 000 questions asked by primary teachers.

Another significant area of interest was how teachers manage the subject matter of their lessons, especially in fields where they do not feel especially competent. As was mentioned in Chapter 1 there is an enormous range of subject matter to be mastered during the compulsory years of schooling. Many primary teachers have found problems coping with the subject knowledge required in fields like science and technology. A later chapter describes two large-scale national surveys we conducted of over a thousand teachers in which we asked them how competent they felt to teach the different subjects and also the extent to which they could teach specific topics in subjects like English, mathematics and science with their existing subject knowledge. There is also a study of teachers teaching what to them was unfamiliar strategies they employed and what problems they encountered.

Finally we focused specifically on student teachers learning this array of management skills. During the project we observed and interviewed numerous student teachers and a later chapter brings together the work we did on teaching strategies, attitude change during teaching practice, and views on disruption in the stand of the project which I directed. There is also a great deal of relevant information about trainees in *Learning to Teach,* the parallel book of research findings to this one written by Neville Bennett and Clive Carre (Bennett and Carre, 1993). A later chapter gives an overview, in the light of the Leverhulme Primary Project research, of the skills primary teachers need for the present and the future, and the sort of training that might be necessary for both beginners and experienced teachers.

3

First Encounters with a Class

Every September a traditional set of rituals is repeated in thousands of primary schools: 5 year olds commence school for the first time; 6 year olds return to find they are no longer the novices of their school; 7 year olds move on to the junior school, or to a higher class in their present school; other classes meet their new teachers; parents wonder whether their children will settle in; teachers establish themselves with their new class, meet new pupils, renew acquaintance with others they have taught before. Not surprisingly, these first encounters have been less well documented and analysed than later phases in the year. It is common for researchers seeking to visit and observe classes early in the year to be asked to come back in late September or early October 'when things have settled down'. First encounters can be private affairs, even in schools which are normally open to observation and scrutiny.

Yet patterns can be laid down in these first few days, rules and relationships established, which, for good or ill, will affect both children and teachers, possibly throughout the year, so we felt it was very important to undertake case studies of a number of student and experienced teachers to see first of all what their aspirations and intentions were and, secondly, what actually transpired when teachers and pupils met for the first time. Such research is much more labour-intensive in the primary school than in the secondary school. When we analysed several hundred lessons in secondary schools as part of a first-encounters' study (Wragg and Wood 1984), it was possible for one observer to watch the lessons of three or four different teachers. Secondary teachers may take five or six different classes each day, sometimes even more, so it is possible for an investigator to see several different teachers, each meeting a new class for the first or second time. In primary schools it is much more likely that each teacher will only have one class, so a separate observer is required for every teacher studied.

A number of social psychologists have looked at first encounters between human beings in a variety of social settings. Goffman (1971) has described the process of impression management which commences at first meetings and continues through subsequent encounters:

> The individual's initial projection commits him to what he is proposing to be and requires him to drop all pretences of being other things. As the interaction among the participants progresses, additions and modifications in this informational state will of course occur, but it is essential that these later developments be related without contradiction to, and even built up from the initial positions taken by the several participants.

Argyle (1967) has described the rapidity with which people reach conclusions about those they meet, the difference in sensitivity of acute observers, like Sherlock Holmes, and the mental patients whose perceptions appear distorted, and the growth of relationships in the early period of acquaintance:

> A will categorize B in terms of social class, race, age, intelligence or whatever dimensions of people

> are most important to him, and this will activate the appropriate set of social techniques on the part of A. It is found that people vary widely in what they look for first in others.

It is not merely the individual personalities which are important when people meet. The social setting is also a powerful influence on events: whether one person meets another as a colleague, employer, supplicant, whether someone holds a certain rank or status, wears a uniform, whether the encounter is in private or in public, between two people or several, takes place informally on the street, in a home, or formally at a gathering, in an institution or workplace.

When teachers meet a new class of pupils, a variety of social, environmental and institutional factors are at work in addition to the effects of the several individual personalities involved. Teachers, whatever their individual style, are known to be legally *in loco parentis*. They are inescapably part of a national, local and professional culture, even if they personally reject a number of aspects of it.

When teachers have been in a school for some time their reputation will precede them and pupil folklore will have told their new classes a great deal about what to expect. Experienced teachers who have moved to another school frequently express surprise during their first few weeks about the difficulty of establishing their identity in a new location after their previous school in which so much could be taken for granted. Supply teachers in particular have to become adept at managing first encounters in new and varying locations because they have so many of them, and our case studies of twenty supply teachers are not included in this chapter.

Evertson and Anderson (1978) studied twenty-seven

teachers of third-grade classes in eight American elementary schools for the first three weeks of the school war, followed by occasional visits later in the school year. They used a mixture of interviews and observations of lessons, concentrating largely on pupils' engagement in their task. Those teacher who secured highest pupil involvement as measured by their schedule showed more evidence of having thought in advance about rules and procedures, gave more time to clarifying rules and procedures, and introduced their pupils gradually to independent work. This kind of study is of considerable interest, but is sometimes criticised for being self-fulfilling, that is, by setting a premium on task involvement, finding that formal and carefully structured teaching is 'effective'.

Eltis (1978), in an Australian study, concentrated on the extent to which impressions formed in early lessons influenced subsequent events. He found that both experienced and student teachers' perceptions of pupils were influenced by speech, appearance, voice and written work. Pupils' accents were thought to be particularly influential on teachers' early and subsequent judgements. He also found that both beginning and experienced teachers were reluctant to discuss pupils' progress and attributes during this early phase.

Eisenhart (1977) concentrated on teachers' methods of establishing control in her two-year study of fifth- and sixth-grade classes in a city in the southern United States. Most teachers assigned seats to pupils rather than let them choose one, and several developed their own distinct style of control from the beginning. One teacher capitalised on the impending arrival of autumn by writing each pupil's name on a leaf which was pinned to a large picture of a tree. Children were exhorted to keep their leaf from failing, and miscreants found their personal leaf removed from sight.

Soar (1973) followed the progress of a cohort of children in 289 kindergarten, first- and second-grade classes for three years. In a smaller-scale study of twenty teachers who were especially high or low in class control, he found that teachers with a high degree of control had started by permitting little pupil freedom and then increasing it, and teachers with a low degree of control had begun with high pupil freedom which they then attempted to decrease.

Some investigators have concentrated on the establishment of classroom rules. Buckley (1977), in an ethnographic study of one classroom, identified thirty-two rules, of which twenty-two had been spoken of in some form by the teacher within the first six days of the school year. Of these thirty-two rules some fifteen came from outside the classroom, mainly from the principal. A number of rules emerged after the initial period, such as when a pupil in the third week played in a certain courtyard during break and was total by the teacher on duty that this was not allowed, even though no formal announcements had ever been made. Some rules were established indirectly and by euphemism. The teacher, rather than state that cheating was not permitted, proclaimed that some pupils 'had big eyes'.

In a study of forty-one secondary teachers and trainees Wragg and Wood (1984) analysed over 300 lessons given at the beginning of the school year or of teaching practice. It was found that many experienced teachers established a big public presence in the very first lesson, making extensive use of their eyes to sweep the class or engage individuals. The most common classroom rule noted was 'no talking when the teacher is talking' (in public situations), followed by 'no disruptive noises', and rules about entering and leaving the classroom and not interfering with the work of others. Student teachers concentrated on the subject matter of their first lesson, on 'making an impact', and were less likely to use their eyes to sweep the class. Experienced teachers tended to focus more on establishing a climate, and stressed rules that had a moral dimension, like the 'proper' way to set out work, or respect for property. They were also much clearer than students, in interview, about what they expected and how they would conduct their lessons, whereas some students said that rules would be established as the need arose, rather than predetermined.

Several investigators into aspects of teacher or pupil expectancy and the way people typify each other have also identified factors which can be of concern during initial meetings. King (1978) observed infant teachers in three schools, and described how they typified children mainly from their own perceptions in the classroom rather than from written reports of other teachers, and how their typification changed as the school year proceeded. Nash (1973) used personal construct theory to study what constructs eight junior school teachers had assembled about the children they taught. He found that teachers based their perception of the children they taught largely in terms of personality and behaviour rather than ability. Hargreaves (1977) identified three models of teacher typification from the literature, an ideal-matching model whereby pupils are set against some imaginary paragon, a characteristic model which is like an identikit, and a dynamic interactionist model, favoured by symbolic interactionists, which tries to reflect the effects of context and the changes in perception which occur over time as a result of events. Anderson *et al.* (1980) and Emmer (1985) have also summarised some of the findings on the first part of the school year.

The Study of Experienced Teachers

We decided to undertake a study of twenty experienced

teachers and both to interview them in July about their intentions in the following September, and then to observe them for the first three days of the school year. In order to recruit sufficient observers primary specialist student teachers in the final stages of their course were trained as interviewers and classroom observers, using specially devised interview and observation schedules. Contact was made with schools in different parts of the country near to the students' homes, so that travel was minimised, A choice was made in each case from the local list of schools and in all cases the first or second randomly selected school agreed to participate. The twenty teachers were interviewed extensively in July and then observed for the first three days of the school year in the following September. Field workers used three schedules altogether, an interview schedule, a first lesson observation schedule and a subsequent lessons observation schedule. Several group and individual training sessions were held, using videotapes to train the twenty field workers. The schedules concentrated on qualitative data, and so every item was discussed in detail and a high level of agreement on principles and conventions was reached before observations and interviews began. Observers were given considerable help with the nature of field notes that would be needed, with numerous specific exemplars.

Of the twenty case studies six teachers were male and fourteen female. All were very experienced, with from eleven to thirty years of teaching with a mean of 19.3 years. Half had originally qualified exclusively as primary teachers and half as secondary only or primary and secondary. Nine were deputy heads with full teaching programmes. Preliminary interviews showed that most were satisfied with their job, were appreciative of the quality of relationships, the facilities available, but were more critical where facilities were poor, as they were in several schools. Twelve were critical of the quality of accommodation and felt that this hindered them in their work. Sixteen operated in traditional closed classrooms, two in open-plan and two in what they described as 'semi-open-plan'. Much concern about the beginning of the year concerned the poor layout of the school, lack of space for storage and display, lack of sinks, hot water, bookcases, poor decoration and other features which they felt made a bad impression on incoming children. Expressions like 'diabolical', 'barely adequate' and primary schools being 'the Cinderella of the education system' confirmed this concern and shame over the working environment. Few teachers had extra help, though fourteen made use of parent helpers in the classroom. Class sizes observed ranged from fifteen to thirty-nine with a mean of twenty-nine, and most classes had roughly equal numbers of boys and girls.

Preparation and Planning Intentions

Only seven teachers said they knew all or most of their new pupils, but most claimed they would not know their new pupils other than from playground duty or perhaps from occasional first aid or deputy head duties. When asked whether there was anything they wanted to know about their new class which would help them teach well or hinder them, fifteen mentioned features such as the reputation of the class, whether they worked well or badly together, what able or special-needs children they would be teaching and who might have behavioural difficulties. One teacher said she was really looking forward to taking her new class simply because it was known to be a difficult one: 'Every school has one class no teacher would like to teach. This is one of them.'

When asked about differences in style between their approach and that of the previous class teacher, thirteen thought there would be a significant difference, two a slight difference and five said no difference at all. Amongst features mentioned most frequently were being more formal, more structured, more organised and more strict, with higher standards and a closer 1 check on children's work. Eight of the twelve who commented mainly on these features stressed their intention to be deliberately mote firm and structured than their predecessor. It is difficult to say whether this tendency might be widespread, but it is noteworthy that, at the intention stage at least, there is such a conscious emphasis on greater firmness and less tolerance of low standards. It is one of the shortcomings of the present study that we were not able to monitor these particular classes throughout the year to see if stated intentions were implemented.

We also asked teachers about their preparation for their very first lessons, what they would prepare, what they would do and think about an hour before and five minutes before meeting the, children. A diversity of responses was noted. An hour before the first meeting many would be concentrating on actual preparation, checking and actually rehearsing in their minds what they would be doing, down, to going through their intended opening words mentally in some cases. Questions in teachers' minds varied from immediate ones like 'Will all the children expected actually turn up?' and, from a teacher of younger children, 'How many children will cry?' to the longer-term 'How will this class develop during the year?'. Some of the deputy heads also had to consider general school issues like 'Have the steps been repaired?' About half expressed general feelings of hope or excitement. In the last five minutes before the children entered the class most said they would have completed their preparations and would try to relax, one with deep breathing exercises, another with a cup of coffee. Some of the deputies were aware that they would probably have general duties, like seeing all the children in from the playground and then meeting their own class. Other likely activities mentioned were talking to parents, wondering how the children would be feeling, and dealing with problems. Four of the teachers taught infant age classes and the other sixteen juniors. Twelve of the teachers taught children in the 9-11 age group.

The Very First Encounter

A separate schedule A was devised for the very first encounter. Most of it was the same us schedule B, which was used for all subsequent lessons, but there were additional sections in which to record whether teachers introduced themselves, showed or talked about different areas of the room, or talked about school or classroom rules. The first session observed occupied typically ninety to 100 minutes and included an assembly. All teachers were well prepared for the children's arrival, and in sixteen cases there were specific worksheets or assignment cards for children to do in the first session. In only four cases did pupils enter the classroom before the teacher. Of the others, eight were already there waiting for the class to arrive and eight accompanied the pupils into the room. Both the formality of the actual entry into the room and the subsequent degree of 'chaos' were coded by the research team on a 1-5 point scale, with 1 being the most formal room entry and 5 representing a very unorganised arrival, and similarly for 'chaos', with' 1 representing none and 5 a great deal. The word 'chaos' here should be dry-cleaned of its usual pejorative overtone. That a particular classroom was in some disarray during the first few minutes of the school year, as parents and children arrived, did not necessarily mean that no effective learning would take place during the rest of the day, as the account in this chapter shows.

It is possible for the two scales to differ, in that an entry may be informal hut not necessarily followed by chaos. Two extracts from observers' logs reveal the range:

Formal entry (scoring 1 for formality and 1 for lack of chaos) The class (of 10-11 year olds) were assembled outside (the room) and told to get their dinner money ready and line up. The class were then told to lead in, wait across the front of the room and await further instructions as to where they should sit. A reminder was given not to talk. The class did as they were told.

Informal entry (scoring 5 for informality and 5 for chaos) The (5-6 year old) pupils came into the room informally along with some parents. The teacher was in the room trying to converse with a worried parent. The children were told to sit on the mat, but few obeyed the instruction. There was a lot of excited chatter and confusion - a state which continued until the bell went and parents left.

Table 3.1 shows the very mixed pattern of entry for the twenty teachers.

Once children had entered the classroom and been seated the degree of orderliness tended to remain steady or increase. In only three classes did observers record greater disorder. Teachers used various devices for establishing or maintaining order. One teacher of 7-8 year olds calmed down noisy children who were sitting on the carpet by saying they were to be quiet so that they would be 'the best class in the school'. An older class of 10-11 year olds became more aggressive post-entry, fighting over where to sit, confused in some cases, walking around wearing coats and carrying bags, as the teacher had not arrived and chairs were on tables, so no one could sit down.

TABLE 3.1

Degree of Formality and Chaos on 1-5 Point Scales During Opening Session of the Year (1 = Highest Degree of Formality, 1 = Least Amount of Chaos)

Formality score	*Chaos score*	*Number of teachers*
1	1	1
1	2	2
2	2	3
3	2	3
3	3	2
3	4	1
4	3	1
4	4	2
4	5	1
5	2	2
5	4	1
5	5	1

Observers noted down what happened when teachers first sought to gain the attention of their class. Only three made a formal attempt to greet their class, saying. 'Good morning class 7,' 'Good morning, everyone. I hope you had a nice holiday.' and 'Good morning, everyone. Did you have a good holiday?' respectively. However, observers' notes show that few actually needed to introduce themselves as they were known to the pupils, having taught them previously or met them in a previous term's induction session. One teacher said to the class, 'Everybody knows me. I don't know you all yet, but by the end of the day I will.' Some teachers used non-verbal signals, a male teacher of 11 year olds, for example, being described as standing hands on hips until pupils fell silent. Most common attention gaining words were 'Right' and variants of 'Could you all please listen.' This was usually followed by instructions about seating, register calling and talk about lunchtime arrangements. In the majority of cases children became immediately attentive, but observers recorded non-attentive behaviour in seven classrooms: that pupils carried on whispering excitedly, continued conversations begun in the playground or fiddled with artefacts like pencil cases or bags. Usually this non-attention was picked up, except in two cases, by the teacher naming the child, asking for silence or directing questions specifically at those not attending. In half the classes there was sonic introduction to the classroom and its resources—the reading corner, for example.

One feature of the first session of the first day, usually with older pupils, was a strong moral exhortation. This confirmed to some extent what teachers had said in interview the previous July about wanting higher standards than the previous teacher. Instances recorded by observers included a statement by one, teacher of top primary pupils that they were 'VIPs' who should set an example, 'image setters' for the whole school. Other teachers made similar appeals and assertions. Some schools were to take a selective 11+ test later in the year to determine which secondary school they should attend, and success in this was sometimes linked to a responsibility to 'have a good year and reap the rewards'.

This moral exhortation was often reinforced in the first school assembly, which frequently took place on the first morning. In addition to the hymns and prayers there were examples of several explicit or implicit purposes, such as establishing control, inspiring, informing, laying down of rules, outlining of expectations, establishment or reinforcement of the school ethos, 'making a fresh start', assertion of community values, as the following recorded incidents reveal:

1. The head praised pupils oh how smart they looked and asked them to keep it up.

2. When you come into assembly, imagine a zip across your mouth. It is your responsibility to keep it closed.'
3. Class 7 (the oldest pupils) had had a poor reputation the year before. The head told them they would be expected to behave well and show a high degree of responsibility, now they were the top class.
4. A theme, 'the importance of friendship', was introduced.
5. The children were told the story of Robert the Bruce, and the moral message it contained, to keep on trying, was emphasised.
6. The head said That the school rules were based on 'common sense, such as taking care.of people'.
7. Children were told not to come to school before nine o'clock as they would not be allowed into the building.
8. The head asked pupils to look at her during assembly when she was talking. One small group of pupils did not do this, so she stared at them until they did.

What characterises this very first encounter at the beginning of the school year is the very multiplicity of purposes it must fulfil. A significant part of this is children's socialisation into a new yet, in most cases, familiar environment. There are conventions to learn - how the register is called, what happens about school dinners, where one sits, hangs clothes, puts bags. In addition, there are rules specific to the new teacher - where free movement is permitted, how to set out work, what noise level is tolerated, what happens when pupils misbehave and, indeed, what constitutes misbehaviour, a topic which will be dealt with again in chapters 4, 5 and 7. An interesting aspect of this initial socialisation occurred when choice of seating was analysed. The continuum was from high teacher direction to completely free choice. Three teachers simply assigned each pupil to a seat, there was no choice: eight offered a partial choice, some permitted pupils to select a seat, others told them where to sit because of specific circumstances or known bad behaviour: three teachers offered free choice, but warned that it was a privilege dependent on good behaviour and that miscreants would be reseated at the teacher's behest; finally, six teachers offered a completely free choice of seat with no conditions attached, though in some cases this was for the first session only, while other matters were sorted out.

Teachers' reasons for their seating policies were sometimes stated explicitly and sometimes concealed. One teacher of 10-11 year olds began in a highly directive manner:

> Now I have decided on places for you this half-term. This is based on maths groups. There is no point in sitting next to children on different books. I change places regularly. The set places I have decided on are ...' [naming each child and indicating assigned seat].

The surface reason here seems to be an ability grouping, but the teacher explained that this was a class which had acquired a bad reputation and she was determined not to let it continue. In practice each group consisted of similar numbers of boys and girls. A number of teachers in the 'semi-directive' category specified a gender mix, as in the case of the teacher who began. 'Sit where you like, but I want a mixture of boys and girls on each table.' The general convention, with these exceptions, appeared to be conditional freedom of choice, contingent on what the teacher regarded as responsible exercising of that freedom.

With so much attention to socialisation and administrative routines, the academic content of the very first session of the year took second place. Some kind of reading or writing activity was the most common focus noted by observers, a handwriting exercise, writing about what children had done on, holiday, silent reading being noted in half the cases. Three examples of maths (one as assessment test), two of art and one of music (hymn practice) were also recorded. The tasks were generally common to the whole class, though a small number of teachers began immediately with group work. The majority of classes settled down to the task in hand immediately, and only in four cases was more than two minutes needed before children commenced their work. The longest recorded settling-down and starting point was four to five minutes for a group given a writing assignment. Early signs of classroom rule establishment often occurred at this stage and teachers usually commented on noise if it occurred, saying, 'I want no talking when I'm talking,' or 'Only the occasional chat with your neighbour. No more.' In nineteen out of twenty classrooms there was no recorded comment about excessive noise. In the remaining class the observer noted that the level of noise did appear to be distracting, especially when the teacher left the room.

In order to take stock of this very first session, observers were asked to make a 'dipstick' report at roughly the half-way stage, recording what was happening some forty-five or fifty minutes into the first day. By this point in the day, fourteen out of twenty classes were expected by the teacher to be engaged on some specific task. Of the remaining six, three were sorting out resources, one was engaged in registration and dinner money one was mid-way in transition between two assignments, and the other was returning from assembly. Many of the teachers were walking round the mom monitoring work, checking progress, collecting dinner money, talking to individuals, or engaging in several of these activities. Only two remained seated at their desk and another two stood at the front of the class.

Observer frequently commented on the nature of individual interactions. These often. reflected the 'firm but friendly' manner that teachers had described in their interviews the previous July, with emphasis on personal understanding:

> the teacher knew something about every child. In some cases 'she, had taught other members of their family, even some parents, [she took] time to chat about each family and check whether they [the children] liked a shortened or full version of their names . . .

A teacher of 6-7 year olds was described as 'very friendly towards children, although she expects what is said to be done. [She is] well prepared, both with activities and resources. No need for much checking from the teacher, as the children are very quiet and apprehensive.'

There was only one exception to this generally businesslike first session, when one teacher did not leave enough time for children to carry out an activity involving their new trays—'disorganisation and chaos set in, with a resulting increase in the amount of noise and too many children moving about in a narrow area'. Although observers were asked specifically to record behaviour judged to be 'inappropriate', there was very little of it in this first session, after the occasional chaos of the first few minutes. Some classes were excited and had to be quietened, but it was more likely that, as one observer described it, 'the children were playing safe and responding with care'. Such mildly deviant behaviour as was recorded tended to occur towards the end of the first session or when the teacher left the room or was occupied with some administrative task.

At the end of these first sessions, usually at playtime, or going to assembly followed by playtime, few instructions were given, as most pupils were familiar with the school's routines for assemblies and morning break. Six classes were given a five or ten-minute warning. Actual dismissal of the class was, however, quite tightly organised in sixteen of the classes, though four classes simply left the room informally. Nine of the classes were lined up at the door, six were dismissed group by group, and the dismissal of the remaining class was not recorded by the observer.

General comments were made by observers at the end of this first session on aspects of class management that seemed worthy of note. Many of these reinforced and restated the generally businesslike nature of what had been a mixture of administration, familiarisation and a certain amount of writing or leading work, mostly done in a friendly manner. One teacher's use of both voice and non-verbal communication was described, showing her use of eye contact for control, something identified by other observers as a notable lecture:

> She regains attention by raising the tone of her voice. Her basic attitude is a very friendly one. She uses her eyes a lot and smiles. She talks a lot but tolerates orderly interruption. The situation is controlled by her looking at the child she wishes to speak to. The others stop talking and everyone given a fair chance.

This predominant image of the very first session in the primary school year is in marked contrast to the study we conducted of secondary teachers' first encounters (Wragg and Wood 1984). Whereas a friendly smile, businesslike manner and benign firmness characterised the presentation of self by the twenty primary teachers in this present study, the twenty secondary teachers' in the earlier study were more aggressively assertive. Most of them stressed in interview the need to project a larger-than-life image in order to establish social control over potentially disruptive adolescents, summed up by one teacher as 'I'm very stern and very hard. I am consciously being a little harder than I am.' Observation of secondary teachers' lessons showed a similar use of eyes to sweep the whole class or engage in eye contact, but the use of a harsh voice, a higher degree of public reprimanding and a very territorial manner (my classroom, my lab) were much more in evidence. Primary teachers used a much gentler manner, orientated towards the individual pupil, with little angularity and no example of public shaming in these first sessions. Social control was certainly established in almost every case, but with none of the overt dominance and aggression noted in the earlier study of secondary teachers.

Establishing and Maintaining Rules

A significant feature of the first three days of the school year which were observed in this study was the establishment, maintenance or reaffirmation of rules. Many human activities are governed by rules of conduct, and learning what these formal rules or informal conventions are, when to follow and when, perhaps more occasionally, to break them, and about the consequences of conformity or dissension, are commonplace both in childhood and in adult life. In school there are the *national rules*, many incorporated in Acts of Parliament, which govern attendance, parental rights and duties, or the use of punishment: there are *local authority rules*, perhaps a code of conduct in physical education lessons or on field trips; there are *school rules*, concerning dress, behaviour in classroom and playground; and finally there are *individual teacher rules* about talking, moving and setting out work or behaviour.

Interviews with teachers in July showed that about three-quarters said they expected to introduce rules from the first session and one said the first session would be devoted largely to rule setting. Others were less explicit, feeling that rules would emerge more as the need arose, and one saying that there was little point in giving too many at any one time as 'they wouldn't remember anyway'. Analysis of interview responses showed that rules could be grouped under several headings, such as movement, talking or work-related. The following nine categories of teacher rules were identified:

1. Movement

Walk quietly.
No running.
Ask first if you want to go to the toilet.
Don't just wander around the room unless you're getting something.
Stick to chosen seat.

2. Talking

Don't talk when I'm talking to you.
You should only be talking to each other if it's about your work.
Don't talk when someone is answering a question.
Only one person talking at a time.
No shouting out.
Put your hands up if you want to ask a question.
Silence during registration.
Silence in the library area.
Listen to the teacher and other pupils.

3. Work-related

Being able to work independently on your own.
Being able to work harmoniously in a group.

Working quietly even if the teacher is out of the room.

Getting out your own tray at the beginning of the day, after lunch or after playtime, and then starting work without having to be told.

Not distracting or spoiling the concentration of others when they are working.

4. *Presentation*

Knowing how to set out work and when to hand it in.

Taking care with content.

5. *Safety*

Care with cupboards, sinks.

Care with scissors, rulers, pencils.

No swinging on chairs.

No playing on slippery banks in wet weather.

6. *Space*

Not allowed in classroom at break.

During wet weather being allowed in school or classroom to read, play games or sit quietly.

This classroom is a work area, not a play area.

7. *Materials*

Equipment to be handled carefully and kept in its proper place.

Keep library books tidy.

Know the correct place for returning equipment or unused materials.

Put things away properly at the end of the day.

Clothing and PE equipment to be kept on pegs.

No writing on desks or book covers.

Return borrowed items to their owner.

Stack chairs on or under tables or desks at the end of the day.

8. Social Behaviour

Show consideration for others.
Be willing to share things and co-operate.
Don't go into someone else's tray unless you've been told to.
Be polite and thoughtful: treat others as you would like to be treated yourself.
Show good manners.

9. Clothing

Clothing to be neat and clean.
Wear uniform properly (i.e. school tie).
All clothing to be labelled.
During hot weather sleeves may be rolled up and cardigans, jackets, pullovers and tie removed.

It is one thing to be able to express a set of rule expectations in a quiet interview in July, but quite another to implement these aspirations amid the rapid-moving novelties of the first session of the school year. Analysis of first sessions showed that sixteen teachers did talk explicitly about classroom rules and that the others also made children aware of rules without describing them in detail, saying, for example, 'You know what we expect of you,' or 'You know what to do.' This taken-for-granted approach to rule establishment or maintenance was particularly noticeable with older pupils. Most of the rules noted in classroom time were teacher rules, sometimes specific to the particular teacher's preferred way of working, whereas in assembly the heads tended to mention school rules about entry and departure or playground behaviour. There was general consistency between what teachers had said in interview and what happened in the classroom, but not exact congruence. For example, one teacher who had expressed in interview a 'no writing on desks' rule did not react when a pupil did write on a desk, as she appeared preoccupied. The numerous demands on a teacher's attention can act as a constraint in rule enforcement.

During the first classroom sessions observed there were fifty examples noted in observers of rule establishment or maintenance. A third of these were related to equipment, materials and resources and involved pens, pencils, notebooks, trays or chairs. A further quarter involved general classroom procedures and sixteen per cent concerned noise levels. Between them, these three aspects covered over three-quarters of all rule-making observed. The remainder dealt with 'dinner money, parental access before school, dress and appearance, movement and personal property.

There were different strategies for the introduction and reiteration of rules. Most frequently, teachers used direct commands, often expressed in precise terms: 'Always bring a book to class,' 'Don't eat pencils,' 'Always underline your work with a ruler - it looks neater.' This last instance is an example of a command plus an explanation, like 'Bring exact change for dinner money, to make life easier.' Some commands were accompanied by a warning: Don't talk when I'm talking, or by the end of term we won't like each other.' Table 3.2 shows the distribution of the fifty rule-setting examples over different categories of strategy:

Rule making is only a first step in the establishment of classroom order and effective working relationships. The first test of teachers' rules comes when they are broken. The major strategy in rule making, as table 3.2 shows, was direct command, the do's and don'ts of classroom life. Observers were asked to made notes about teachers' responses to breaches of their rules, what happened, whether the teacher responded and what the outcome was.

TABLE 3.2

Strategy	*No. of Examples*
Direct command	23
Explanation	5
Statement with expectation	4
Command with warning	3
Command with warning	3
Expectation	2
Statement	2
Question	2
Statement with command	2
Unspecified	2
Expectation with warning	1
Expectation with question	1
Total	50

Only one serious incident occurred, when a newly arrived 5 year old, who was in a highly emotional state, kicked a supply teacher on the shin. The worst incident, apart from that, was when a girl slammed a book on the desk while answering a fellow pupil's question, and scattered some crayons. Chapter 5 deals with pupil disruption in more detail, so, at this stage, the analysis of 223 incidents of what is usually minor misbehaviour during first lessons will be considered. Of these, sixty-five were described and analysed in greater detail by observers and analysts as being particularly illustrative of misbehaviour occurring. The largest category involved talking either too noisily, out of turn, or failing to listen. The other two most common categories were fiddling with items such as rulers, pencil cases or bags, and being out of seat and/or distracting other pupils. There was no physical aggression between pupils, other than two instances of pushing each other. Most of the illicit talk was between pairs of pupils rather than larger groups. Fidgeting and fiddling with artefacts was mostly associated, in the comments of observers, with children losing interest when passive for too long. In about two-thirds of cases teachers checked, by comment, reprimand or statement of a rule, the noisy chatter, usually reacting before it had escalated. Eye contact, moving over to the pupils concerned, touching lightly and moving pupils to another seat, were also recorded as response strategies. The assertions of authority were firm but not as hard and aggressive as had been noted in earlier studies of both male and female secondary teachers: 'Hands, please. Let us have manners at all times,' 'For the moment, I'm the boss. No talking when the teacher is talking.' Reprimands were administered slightly more to individuals than to small groups or the whole class. In 90 per cent of cases the misbehaviour ceased immediately. Only rarely did it not stop at all. This picture confirmed that teachers appeared to follow the rule-making and rule-enforcing behaviour they had described in interview, though demands on their attention, and pressure of objectives to be achieved, sometimes acted as a constraint.

Later Encounters

The patterns of the first week of the school year in the twenty schools we studied were very varied. Even the school day varied in length by fifty minutes, or four hours ten minutes per week. The longest school day recorded was 415 minutes, the shortest 365 minutes. Time spent in the classroom, as opposed to the playground or dining room, also varied by fifty minutes, from 315 minutes down to 265 minutes. Both extremes were witnessed in older junior classes. All except one school operated two morning sessions, the remaining school had just one with a flexible break. A quarter of schools had a single continuous session in the afternoon, the others ran two sessions. Observers commented on the loss of concentration during the late afternoon in schools that had no break.

After the first day teachers' patterns of behaviour did change. The entry routine at the beginning of the day would obviously be different when there was no need to make pupils sit, but registration followed whatever the teacher regarded as her standard pattern. Entry to class at other times did change, however, and it became less likely that the teacher and pupils would enter the room together. More commonly pupils arrived first, often because their teacher had lunchtime or break duties in the playground or elsewhere. Some teachers who had stated in interview their desire to be more formal or not allow misbehaviour were amongst the ones more likely to be in the classroom when the class arrived. Table 3.3 shows a summary of entry behaviour over the three days observed. The later entries were also generally much less formal than on the first morning, with few classes lining up outside. In several cases girls were seen to enter the room first. Although entry was informal it was rarely described as disorderly.

On the first day most teachers had had all necessary materials to hand for the beginning of the session and there were few instances during the day of these not having been prepared by the beginning of the session or of teachers still assembling the necessary equipment or materials as the class arrived. This general pattern of preparedness continued almost unaltered, apart from a very slight tendency for more examples to be recorded of preparation going on as pupils arrived, an increase from two instances on the first day (out of seventy-seven sessions) to five on the third day (out of seventy-one sessions).

Analysis of the first few minutes of each session showed that in most cases work began quickly. Occasional boisterous entrances were recorded, but these were usually followed by orderly work. There was just one exception, a teacher whose lessons always began in an unruly way, and the observer recorded on the first day, 'Entrance noisy . . . fighting over desks and when putting school bags and jumpers into classroom'; on the second day. 'Turbulent pushing and shoving'; on the third day, 'Half the class in by 8.50. Remainder enter in various ways. Much movement between 8.50 and 9.00. one group looking at a book, one group fighting, two children helping teacher. When a bell rings pupils sit down noisily . . . talking, pushing, bickering over a ball.' The children did then get on with some work, but interventions from the teacher were not noted, and no task demand was recorded. A much more typical first few minutes, however, would show pupils entering in an orderly manner but talking to other pupils, sitting down after hanging up coats and beginning to work fairly promptly, usually without the need to be directed, as teachers had made it clear that this was what was expected. In one classroom parents (of 7-8 year olds) came in with the children each morning and the teacher encouraged this. There could delays as a result, one parent, for example, explaining to the teacher about child's medicine, but on another occasion -the day began with a parent showing the class how to make a French plait. Application of the 1-5 'chaos' scale, described earlier, at the outset of the session and after children had taken their seats, showed that usually there was no change or the classroom had become less Chaotic. Table 3.4 shows the analysis of these early minutes of each session. There is very little difference in the three daily patterns. Individual teachers' patterns were also quite consistent. Fourteen teachers' lessons showed a predominant pattern of no change or less chaos, two teachers a pattern of no change or more chaos, and four had mixed patterns.

A further example of rapid socialisation of pupils was shown by the decline in the number of acts of inappropriate behaviour observed during the three days. The following findings must, however, be interpreted with some caution. Although every effort was made during training, through videos, discussion and analysis of lessons, to ensure consistency in what was regarded as 'inappropriate'—for example, distracting others, talking illicitly, fiddling with pencil case instead of working - there were twenty different observers, and it is never possible, with such numbers, to guarantee absolute consistency. With this caveat, it does seem that instances of inappropriate behaviour declined after the first day. Almost all inappropriate behaviour observed was trivial. There was one incident, referred to above, of a distraught 5 year old kicking a supply teacher on the very first morning, and there were examples of pupils fighting for desks or chairs, but most other inappropriate behaviour was noisy chatter and this was almost always reprimanded by the teacher, whereupon, in most cases, it ceased. Table 3.5 summarises some of the inappropriate behaviour data.

There were fifteen teachers whose patterns showed less inappropriate behaviour on day 3 compared with day 1, and five whose sessions showed more, but the general trend was down. Given that the average length of a session was seventy to seventy-five minutes, and some classes were over thirty pupils, the overall mean of fifteen instances per session seems relatively low, and observers' field notes constantly confirm the orderly nature of the classrooms they observed.

TABLE 3.4

Degree of Chaos Post-entry Compared with Actual Entry in 222 Sessions Observed During First Three Days

Nature of change	*Day 1*	*Day 2*	*Day 3*	*Total*
More chaos	15	12	12	39
Less chaos	34	37	33	104
No change	24	18	19	61
Not recorded or unknown	4	7	7	18
Total	77	74	71	222

TABLE 3.5

Number of Instances of Inappropriate Behaviour Per Session

Overall mean number of instances of inappropriate behaviour per session	15.0
Mean number of instances of inappropriate behaviour per session, day 1	16.3
Mean number of instances of inappropriate behaviour per session, days 2 and 3	14.3
Teacher with highest mean number of instances per session	27.4
Teacher with lowest mean number of instances per session	3.8

Relationships continued to be friendly, with most teachers fine-tuning classroom rules by restating them or by commenting on an event. On one occasion, on the third day, for example, several children who had finished rushed towards the teacher's desk, something which had not happened on the first or second day. She told them there was no need to rush once they had completed a piece of work and no further instance was noted. Though the formality of the first morning was reduced in most cases on the second and third days, it was noticeable that those teachers who, in interview, had said they would be more strict than the previous teacher were usually quickest to react to inappropriate behaviour, except for one teacher who made no such efforts.

There will be further comment on these first encounters in chapter 11 when our research into student teachers is described, as they were also studied for he first few days of their block teaching practice, and some interesting comparisons can be made. It is a pity there have been so few studies of first encounters, as it is a fascinating area of classroom research. Skilful teachers observed in this study were able to receive as many as thirty-nine children, in the case of the largest class observed, a group of 9-10 year olds, and, despite the boisterous excitement, apprehension and noisy chatter of the first arrival, set them to work in an orderly manner within a short time. This was almost always done in a friendly but firm manner, with rules made explicit, in most cases, from the beginning. There was much exhortation in assembly, as well as in class, about the need for higher horizons, good behaviour, good standards of work, but there was very little of the harsher-voiced authoritarian stance taken by secondary teachers in a similar study (Wragg and Wood. 1984) by the present writer. The rapidity with which even children with difficult behaviour problems or anxieties became absorbed in activity is illustrated by these extracts from a researcher's notes of a reception class on the first day of the year.

The school is a large nursery and first school for 3-8 year olds in the middle of a huge working-class estate. From 8.30 onwards children arrive, some alone, some in twos and threes, sometimes with sometimes without their parents. Whole families appear - mother. Grandma, Granddad, the child starting school, often a younger brother or sister, maybe two, with one in a pushchair, even the family dog. It is a big family occasion. By nine o'clock most children are in school and the street outside is deserted apart from the occasional passer-by or late arrival. Mrs A. has about two-thirds of her class present. She sits in a chair with the children around her feet. They talk about dinners, classroom rituals, who knows who in the class and where children might sit. Every five minutes or so a parent appears at the door with a child. An extra teacher, brought in for the first week, is on hand to feed in the latecomers. By 9.30 the class appears to be complete and children are assigned to tables where they choose an activity from several possibilities ...

... at 10.20 there is an ear-splitting yell from down the corridor. The last arrival has appeared. She is clearly not enamoured of the idea of coming to school and her cries of 'No, Mummy, I don't want to, go,' are joined in counterpoint by her mother's audible threats, bribes and oaths, `I'll come and fetch you at tea time,' 'You've *got* to go to school or I'll get into trouble.' Outside Mrs A.'s classroom the extra supply teacher attempts to soothe parent and child. 'What's her name? Tina, is it? Well, come with me, Tina, and I'll take you into Mrs A.'s room.' Tina kicks her violently on the shin.

The supply teacher brings Tina and her mother into the classroom. She sits Tina down at a table and starts to do a jigsaw with her. 'I'm just going to have a word with Mrs A., I'll be back in a second.' Meanwhile, Tina's mother slips gratefully out of the room. A brief ten-second conversation between the supply teacher and Mrs A. follows, in which the supply teacher says she will leave Tina to get on with the jigsaw. She returns to the table and crouches alongside Tina. 'Oh, well done. You're good at jigsaws, aren't you, Tina?' With that she mutters a vague 'I'll be back soon' and leaves the room. A couple of minutes later Mrs A. goes over to Tina. 'You've nearly finished that,

Tina, well done. Here's a box of building bricks. When you've finished see if you can build something nice and then I'll come and have a look at it...

For the whole of the day Tina worked assiduously alongside the rest of the class, slightly reserved, but indistinguishable from the others, doing the activities, taking her lunch, playing in the playground during breaks.

The supply teacher made a brief return visit to see how she was, but by then she was immersed in constructing an elaborate arrangement of building bricks and barely looked up. At 3.15 she listened attentively as the teacher read the class a story, congratulated the children on their good behaviour and said she was looking forward to seeing them all the following day. At 3.30 the bell rang for the end of school and parents clustered outside the classroom to collect their children. Tina's mother appeared, pale-faced and anxiously asking how she had got on. 'Fine.' replied Mrs A. 'See you tomorrow, Tina,' whereupon Tina burst into tears. Her mother may well have been convinced that she had spent the day on the rack. The following day, however. Tina came to school on time, was calm in appearance and manifested no outward signs of distress about school.

4

Systematic Studies of Class Management

Managing the very first encounters with a new class is an important aspect of teaching, but sustaining and enhancing rules, relationships, application to the task in hand, preparation and planning must go on throughout the time that teachers and pupils are together. In order to monitor what happened in these more mature phases of the school year or term, once daily routines had been established, we decided to study the classrooms of a sample of experienced and novice teachers in different kinds of schools. Schools in ten local authorities were approached as being representative of a variety of large and small urban and rural schools. Thirty schools agreed to participate, and between one and nine teachers were observed in each school, giving a total of sixty teachers and students, of whom fifty-one were female and nine were male. Each was observed for four sessions, except for one teacher who was ill for several weeks and so was only observed for three sessions. The distribution of teachers and lessons is shown in table 4.1. This chapter concentrates on the quantitative data from these observations.

A mixture of observation methods was used, some structured and quantified, others semi-structured, yet others

TABLE 4.1

Number of teachers and lessons observed in present sample

Region	*Teachers*	*Lessons*
North-west	25	100
London East End	9	35
South-west	14	56
Student teachers in South-west	12	48
Total	60	239

freehand. There were interviews with the teachers as well as observations of their 'lessons'. For this purpose a session, which usually lasted between half an hour and an hour, was termed a 'lesson', though it may have consisted of more than a single type of activity. The observer used first of all a version of the Nottingham Class Management Observation Schedule (Wragg 1984). This *is* a category system in which the researcher ticks any of seventy activities which occur in each observation period: what teachers do, what pupils do, what the outcome is, as well as the degree of deviance. This is done for five separate lesson segments lasting ninety seconds each, once the session has begun. Thus 1,195 lesson segments were analysed from the 239 lessons observed. Most of the categories in the Nottingham Class Management Observation Schedule were used, but several were dropped, as primary classrooms are more complex to observe than secondary, so, for example, the three pupil movement categories of the original 'at wrong time', 'at wrong speed', 'to wrong place' were put together as 'inappropriate movement'. The principal focus in the schedule is on the teacher's handling of misbehaviour.

The definition of 'deviance' in classroom observation is not an easy matter. To some extent it is defined by the teacher. One teacher may permit free movement, another forbids pupils to leave their seats without permission.

However, observers do have to make a number of personal decisions about what constitutes deviant behaviour, for a teacher may ignore, albeit rarely, one pupil hitting another, and though this may appear to legitimate such behaviour in one classroom, it would not constitute acceptable behaviour in most. Observers took what were perceived as the teacher's rules of conduct as a starting point, but had to exercise judgement about misbehaviour that would have been perceived as deviant in most other classrooms. It is a judgement between the individual and the norm which is by no means perfect, but observers did reach a high degree of agreement about interpretations before the research began, and maintained it through the duration of the study, as described below.

The second part of the schedule involves a sweep of every pupil in the class. The observer studies each pupil in turn for twenty seconds and then makes two decisions about on-task behaviour and deviance. The on-task behaviour category involves a decision as to whether the child being observed spends roughly 0-6 seconds, 7-13 seconds or 14-20 seconds on the task in hand. 'Mild' deviance is defined as misbehaviour like noisy or illicit talk, distraction of others, or wrong movement, whereas 'more serious' deviance includes violence to another pupil or to the teacher, insulting behaviour to the teacher, or damage to property. An involvement and a deviance index are then calculated by the following formula:

$$\text{Involvement or deviance index} = \frac{\text{Factor A} \times 100}{\text{Number of pupils} \times 2}$$

In each case, factor A is calculated by weighting each of the three observation categories 0. 1 or 2 and multiplying by the number of pupils in each category. Thus if, out of twenty-eight pupils, two were 'low' on task, ten were 'medium' and sixteen were 'high', then factor A would be

(2 x 0) + (10 + 0) + (16 × 2) = 42. Inserted into the involvement equation, this would give an index score of 75, that is, 42 divided by 56 (twice the number of pupils, times 100. The deviance index score is calculated in a similar manner. The possible range, therefore, is from 0 to 100, a score of 0 being obtained if all pupils were low on-task and not deviant, and a maximum score of 100 achieved if all were on task and behaving in a more seriously deviant manner. This is inevitably a rough-and-ready estimate, as the categories could be weighted in different ways, or not weighted at all, but it was used consistently in each lesson, so despite its limitations it is of some interest.

Two trained observers carried out the observations and, in order to checks the extent to which they agreed or disagreed with others, two inter-observer agreement measures were taken, before and after the fieldwork. A percentage agreement figure was used, that is, the percentage of times the two observers agreed with each other on all the categories for five lesson observation segments. Observations were done on videotapes so that observers' ratings could be compared before and after the fieldwork. The use of percentages would be open to criticism if there were many unlikely categories like 'teacher flies through window' or events that never occurred, but the schedule consists of categories of behaviour all of which have been observed in classrooms. Agreement between observers was very high. Inter-observer agreement (comparing one observer with another) was 95.2 per cent before the fieldwork and 88.6 per cent after completion of all observation. Intra-observer agreement (the extent to which observers agree with themselves on two different ratings of the same videotaped lesson) was also very high, with observer A scoring 87.6 per cent, and observer B 88.1 per cent. The observation schedule does, therefore, seem to have been applied with a high degree of consistency.

Qualitative data were collected using two different approaches. The first involved the collection of 'critical events', that is, instances of classroom, behaviour which the observer judged to be illustrative of some aspect of the teacher's class management, perhaps a rule being established, observed or broken, an aspect of interpersonal relationships or some other indicative event. The 'critical events' approach is based on the 'critical incidents' technique developed by Flanagan (1949). The observer wrote down what led up to the event, what happened and what the outcome was. After the lesson, teachers were interviewed and asked for their perception of what happened. The interviewer used neutral language like 'Can you tell me about . . .?' rather than loaded or leading questions, such as 'Why didn't you ...?'.

The second source of qualitative data was through the use of three photographs in the interviews with teachers. These were employed in other parts of the Leverhulme Primary Project to interview student teachers, class teachers, supply teachers, and pupils. Photograph 1 shows two pupils pushing each other, photograph 2 is of a class bursting into a room after break, and photograph 3 shows a girl, who has been told off for scribbling on a pupil's book, standing at the front of the class and muttering. 'Old cow.' under her breath. These photographs (figure 4.1) were selected from a larger sample of pictures which had been piloted, as being illustrative of different types of deviance: a common piece of group misbehaviour (rushing into the room), a quarrel between a small group, with minor aggressive physical encounter, and a more serious piece of misbehaviour involving damage to property and audible insult to the teacher. Teachers are asked how they would react were these events to happen in their own classroom.

We obtained, therefore, a considerable amount of data from the sixty teachers in the sample: structured lesson observations, critical events' and interview statements. These responses are reported in this and the following chapter, and also in chapter 11, which deals specifically with student teachers and their class teacher supervisors.

Strategies Observed

A wide range of lesson settings was covered for the whole sample. Most of the lesson segments, 58 per cent in all, covered mixed subject matter. Of the rest, 13 per cent were exclusively maths, 13 per cent English, 8 per cent humanities, 5 per cent science, and one per cent art, physical education and technology. None was exclusively music. The ages of classes ranged from 4 up to 12, with 18 per cent in reception or year 1 classes, 28 per cent in years 2 and 3, 28 per cent in years 4 and 5, and 26 per cent in years 6 and 7. In each lesson segment, the predominant type of activity was recorded, and table 4.2 shows the breakdown according to whether the teacher was acting solo, for example addressing the whole class, whether there was teacher-pupil interaction, if the pupils working with or without the teacher monitoring, or if there was a transition from one activity to another. In each case, the one predominant activity during the period of observation was noted.

The principal choice of working strategy by primary teachers in this sample, therefore, is for a two-thirds to one-third split between individual or group work and whole-class teaching. Of the larger category — that is, pupils working singly or in groups - almost all of it was being monitored by the teacher. In the case of whole-class teaching, about two-thirds involved teacher-pupil interaction and the remaining third usually the teacher addressing the class, often explaining the topic, telling a story or presenting information.

TABLE 4.2

Predominant type of activity in each of 1,195 lesson segments observed for the whole sample (forty-eight teachers and twelve student teachers)

Activity	*Percentage of occurrences*
Teacher solo	9.7
Teacher-pupil interaction	20.6
Pupils working, teacher monitoring	63.4
Pupils working, teacher not monitoring	2.3
Transition with movement	1.5
Transition without movement	2.5
Total	100.00

When we looked at misbehaviour, we found that very little of what was observed was serious, only 2 per cent deviant behaviour being coded in that category, the other 98 per cent being coded as 'mild'. What tended to happen was that in just over half the lesson segments analysed there was some minor misbehaviour. Coding was done quite strictly, so if, out of thirty pupils, one distracted another, that would have been registered under the one pupil' category. Table 4.3 shows the number of pupils involved when misbehaviour was noted.

In about a fifth of cases, two to four pupils were involved, and in another fifth of cases it was five pupils or more. Very often this would be a single group: frequently, though not always, boys sitting round the same table. The most common form of misbehaviour was noisy or illicit talk, which was noted in just under a third of lesson segments. Inappropriate movement, like leaving the seat without permission, when it should have been requested, or running, was the second most frequent form of misbehaviour, occurring in just over a quarter of lesson segments. Inappropriate use of materials - for example, twanging a ruler - occurred in 10 per cent of lesson segments. Defiance of the teacher, in fourth place, was observed in 8 per cent. Table 4.4 shows these and some minor categories of misbehaviour.

TABLE 4.3

Number of pupils involved in misbehaviour during lesson segments (whole sample = forth-eight teachers and twelve student teachers)

Number of pupils involved	*Percentage of occasions*
No misbehaviour	44.6
One pupil	16.5
Two to four pupils	19.5
Five or more pupils	19.4
Total	100.00

TABLE 4.4

Percentage of lesson segments in which various kinds of misbehaviour occurred (total sample = 1,195 lesson segments)

	Types of misbehaviour	*Percentage of occurrences*
1.	Noisy or illicit talk	32.9
2	Inappropriate movement	26.4
3	Inappropriate use of materials	10.3
4	Defiance of teacher	8.3
5	Taking something without permission	1.8
6	Physical aggression towards another pupil	1.4
7	Illicit copying	0.6
8	Damage to materials/equipment	0.3
9	Insult to teacher	0.3
10	Illicit eating or drinking	0.3
11	Refusal to move	0.1

Almost always when misbehaviour did take place the teacher responded, usually before the deviance had

TABLE 4.5

Teachers' responses to misbehaviour (total sample = -1,195 lesson segments)

	Teachers' responses to misbehaviour	*Percentage of occurrences*
A1	To whole class	26
A2	To group	38
A3	To individuals	36
B1	Before escalation of misbehaviour	94
B2	After escalation of misbehaviour	6
C1	Order to cease	72
C2	Pupil named	68
C3	Reprimand	45
C4	Involve pupils in work	26
C5	Proximity (going over to pupil)	22
C6	Touch	16
C7	Facial expression	15
C8	Gesture	13
C9	Pause	7
C10	Pupil moved	5
C11	Praise/encouragement	4
C12	Humour	4
D1	Teacher response brief	78
D2	Teacher response sustained	22

escalated. Only in 9 per cent of cases was there no response. The most common responses were an order to cease or a reprimand, sometimes both, usually involving one or more pupils being named. Table 4.5 shows the distribution of teachers' responses and the most common as well as some less frequently occurring categories. Al to A3 figures show the targets of the response, Bl and B2 the times, Cl to C12 actual strategies, and Dl and D2 the length of the response.

Reprimanding the pupils who were misbehaving, often to re-involve them in their work, was a common strategy, as were other non-verbal forms of behaviour like gesture and facial expression. Touching was usually to steer pupils away, tap them on the shoulder or turn them round, not physical punishment, which was not observed once. Confiscation of objects, ridicule, detention and the involvement of other teachers, including the head, were all rare, occurring on one per cent or less of occasions. The involvement of another teacher was only seen seven times in the whole set of observations. The outcome of these interactions can be seen in table 4.6, in which Al to A3 give pupils' reactions, B1 to B4 reveal whether the misbehaviour increased, decreased, remained the same or not, and C1 to C3 show whether the teacher appeared calm, agitated or angry.

TABLE 4.6

Outcomes of teachers' interactions, shown as a percentage of all responses (total sample = 1,195 lesson segments)

	Outcome of teacher interaction	*Percentage of occurrences*
A1	Pupil(s) silent	90
A2	Pupil(s) accept(s) teacher's action	6
A3	Pupil(s) altercate(s) or protest(s)	4
B1	Misbehaviour ends	79
B2	Misbehaviour lessens	15
B3	Misbehaviour is sustained	5
B4	Misbehaviour increases	1
C1	Teacher calm	90
C2	Teacher agitated	8
C3	Teacher angry	2

The summary of outcomes confirms the general orderliness. Mostly teachers dealt calmly with the minor deviance which occurred, like noisy talk or unauthorised movement. In most cases the immediate outcome was that misbehaviour ended or lessened, though other acts of minor deviance might recur later. Relatively few pupils challenged the teacher, only 4 per cent occurrences of altercating or protesting were observed. In about 7 per cent of lesson segments, the level of deviant behaviour was labelled 'high', which was interpreted as five or more witnessed acts of misbehaviour. The overall picture of primary classrooms observed in this particular study, therefore, is one of several minor irritations that affect harmonious working, rather than large insurrections or mayhem.

Classrooms in Different Contexts

Lessons were observed in a variety of contexts, some with older pupils, others with younger, some in city schools, others in more rural areas. It is worth considering what, if any, differences were found in these various circumstances, though it must be stressed that any descriptions in this chapter are of the present sample only. It would not be wise to generalise what is reported here to all classrooms in the regions or according to various age groups. This is strictly a report of one study. The classrooms of student teachers, compared with those same classrooms when the regular class teacher was in charge, so all tables and discussion in the remainder of this chapter refer to the sample of forty-eight experienced teachers only.

As shown in table 4.1, there were 100 lessons observed in the North-west, fifty-six in the South-west and thirty-five in the East End of London. Table, 4.7 shows the distribution obtained in each of those three locations on

TABLE 4.7

Percentages of different categories of teacher and pupil behaviour of experienced teachers in three regions (experienced teachers only, students excluded)

Category	*North-west*	*South-west*	*London*
Teacher solo	12	5	5
Teacher-pupil interaction	13	20	30
Pupils working, teachers monitoring	69	66	59
No misbehaviour	43	50	50
Noisy or illicit talk	29	25	36
Inappropriate movement	33	24	15
Inappropriate use of materials	9	9	10
Defiance of teacher	9	8	7
Order to cease	69	68	66
Pupil named	67	67	71
Reprimand	44	36	56
Involve pupils in work	29	44	10
Pupil(s) silent	94	84	85
Pupil(s) altercate(s) or protest(s)	2	3	12
Misbehaviour ends	86	78	84
Misbehaviour sustained	4	8	0
Teacher calm	89	94	93

some of the major categories from the classroom observation schedule. The overall patterns in the three regions are more notable for their similarities than their differences. Categories of misbehaviour such as 'defiance of teacher' and inappropriate use of materials' occur on a virtually identical scale in each of the three locations. Teachers' strategies such as 'order to cease' and 'pupil moved' are also similar in distribution. The results have not been subjected to analysis of variance or any other statistical procedure for determining whether the differences between groups are statistically significant, as this would make them look more precise than they are. In the London

TABLE 4.8

Percentages of different categories of teacher and pupil behaviour with three age groups: reception class, year 1, year 2 (4-7 year olds), years 3 and 4 (7-9 year olds), years 5, 6 and 7 (9-12 year olds)

	Age group		
Category	*4-7*	*7-9*	*9-12*
Teacher solo	7	9	14
Teacher-pupil interaction	22	22	18
Pupils working, teacher monitoring	65	65	61
No misbehaviour	46	32	54
Noisy or illicit talk	32	46	25
Inappropriate movement	27	36	18
Inappropriate use of materials	8	15	8
Defiance of teacher	6	12	5
Order to cease	70	76	69
Pupil named	62	69	61
Reprimand	43	51	39
Involve pupils in work	34	26	20
Proximity (going over to pupil)	23	23	19
Touch	30	15	7
Facial expression	13	19	11
Pupil(s) silent	95	90	85
Pupil(s) altercate(s) or protest(s)	4	5	4
Misbehaviour ends	87	69	85
Misbehaviour lessens	10	22	11
Misbehaviour sustained	2	9	4
Teacher calm	96	84	94

schools there is a tendency for slightly more teacher-pupil interaction and a lower frequency of pupils working alone or in groups, with the teacher monitoring. than in the others. Noisy or illicit talk is slightly higher in London, but inappropriate movement is lower, the North-west showing highest incidence of this. South-west teachers were less likely to use reprimand and most likely to re-involve pupils in their work, a strategy more rarely used by the London teachers. London children were more likely to altercate or protest at the teacher's action than pupils in the other two places. However, it is worth repeating that these tentative findings refer only to the present sample and should not be generalised to whole regions, until significant numbers or other research projects report similar trends, and regional comparisons are very rare in classroom observation research.

Another aspect of context worth exploring is the similarities and differences in patterns across age groups. Table 4.8 shows the sample split in three different age group's, infant age, covering the reception class, and year 1 and 2, that is, children aged 4 to 7; lower juniors, which consisted of year 3 and 4 with children aged from 7 to 9; and upper juniors, which was classes 5, 6 and 7, children aged from 9 to 12, as there were some older middle school groups in the sample. The three groups made up 28, 32 and 40 per cent of the sample respectively. Some very interesting trends and differences can be seen when different age groups are compared. The first striking feature is that there is more misbehaviour in the classes of younger junior pupils aged 7-9 than there is amongst infants or older primary pupils.

Whereas misbehaviour occurred in about half the lesson segments we analysed for infant and older juniors, in year 3 and 4 classes of younger juniors it was observed in about two-thirds. Consequently, table 4.8 shows a noticeably higher incidence of noisy or illicit talk, inappropriate movement or use of materials, defiance of the teacher, as well as more reprimands, orders to cease and naming of pupils. Misbehaviour is less likely to end, though more likely to lessen, and also more likely to be sustained at the same level as before the teacher's intervention, and teachers are less calm. In order to check whether a degree of distortion may have occurred because of one or two especially badly behaved classes in a particular year group, we compared the separate profiles for 7-8 year olds and 8-9 year olds. They were virtually identical, noisy or illicit talk being 46 per cent for both year groups, no misbehaviour 32 per cent for both, defiance of the teacher 12 per cent for both, and reprimand being 51 and 49 per cent respectively.

Least misbehaviour was recorded with the oldest pupils and there were certain interesting trends across age groups. The most obvious difference in teachers' responses to misbehaviour is the sharply diminishing occurrence of touch from 30 to 15 to 7 in the three groups. Touch is not always a hostile act, like pushing someone into place or tapping them sharply on the shoulder. With younger children it was sometimes an affectionate hug or an arm around the shoulder. Touch and proximity were often observed together in infant classes. The teacher would go over to a misbehaving pupil and steer the pupil gently hack to the task in hand, hence the higher incidence of the category 'involve pupils in work' with younger children. With older pupils there is much more of a touch taboo.

Another feature we decided to investigate was whether there were differences between morning and afternoon activities. Some primary schools prefer a 'drills' and 'frills' approach, with more structured work or basic activities in core subjects like English and mathematics in the morning, and more project work and choosing in the afternoons. Others make no such distinctions. Inevitably we observed more morning lessons than afternoon sessions, about three-quarters of the observations being before lunch, as in all the schools we studied the morning half-day was longer, often much more so, than the afternoon period. We were also interested to see, as teachers sometimes said in interview that children were more tired in the afternoon and more likely to misbehave, whether this really was the case. Table 4.9 shows some morning and afternoon comparisons.

TABLE 4.9

Percentages of different categories of teacher and pupil behaviour in morning and afternoon sessions

Category	*Morning*	*Afternoon*
Teacher solo	9	12
Teacher-pupil interaction	19	27
Pupils working, teacher monitoring	66	53
No misbehaviour	46	39
Noisy or illicit talk	31	40
Inappropriate movement	26	27
Inappropriate use of materials	9	13
Defiance of teacher	7	12
Order to cease	71	76
Pupil named	67	69
Reprimand	42	55
Involve pupils in work	29	16
Pupil(s) silent	90	90
Pupil(s) altercate(s) or protest(s)	4	6
Misbehaviour ends	81	74
Misbehaviour sustained	5	5
Teacher calm	92	86

The profiles of morning and afternoon sessions are quite similar. There is slightly more teacher solo or teacher-pupil interaction in the afternoons and slightly less misbehaviour, though the incidence of noisy or illicit talk, inappropriate use of materials and defiance of teacher are all a little higher. Teachers tended to use more reprimands and were less likely to re-involve the pupils in their work; and misbehaviour was less likely to end after a teacher intervention, but these differences were all relatively small rather than dramatic. Nonetheless, the evidence here does corroborate, to a moderate degree, some teachers' belief that afternoon sessions contain more misbehaviour.

The evidence we obtained from the individual pupil studies, which allowed the calculation of task involvement and deviance levels, largely confirmed what has already been described in this chapter. Involvement and deviance index scores can, in theory, range from 0 to 100, but in practice the range is much smaller. During each observation period, every pupil in the class was observed in turn for twenty seconds. The average scores tor the whole sample were 71 for involvement and 5 for deviance. What this means in practice is that if, during the lesson observed, there were thirty children in the class, average scores would he obtained for involvement and deviance as follows: the average involvement score of 71 would mean that about sixteen of the of the class would be engaged in the task in hand, whatever that might be-working individually, listening to the teacher, answering a question - but about three or four pupils, often in the same group, might be not working on their task, or be engaged in mild misbehaviour, most frequently talking to their neighbours instead of working, or moving round the room when they should have been at their place. The range of involvement and deviance scores is shown in table 4.10. This reveals that individual lesson scores would range from as low as 0 up to 26 for deviance, and from 28 to 100 for involvement.

At the extremes a score of 0 for deviance means no one misbehaved at all during the period of observation and 100 for involvement meant that every child observed was fully devoted to the task in hand. A score of 26 for deviance would be obtained in a class of thirty if sixteen pupils were misbehaving in a mildly deviant fashion and the other

TABLE 4.10

Range of involvement and deviance scores obtained for total sample

Measure	*Involve-ment score*	*Deviance score*
Average of whole group	71	5
Lowest average for individual teacher (four lessons)	38	0
Lowest score for individual lesson	28	0
Highest average for individual teacher (four lessons)	92	20
Highest score for individual lesson	100	26

fourteen were behaving well, and an involvement score of 28 would result if, for example, five pupils were seen to be highly involved in the task, seven were medium involved, and the other eighteen were not involved in what they were supposed to be doing. Involvement and deviance scores alone are not, it must be stressed, measures of effective teaching and learning. After all, it would be possible to obtain a deviance score of 0 and an involvement score of 100 by terrorisng children into copying out telephone directories. They are rough-and-ready estimates of attentiveness to the task and pupil behaviour. As will be shown in the next chapter, some teachers teach in very difficult inner-city schools with large classes of unruly pupils, and others are in smaller orderly communities. These figures may well be related to the quality of teaching, but they are not absolute measures of it. One would expect there to be a high inverse correlation between attentiveness and deviance, the more of the one the less of the other, and indeed the highly significant correlation obtained.

Teachers' Decision-making

Teachers were asked in interview to say how they would react to the situations seen in the three photographs shown to them, as described earlier in this chapter. The most common replies, in descending order of frequency of mention, are given below. Some teachers gave more than one response to a situation.

Picture A (Two children seen pushing each other)

Introduction 'You're sitting with your back to this group when you hear a noise. You turn round and see two children messing about. You have told them off once that day for not getting on with their work. What if anything do you do?'

1. Separate the two children.
2. Find out what has happened (many of these also included movement, either by the teacher or the teacher calling the pupils over).
3. It would depend on the children/their expectations/children's response/school sanctions.
4. Look at the task the children are supposed to be doing and reassess it, check it or discuss it.
5. Tell them off/comment on the behaviour.
6. See it as time-wasting and so get them back to work.
7. Punish (this usually meant keeping the children in if they hadn't finished the work or because they had already been told off).
8. Threaten punishment or warn the children.

Other mentions Shout or express emotion, send to the head, seat them next to the teacher, keep an eye on them, ask the class to reflect, throw them a glance/stare.

By far the most popular response, with almost two-thirds of teachers choosing this strategy, was to separate the children in some way. A number of these mentioned that this course of action would be taken because the children had already been warned:

I'd separate them immediately, because if they'd already been warned, they'd had their opportunity to behave ... I would just separate them, one at one end of the room and one at the other end of the room.

If I'd already told them off once, I'd probably separate them straight away, either take one off the table . . . move them to the front of the class, whatever the system is. ... I might be tempted to say, 'Look, what's going on?' but if I'd already told them off once that day I don't think I'd question them, I'd just separate them ... to stop the distraction.

Picture B (class rushing into the room after break)

Introduction. 'This class has just been out for break. They come running back into the room, pushing each other, squealing and laughing. What, if anything, do you do?'

1. Send them outside and make them come in again.
2. Stop them as they come in.
3. Talk about their behaviour, which included pointing out the dangers of rushing into the room.
4. Seat the children.
5. It depends on the circumstances.
6. Tell off/pass comment on behaviour.

Other mentions. Get them to return to work, ignore it, keep them in, reassess the room's layout, shout at them.

The overwhelming response, given by nearly 80 per cent of respondents, was to send the children out. Many teachers gave reasons for their reaction, explaining that they wanted to calm pupils down or that they felt the class ought to know better:

> I would probably get them all to sit down in an area like this [pointing to one part of the classroom], an area where they can all sit down, and tell them that they are going to calm down and that break time is over, and if that isn't effective, I'd probably read a story to them to get them calmed down. . . .

Others merely saw their action as punitive in a self-explanatory way:

> I'd make them all sit down and be quiet and then I'd say, 'Right! We're going back into the playground, and when I blow the whistle, line up at the door and walk in quietly.' And we'd just keep doing it over and over again, really, just wasting time, until they managed to come in quietly and sit down.

Picture C (girl scribbles on books and calls teacher 'old cow')

Introduction. 'You have caught this girl scribbling on someone else's book. You have told her off in front of the class and you hear her mutter "old cow" under her breath. The children near by snigger. What, if anything, do you do?'

1. Speak to her on her own, now or later, to discuss her behaviour.
2. Show emotion - anger, sarcasm, upset, humour.
3. It would depend on the child.
4. Send to the head.
5. Involve the whole class in some way.
6. Punish the girl.
7. Ask her to repeat it.
8. Tell her off.
9. Ignore the behaviour.

Other mentions. Withdraw her, make a joke of it, be seen to deal with it, get her to rub out the scribbling.

About half the teachers gave the most common response, which was to avoid public confrontation by seeing the girl on her own:

> I would certainly take her somewhere and speak to her quietly. I wouldn't want to have a confrontation with her in front of the other children. I would deal with it (myself)... I would either take her aside, or take her to a quiet part of the classroom, where I could speak to her softly and sort it out from there.

About a quarter of respondents described how they would give some emotional reaction to signal to the girl and the class how they felt:

> I'd put her in a withdrawal situation. It would all depend on how I was feeling at the time. If I was level-headed and taking it very calmly ... I'd say. 'You go over there and I'll talk to you later on. At the moment if I talk to you I'll get too angry' and I'll explain to the others there may be reasons behind why she's doing this.... The group make themselves an audience and could send her up to be more of an actress than she need be ... (I'd) talk about being more understanding (to the class). ... I might know what the child's like . . . there's certainly a lot of investigative work can be done there.

Most teachers responded quickly and without hesitation to each of the pictures, and this confirmed not only the conclusions in the research literature speed of decision-making but also the findings of our own research, that teachers usually responded before the escalation of lance. Teachers make thousands of decisions every week, often with only a second or so in which to sum up a vast amount of visual information, past histories, precedents, consequences, context factors and individual differences, so it is not surprising that most responded fairly quickly. Many of the popular strategies involved some degree of confrontation rather than evasion, though the exact opposite was the case in the third picture when personal insult to the teacher was involved.

The most common inclination in the first two pictures was to engage in a mild to medium confrontation of the situation, with immediate counter-measures: separate quarrelling pupils, send the class outside. In the case of the personal insult, it is a delaying strategy, a private conversation rather than a public harangue, possibly held later when the emotions on both sides have subsided. Occasionally, the suggestion was to ignore what had happened, but this was relatively rare. Telling off is the most common reaction predicted by pupils, but it is lower down the list in teach minds.

Another strategy proposed with the pictures, but not always observed so, frequently in the classrooms of the teachers who advocated it, as described in this chapter and the following one, was that of reasoning and negotiation. Looking lor explanations, asking children why they did something, was indeed a feature of some teachers' lessons, but the immediate pressure to respond to misbehaviour sometimes meant that such intentions evaporated in the heat of real classroom aggravation. On the other hand, the events in the photographs are a little more dramatic than the illicit chatter and movement which make up most classroom misbehaviour, so one cannot expect complete congruence. Many teachers did show, in their responses to these photographs, glimpses into their behaviour which mirrored their actual classroom practice. In a small number of cases there was a large gulf between armchair, decision-making and the real thing. The responses to the photographs by experienced teachers, supply teachers, pupils and student teachers will be discussed again in later chapters.

5

Managing Children's Behaviour and Work

It is 8.20 a.m. in the downtown area of a large Northern city. As the bleak morning light flickers across the broken tiles and the for years unpointed brick work of the grim terraced houses round about, the first few pupils and teachers are arriving at school. In the playground lies a dead rat. How had it perished? There is speculation among pupils and staff. Perhaps someone had short it with an air rifle, or may be it just finally breathed its last in the grimy environment in which it had spent its brief existence. It lay there, another symbol of decay and neglect in a crumbling inner city. Meanwhile the head greeted our project researcher with the news that this was a tough school in a tough area. There had been thirteen break-ins in the last thirteen months—even the few plants in front of the school had been dug up and removed. In a nearby school we visited, a pupil proudly told his teacher that his father had been on television. Pleased at this mark of recognition of an otherwise ignored sector of society, she enquired what programme he had appeared in. The answer was BBC national news. He had been shown throwing slates from the roof of a prison during a jail riot.

In a pretty town in another part of the country it is also 8.20 a.m. This is no wealthy commuter belt community, just a small market town in the south of England with a low crime rate and a more rural aspect. An abundance of green surrounds the local school, with small gardens, mainly well tended, a patch of grass and several trees. The children arriving are certainly not from rich families, quite the reverse, nor do they look sedated as they walk or jog into the playground, but the contrast with the city environment described above is a sharp one. The head greets our project researcher with a friendly welcome. She has a big problem today, she tells him, as the caretaker is away and he normally carries the heavy television equipment across to the temporary classroom in the playground. It seems a million miles away from the inner-city school charged with educating children in some of the most desperate circumstances found in our society.

Yet just as some classrooms fill out the stereotypes, others belie them. During the Leverhulme Primary Project we occasionally observed badly behaved classes in what looked to be idyllic surroundings and orderly classes in the most unpromising environments. As will be described below we sometimes saw two teachers in the same school, one with a high degree of task involvement and orderliness, the other with lower pupil application and more misbehaviour. Social conditions certainly do affect class management, but they are not the sole determinants of it. This chapter will give some further detail to flesh out the quantitative data described in the previous chapter.

Maintaining Classroom Rules

Classroom rules and conventions establish the framework within which learning takes place, how teachers assert, establish or negotiate these in their first few lessons. Once the school year is under way many rules are so firmly established they need no further reiteration. Others demand constant fine-tuning, especially those to do with noisy or illicit pupil talk, which was shown to be the most frequent form of deviant behaviour. What constitutes 'noise' rather than normal conversation is a variable rather than a fixed concept. Some teachers' tolerance is quite high, whereas that of other teachers may be low. Young children in particular, partly because their voices are at a higher pitch, partly because they are not always fully socialised in whatever passes for 'acceptable' levels of excited conversation, were reminded frequently about the issue, sometimes with a dramatic display, as in the case of a reception class taught by an experienced teacher in a London school where we observed:

> *Teacher* (in a loud public voice, sounding shocked) Stop! (The class falls quiet. Pause). All the children in the home corner come out! (Children playing in the far corner of the classroom come forward sheepishly). Why do you think I've asked you to come out?
>
> *Pupil* Because we're shouting.
>
> *Teacher* That's right. Now please go back and work quietly. (Children return to their corner and the noise level remains lower).

In this particular instance the teacher chose a minor public shaming. She could have gone over to the children concerned and spoken directly to the small group involved, but she felt a rule was being broken that children were expected to know, as they revealed when they answered her question correctly. The minor public shaming was a demonstration and reaffirmation of the rule, and the likely consequences of breaking it, to others in the class. It illustrates a common sequence of events well understood by pupils, as will be described in chapter 7: talk to loud = get told off in public. As a strategy it was in this instance, 'effective,' if the chief criterion is whether it led to more tolerable levels of noise enabling others to work unimpaired 'skilful' if the criteria are first of all exercising the vigilance necessary to pick up possible disruption before it escalates, and secondly to deal with it in a way that is understood and complied with by the pupils, and 'acceptable' if one takes as indicative of that term the pupils' apparent lack of resentment or hostility to the teacher's action:

Some rules have been made explicit, but children do not subsequently generalise them to every situation, so the teacher may then make the specific instance public. In a London class of 6-7 year olds there was a rule that equipment and materials must be put away. In one lesson a group of children had been painting and an apron had been left out:

> *Teacher* (calls back the children who had been working at the table concerned). Who was wearing a red apron?
>
> *Pupils* (No reply).
>
> *Teacher* (pause) Will you put it back, please? (Child returns apron to storage space). If you need an apron you need to get it yourself.... and you need to put it back in the right place. I'm not going to do it for you. (Pause.) Now, off you go. (Children return to their tasks).

This reaffirmation of a specific instance of a rule in a specific context occurred frequently with the second most common form of perceived misbehaviour in the present study, inappropriate movement, when pupils left their seat without permission, at the wrong time, to the wrong place, or in the wrong manner. In a class of 7-8 year olds in the North-west there was a rule that children wanting to solicit the teacher's attention were to raise their hand and wait. This rule causes difficulties for pupils, as they may wait for some time if the teacher is engrossed with one pupil, so three children walks over to where the teacher is standing:

> *Teacher* (making a show of counting them). Now why are there one, two, three, people here? (One pupil returns to his seat and raises his hand. The teacher walks past the other two). Peter's got his hand up, so I'm going over to him. (The other two sit down and raise their hands). How many children are out of their seats? One, two..... (Points and counts).

The problem with this rule is that there is a price to pay for it. If children are not to leave their seat frequently to solicit the teacher's attention, then two conditions must obtain. First of all, the teacher must be perpetually vigilant, otherwise several children can sit, arms aloft, for inordinate lengths of time. Secondly, the teacher must establish a high degree of pupil independence which minimises the number of occasions when they will need to approach her. Many of the questions we observed asked by children standing in line to see the teacher, or sitting at their table waiting, were simple to answer, like how to spell a word when there were dictionaries in the room, or what to do next, when the answer was turn the page and carry on, or check your answers.

In a different classroom with 8-9 year olds in the North-west we observed an applications of this rule which revealed the need for consistency. Some children put up their hands, others went over to the teacher. From time to time the teacher would attempt to delineate and reinforce the rule by sending someone away. On one occasion she said to a pupil, 'Go and sit down and put your hand up if you want help.' After thirty seconds she went over to him and answered his question. She then told another child not to interrupt her, but answered the questions of other pupils when they interrupted. One girl sat for over five minutes with her arm aloft and remained unnoticed until she called out, 'Miss,' in frustration. The teacher then went over to ther. It was easy to see what the rule was meant to be: put up your hand if you want help, and don't interrupt. It was much more difficult in practice, however, for children to see a pattern to breaches of the rule, because there did not seem to be one. The details of the rule were diffuse, ill-defined and unevenly reinforced. As a consequence the lessons were full of instances of roaming pupils punctuated by sporadic and largely ineffectual reminders of what the rule was supposed to be.

Successful maintenance of classroom rules, irrespective of how they had, originally been introduced or negotiated, appeared to require clarity of purpose, understanding and assent from the pupils, fair-minded and appropriate interpretation or adaptation in the relevant context, and consistent application and reinforcement. Absence of some or all of these conditions was often accompanied by a higher incidence of misbehaviour by pupils.

Maintaining Interpersonal Relationships

While some teachers continued to make use of some public displays of anger or to use minor shaming, rather than outright humiliation, to keep order, as table 4.5 showed, about three-quarters of teachers' responses to misbehaviour were addressed to individuals or small groups rather than the whole class. Interactions with individual pupils can exert a powerful influence on the genesis and maintenance of personal relationships. Acts by the teacher which had positive or negative effects were noted by observers on numerous occasions. In most classrooms positive affect outweighed negative affect, but the obverse was also seen occasionally. Here are some instances, under several headings, of both positive and negative teacher behaviour which appeared to affect relationships and which was witnessed by researchers during the project:

1. *Academic*
   (a) Explaining patiently to a pupil who does not understand a new concept.
   (b) Making a sarcastic remark to someone who does not understnd a new concept.

2. *Managerial*
   (a) Smiling at and thanking someone who has helped clear away.
   (b) Blaming someone for a mess, choosing wrong pupil.

3. *Social*
   (a) Talking to children as they enter the classroom about what they did at the weekend.
   (b) Belittling someone's hobby.

4. *Expectation*
   (a) Looking for positive qualities and achievements in children.
   (b) Having low expectations or always focusing on the negative side of pupils' work or behaviour.

5. *Home/school*
   (a) Talking positively with parents and members of pupils' communities.
   (b) Showing little or no interest in children's origins and values.

6. Individuals

(a) Taking a personal interest in a child as an individual.

(b) Seeing the class as a group without individual identities.

There were many examples of teachers working in very difficult circumstances who made special efforts to raise the self-image of their pupils. One teacher of 5 year olds in a school in an exceptionally difficult area made numerous positive references to children. A child who arrives in tears and who has had no breakfast is first comforted and then taken to the reading corner. Shortly afterwards her tears have ceased and she is happily engaged in a piece of work. The teacher calls the class her 'smarties' ('Time for my smarties to go to assembly'), the combination of the name of a well-known sweet and the suggestion that the children are all 'smart' being well received by the class.

Some of the most striking examples of a predominantly positive climate of relationships were observed in the classroom which contained children who did not speak English as their first language. In establishing and maintaining interpersonal relationships most people rely heavily on spoken language, even though non-verbal cues and messages may play a part. Touch was noted much more frequently with younger children, especially when children cried or appeared upset, when the teacher would often put her arm round them. Stripped of language, however, the most obvious form of communication, many would find establishing good harmonious relationships very difficult. In the classrooms of all the London teachers we observed, in those of some of the North-west teachers, but very few of the South-west teachers, there were one or two, occasionally several, non-English-speakers. Most teachers made special efforts to establish positive relationships by involving pupils as well as themselves, as this event, noted in a London classroom, reveals.

> There is a new pupil in the class of 11-12 year olds who has just moved to England and who speaks very little English. Often there are fellow speakers in the case of languages like Bengali and the teacher assigns a 'translator' from amongst the pupils, but on this occasion no one else in the class speaks his language. The class is studying Europe, and the teacher is writing the names of European countries on the blackboard. Pupils are suggesting names she can add. The new boy raises his hand and says 'France,' following a whispered conversation with his neighbour. Michael. The teacher praises him fulsomely, 'Well done. Stefan, god boy.' In the interview following the lesson she explains how she has assigned Michael to help Stefan. She had discussed with the class how they could all help someone who did not speak English. Michael had sat beside Stefan and looked at the map with him, whispering to him the names of countries when he had indicated them.

Even well intended teachers, however, can fall short of their own aspirations admit the sustained distractions of classroom life, and risk arousing animosity by a piece of unfairness. A 6 year old boy was seen in one classroom to tidy up voluntarily some pieces of equipment that had been left scattered across the floor. He had initiated this himself, even though he had not been using the pieces. The teacher went over to him and told him to leave them and go and do some printing instead. He did as he was asked, leaving five or six pieces still on the floor. About twenty-five minutes later the teacher came over to where he was printing, took him by the hand to where the remaining pieces still lay on the floor, told him it was untidy to have left them and he should now pick them up. Without protest or altercation he did so and then returned quietly to his printing. In over 90 per cent of cases where we saw a reprimand given to a pupil the target was judged to be fair by the observer, but in those cases where it was not, personal relationships could easily be soured. Unfairness is one of the events pupils resent most deeply.

Some teachers were so concerned about fairness in their relationships that they engaged in extended negotiation with pupils. Negotiated rules were relatively infrequent in our observations, as most were determined either explicitly by the teacher or implicitly by the pupils in terms of what they actually did. In the school in the North-west the extrinsic rewards and punishments, system was built around house points and stars. Pupils doing well or badly could gain or lose points for their house team. One day the teacher gives Patricia house points for a piece of work.

Pupil 1 That's not fair, she shouldn't get that many points.

Teacher All right. I'll give you one point Patricia. Are you all happy with that decision?

Pupil 2 No, it's still not fair.

Teacher. Well, can anybody suggest a way we can overcome the problem?

Pupil 3 Give everybody a point.

Pupil 4 No, that's silly. Don't give Patricia a point at all.

Pupil 5 Give her a star instead. It's worth a star but not house points.

Teacher All those that agree with Mary's suggestion put up your hands. Right, that's virtually everybody. Are you happy with that decision, Patricia?

(Patricia nods, smiles and seems to be pleased).

Just as relationships between the teacher and pupils are regarded as important, so too are interpersonal relationships amongst the children themselves; for all are part of the same classroom culture. Whereas in the case of non-English-speaking Stefan, described above, the teacher had made special efforts to involve other pupils in his reception and accommodation within the class, there were examples when teachers appeared to be less effective at resolving problems between pupils.

In a class of 8-9 year olds three girls were sitting together at the same table. Two of them, Alice and Rachel, would from time to time torment Caroline, the third girl, by refusing to give her a rubber, throwing things at her, preventing her from working. The teacher rarely intervened. Occasionally she would look at Alice's and Rachel's work, but not refer to their behaviour, except indirectly, by saying to Caroline, 'Just ignore them, Caroline, and get on with your work.' Her explanation of this strategy in interview was:

> Alice and Rachel are just attention-seekers. Alice in particular is a very unsettled child. She does the same thing in the playground, picks an argument with somebody and runs up to whoever is on duty shouting about the offence being committed against her when in fact she's started it herself, or telling tales about somebody else doing something to somebody. It's a lot of attention-seeking behaviour.

To some extent, by ignoring what she rightly or wrongly judged to be attention seeking, the teacher was following the tenets of behaiour modification, which decree that 'bad' behaviour should be ignored so that it is extinguished by not being reinforced. However, the corollary to not reinforcing behaviour of which the teacher disapproves is that approved behaviour should be reinforced. The teacher did not appear to find out further information about why Alice sought attention, and this event highlights the dilemma faced by many teachers. Since eliciting deeper-lying causes of anti-social behaviour is not only time-consuming but requires considerable expertise, it is sometimes the case that, during lessons at any rate, misbehaviour is accommodated, contained, treated or ignored, rather than its causes diagnosed.

Disruptive Behaviour

The most common source of disruption of a pupil's work was interruption by another pupil or occasionally by the teacher, for reasons other than to monitor what was being done. Occasionally there were aggressive intrusions into the work of an individual, a small group or the whole class, often by a single pupil. In one classroom the same 5 year old pupil was reprimanded three or four times each time registration was taken and his behaviour dominated the lessons. The teacher usually brought him to sit on the floor next to her during whole class sessions, and as he pulled objects out of the trolley that he wanted to use in the forthcoming activity she would gently take them from him and incorporate them into her explanation of what the children were to do. The demands of this one pupil consumed a great deal of her classroom time, and with twenty seven or twenty-eight others it was often a matter of coping or containing strategies, rather than something which significantly altered his behaviour.

When more than one pupil disrupts, even more time can be consumed. An inexperienced student teacher was seen with a class of 7-8 year olds. Within one minute she asked for quiet seven times, stamped her foot, clapped her hands, named individual pupils, raised her voice, asked pupils to put their hands on their head, but none of these acts reduced the noise level. Once she had given out the maths worksheets, however, the noise diminished and most pupils worked assiduously at them, albeit with occasional conversations. When classes were engaged in work which seemed to them appropriate and worthwhile, such disruption as occurred tended to be caused by individual pupils or occasionally by a small group of two or three pupils.

As was shown most teachers took action before disruption escalated, often revealing a high degree of vigilance, and were able to split their attention between the child or group they were with and the rest of the class by employing the split glance, demonstrating what Jacob Kounin called 'with-itness.' Frequently, noticing potential disruption and nipping it in the bud took place almost instantaneously. One reception class was reading a book together when a child began to fiddle with the laces on a pair of shoes, distracting others. Within seconds of this beginning the teacher called out, 'Sally, what are you doing? If you play with your shoelaces you won't learn the words. Put your shoes away.' The child complied, but before starting to talk about the next page the teacher glanced up and said, in a firm but friendly manner. 'Now, are you listening, Sally?' There was no further interruption.

By contrast, in another class of 5 year olds four children were playing with scales and bricks. One child hit another, unseen by the teacher, then another boy hit one of the girls, who asked him to stop punching her. He hit her again, so she left the table to work elsewhere. The aggressive boy called out the teacher's name several times. Twice she came over to check his work, but never commented on his behaviour, even though he continued to be noisily aggressive towards others throughout the lesson. Disruption caused by distracting behaviour, chatter, minor teasing and attention-seeking were, in general, easily contained by most teachers. It was the individual aggressive child who caused greatest dismay, both to fellow pupils and to the teacher, and the demands made by such individuals on the teacher's time and energy during a lesson could be considerable.

Yet many of the teachers who encountered this more aggressive style of disruption did deploy strategies which appeared successful in resolving or even eliminating anti-social aggression. Some used extrinsic rewards, like points or stars when the pupil had behaved well. Others eschewed this more formal recognition and made use of extensive praise instead. There were examples of assigning responsibility for some logistical operation, like giving out books or collecting in work, but where these are perceived as privileges, there can be some resentment from other pupils if aggression is thought to have been rewarded and good social behaviour ignored.

Touch was rarely used with older children but it was a common feature with younger pupils. For example, when a boy was said by others to have been kicking pupils, one teacher said, in a half joking, half serious manner, 'Would you like me to kick him?' and then seized him by the shoulders and pushed him towards a table. Other pupils laughed but the boy's face was expressionless. This is an interesting example of a strategy which was 'successful' in terminating the disruption, but about which opinion might be divided, given the possible apprehension of the boy concerned.

Another teacher, investigating why a 5 year old girl was crying, found that a boy had hit her. There followed a conversation between the teacher and the two pupils concerned which ended with the teacher telling them to be friends and give each other 'a big hug.' This done, no further aggression was noted. The strategy of looking for the positive was sometimes exemplified by the teacher holding up the disruptive pupil's work for admiration by the rest when he had done especially well.

Classroom Routines

The daily repeated rituals of classroom life, arrival, registration, 'circle time' or 'carpet time', where children sit with the teacher to discuss matters of concern, lesson endings, are in many classrooms the secure framework within which transactions take place. In some classrooms these were highly formalised: lined-up supervised entry, great formality over registration, regimented departure. More frequently they were simply regular occurrences which signalled important messages and established or maintained a particular classroom climate.

Teachers showed considerable variation in their use of time. In some classrooms there was little sense of urgency, assignments were open-ended, to be done in the pupil's own time, even if they was slowly paced. Others made the issue of time more public, using group alerting to tell pupils how long there was left or reminding individuals of when they would be expected to have finished. In one class where 'time' was actually the topic of study, two 7 year old boys had not been working diligently, so the teacher went over to their table, put a clock on it and showed them how long they had to finish the task in hand. When one of the boys had finished, however, he reported to the teacher that the other boy had turned back the clock to give himself more time. The teacher smiled at him, seemed pleased that he had understood time well enough to realise how to create more of it, but then re-set the clock and gave him a fresh target.

Within the major routines there were often minor ones. One teacher of 5 year olds whose lesson endings always seemed to pass smoothly would warn children to be ready to stop, and then, when she actually said, 'Stop working,' all the pupils put their hands in the air and waved them. 'They're all supposed to waggle their arms in the air,' she explained in interview, 'so I can see they've actually stopped, because I only say 'stop!" in order to say something to everybody.' She would then give the class ten seconds to sit on the carpet, which she counted out slowly, taking more than ten seconds so they would not rush, and then announced, 'Give yourself a clap,' when all had complied. Many other teachers had established a formal exit at the end of the day, one insisting on a very precise and straight line before anyone was allowed to leave: 'I've asked you to line up and I can see (points finger as she counts) one, two, three, four, five, six, seven, eight not in line.' Major and minor routines were observed on a regular basis in virtually every classroom observed, other than those of a few student teachers.

More Effective and Less Effective Management

Taking as two criteria of effectiveness the extent to which pupils were involved in the task and the amount of misbehaviour, it was sometimes possible to see two teachers in the same or a similar environment, where one obtained high task involvement and low deviance, and the other the reverse. Although the class itself can sometimes be the main determinant of such differences, especially when one group contains more disruptive pupils than another, there were occasions when it was not major differences between two classes, but noticeable distinctions between the teaching styles of their teachers, that seemed to explain differences in behaviour. Mrs. Abel and Miss Baker taught third-year juniors and second-year juniors respectively in the same school. There were serious social problems in the area, so it was not an easy assignment teaching in that particular school. Yet, as these short accounts reveal, the two teachers were quite different from each other in terms of relationships, amount of quality of work from pupils and classroom climate. Even having a whole-school policy for such maters as discipline cannot always eradicate individual differences in temperament and practice.

Mrs. Abel

There is a sense of benign urgency about Mrs. Abel's lessons, whether she is checking scores on a maths test and discussing children's 'silly' mistakes, or whether the class is engaged in individual and small group work. There is a rule that children waiting for help must get out their reading book, not sit doing nothing. Yet when she asks questions she says, 'Don't panic,' to anyone not sure of an answer and makes extensive use of praise. She seems well prepared and sets tasks which hold and maintain pupils' attention. When there is incipient misbehaviour, she often defuses the situation with quick but pointed humour: 'Jason, it won't help if you're chopping her neck off with a ruler.'

From time to time she alerts the whole class to some matter of principle with specific reference to a particular event. On one occasion a girl has finished maths book No. 4 ahead of the rest. After checking her work she tells the whole class that this deserves a round of applause. In interview she explains that, when she took over the class, they were so far behind what she expected that she has put a high premium on successful achievement: 'We are so far behind in this class with maths.... when I got them two were doing second-year work and the rest first-year work, and they were so far behind ..... so we've made this big thing about every time they finish a particular stage they get praise..... they're really proud of themselves if they do it.' When she asked children to pat themselves on the back, some did it literally. Large-scale display of pupils' work around the classroom reinforced this public recognition of positive achievement.

Mrs. Abel's high task involvement and low deviance scores (see below) seem to be the result of considerable thought about appropriate work for the class and individuals; extensive use of reinforcement, especially in the form of praise, some private, much public; completely consistent classroom rules, enforced in a benign but firm manner, so that calling out is not a problem and, when it threatens to be, children are reminded of the rule; and a considerable amount of good humour, both from herself and the children, which defuses potential trouble and cements positive interpersonal relationships. She also reminds pupils of the time available and regularly monitors their work, especially those with difficulties. When her pupils were interviewed, for the research on pupil perceptions described in chapter 7, many named her as 'the best teacher in the world.

Miss Baker

At the beginning of lessons Miss Baker quickly announces what pupils will do, but there is a long settling down period and children seem to move around the room, often on what seems to be a purposeless perambulation, before commencing work. Task involvement levels are comparatively low and deviance is higher than average (see below). This can be partly explained by two very noticeable elements. The first is that the rules of behaviour are not always clear or consistently applied, and this relates to the second factor, which is that relationships between pupils and teacher are more negative than in Mrs. Abel's classroom.

Some of the instances of misbehaviour exemplify these differences. On one occasion a boy donned a baseball cap.

'Get that hat off. I'm not going to tell you again, young man,' the teacher called across the room. He hurled his hat into the centre of the table. The teacher did not comment, though she clearly saw his response. Afterwards the teacher said she had ignored it because 'he was just being silly.' In another lesson she asked children to put their hands up before speaking. Few did. She also requested them not to walk around the room, but several ignored her. She then shouted at six pupils not in their seats and told one to go out into the corridor. He stayed in the rook and she made no comment.

In interview she says, 'They're wasting their time and they're wasting the other children's time. In the last few weeks what I've actually been doing is saying they can't get out of their seats without permission. They've got to put their hands up to tell me why they want to (move) and ask me if they can. It's really just a disruptive thing that I've got.' The intention was clear but the implementation was unsuccessful.

Alongside this inconsistency in rule enforcement is a harsher style of relationship. Praise is rarely used and Miss Baker is frequently critical of the same two target pupils, Darren and Lloyd, even when they are not misbehaving. On one occasion during a PE lesson she drags Lloyd across the hall floor by his legs, shouting at him to be quiet and sit still. Two children giggle. Later she sends him out of the room. He stands by the doorway. 'Remove yourself from that doorway.' He eventually moves. She sends Darren out. Then, when he is leaving the room, she calls him back. He leaves anyway. In interview she says of Lloyd. 'He tends to put on affection. He comes up and cuddles you, but it's all put on, trying to creep to you, attention-seeking...... otherwise it's conflict with Darren all the time.'

Miss Baker's relatively low task involvement level and higher deviance rate seem to be related to two principal related factors: the inconsistent application of classroom rules—applying them harshly one moment, ignoring them the next—and negative interpersonal relationships, with few examples of good work being recognised. The only occasion she was seen to smile was once at the end of a school day when all but one group of children had been dismissed. Her answers to the questions posed in the photographs were also more diffuse than Mrs. Abel's. For the third picture, where the girl has called the teacher 'old cow,' she admitted that this had happened to her, but said she might ignore it, or try to defuse it by saying she did look like an old cow. Mrs. Abel, by comparison, felt it was natural to react angrily, but that teachers' anger must be expressed in a proper manner.

During a school year children may spend a thousand or more hours in the company of their class teacher. The cumulative effect of patterns of high involvement and low deviance, or low involvement and high deviance, can be considerable. Mrs. Abel's average task involvement score was 84, and her range was from 79 to 94. This means that, typically, out of thirty children, about twenty-three would be observed to be highly involved in their work, about four would be medium involved and two not involved. Given that children must sometimes wait, and that no one concentrates for sixty minutes in every hour, this is a high degree of application.

By contrast Miss Baker's average task involvement score was 38, with a range of from 28 to 53. In practice this means, in a class of thirty, about seven pupils highly engaged in the task in hand, nine would be medium involved and fifteen would not be engaged, a quite different picture. Mrs. Abel's average deviance score was 2, with a range of

0 to 4. This means that one pupil might be mildly misbehaving, say distracting a neighbour. Miss Baker's average deviance score was 20, with a range of from 10 to 26. This would involve say nineteen pupils not misbehaving, ten engaging in minor misbehavior, and one behaving more badly, perhaps hitting another pupil.

So in one room in the school virtually everyone is working on the task in hand and behaving well; a few doors away, with pupils from a similar social background, about half are not involved in their work and a third are chattering or moving around the room when they should not be. Contemplating one such hour multiplied by 1,000 over a school year may help to explain some aspects of the differences in learning achievement by two classes in similar circumstances at the end of a school year.

6

Supply of Teachers

Whereas experienced teachers in permanent posts of student teachers on teaching practice usually have several weeks during which to get to know their new classes, establish and fine-tune relationships and rules of behaviour, and decide which subjects and topics to teach at what time, many supply teachers have little opportunity to operate in stable conditions over a lengthy period of time with the same class.

They are often telephoned at short notice and asked to come in and take over a class, acting as substitute teachers. We decided that it would be interesting to study the approach to class management supply teachers adopted, especially those who had to arrange numerous first encounters with classes they had never met. It seemed likely that, since they had more opportunity than most teachers to establish themselves with several different classes, some might have developed skills which would be of interest to all teachers, even if others had simply learned coping strategies. An opportunity sample of twenty supply teachers was selected from one local authority in the South-west of England. A semi-structured interview schedule was used (Trotter and Wragg 1990). All but two of the interviews, which lasted at least an hour and usually much more than that, were tape-recorded and transcribed, and in the other two cases extensive notes were taken.

There have been very few studies of supply teachers (Loveys 1988), and those that are undertaken are often surveys of teacher absence and the use of supply cover. A one-day snapshot survey of the Inner London Education Authority looked at teacher absence and cover arrangements (ILEA 1989) and found that 40 per cent of that day's absences were covered by supply teachers. The short-term and long-term absence rates were 10.1 per cent and 3 per cent of the teaching force respectively. Supply teachers help maintain and lubricate the system. Without them, some schools, faced with severe absence or recruitment problems, would grind to a halt.

The twenty teachers in the sample were mainly women, only two being men, and had an average seven years of regular experience in schools before taking up supply work, though the actual range was from one teacher who had taught for twenty-three years first, to another who went straight into supply teaching without any other experience. The most common reasons offered for becoming a supply teacher were flexibility, financial advantage, interest and enjoyment, and as a springboard to a permanent post. They had spent about five and a half years on average as a supply teacher, and the range was from one person who had done it for nineteen years to another who was in her first year of it. The median number of different schools they had worked in was roughly six, though the distribution was skewed, with one in particular having experience of 'about fifty.' More typically, teachers had a more restricted number of schools likely to ring them up.

Emmer *et al.* (1981) and Evertson and Emmer (1982) are amongst several investigators who have highlighted the importance of preparation and planning in class management, yet supply teachers often report lack of time for this very matter. In order to elicit what thoughts and strategies supply teachers had developed, the main part of the interview schedule concentrated on their thoughts and actions before meeting a new class; what image, if any, they sought to project of themselves when they met a new class for the first time; what relationships they tried to establish; what and whose rules applied: what they did when disruptive behaviour occurred. In this last case, we again used the photographs of disruptive incidents.

First Meetings

It was quite clear, from amongst all the interviews, that there were many occasions when supply teachers had little time to prepare. One respondent described how she was hired by the had as she took her own daughter to school:

> He [the head] grabbed me and said, 'Someone's not feeling well, can you do it?' So I had no idea that I was going to teach that day and I went straight in. I didn't have anything with me. I just went straight into the classroom.

It is not surprising that, in the circumstances, some teachers develop deft strategies for coping with the lack of preparation time. One teacher told how she kept a bag for infants and a bag for juniors in her bedroom. As soon as she received a phone call and knew the age group she would be teaching, she seized the appropriate holdall and set off to the school. Another told of how she dreaded the 7.40 a.m. phone call, as she knew it would be a head ringing up, since that was the only kind of call she received at that morning hour.

Once supply teachers arrive at school they are award of their marginal status. Some teachers used the expression 'lowest of the low' to describe it, and one described herself as 'one grade up from the dinner lady,' Another said:

> You are at a disadvantage by the fact that you are a supply teacher. You're just a couple of notches above a student, aren't you? Children know that you are a supply teacher..... they don't have the same respect for you as they do for people who are on the permanent staff.

Others complained at being called 'the supply' rather than being addressed by name, and of not receiving relevant information about the national curriculum, about class projects, or school rules and conventions.

This lack of knowledge could lead to problems, especially as the teachers did not know children as individuals:

> I once mad a child who wasn't very bright—and I didn't realise it — look extremely silly and I've never forgotten that and afterwards I felt dreadful..... He was messing about. I'd given them a tables test . . it was a tables sheet and he was messing around and being silly and, of course, when it came to marketing them he'd only got a few. And I sort of said to him, in front of all the class, 'If you hadn't been put in there for a little while and obviously he was being silly, I suppose, to cover up for the fact that he couldn't do it. He really was at the rock bottom for brains—and quite a nice lad, actually—but I suppose I'd put him on the soot unfairly and I hadn't realise that and afterwards I felt terrible....

The supply teachers were asked how they prepared for these first meetings with a new class, given the shortness of notice and lack of familiarity with the people involved. One described how important the image of efficiency was to her:

> Basically, if I'm approaching a new class. I'm getting myself ready to get in there fairly early—I'm usually in a half-hour, forty minutes before I actually meet a class.... because you want to put over the idea that you're well organised and a together person. I think the worst thing that a supply teacher can do is to be dithery in front of a new class—it's important that you are competent and confident with taking a register and you know how the dinner money is slotted in and things like this, even if you are thinking 'Well, they don't do their dinner money like so-and-so; this is totally wrong or something'..... You've got to get a bit of street credibility fairly early on. I think.

Others echoed this need to be as well-prepared as possible in the circumstances. This involved not only preliminary organisation, but also knowing what questions the teachers needed to ask when she arrived about school routines, like assembly or playground duty, so that her own preparation could dovetail with the schools' normal practice:

> I will have planned out exactly what I'm going to do the night before—well that's if you know the day before—if I've had that [notice] then I will have planned out hat I'm going to do with them. So an hour before I would be making sure that I'd got all the materials that I knew [I needed],

> up to lunchtime, I think. I would make sure that I'd got all the paper and the pencils and any books that I was gong to need. I would have found out whether it was playground duty [and] if there were assemblies..... Not all classrooms have a timetable up, but you need to know if you've got any mother-helpers coming in, if there's an assembly or if there's apparatus [or] television programmes. I would have found that out to begin with, and then fitted that in with what I'd planned to do.

One teacher's strategy was to rehearse her first lesson in her own mind about an hour before meeting the class, to go though the children's books to see what level and type of work would be appropriate, to set out paper, pencils or equipment, and then to stand in the room and think through what she was going to do. Four teachers admitted experiencing feelings of panic that rendered rehearsal unlikely, and felt that it was difficult, in the circumstances, to be constructive. Most, however, used early arrival to find out about the normal structure of a school day, the timetable, if there was one, what resources were available, and what the class's regular teacher had done recently.

Although some respondents claimed not to think too deeply about anything other than survival, one saying 'I do work, I don't think,' it was quite clear that a great deal of thought accompanied first encounters, even if teachers could not always articulate it. All were asked specifically what image they would like to project, and sixteen of the twenty had no difficulty at all describing what this was. They were able to describe in detail their vision of how they wanted children to perceive them and what they did to establish this favoured image in a consistent manner.

'Firm but friendly' was a commonly used expression. One who described this as needing to look 'efficient, organised, firm but reasonable.... reasonable/friendly' went on:

> I don't ever want to come over as being too hard, so I tend if I am being harsh or delivering 'rules,' in inverted commas, or the way I feel it needs to be for us to get on, I try to say it in a very reasonable sort of voice because I think if you're delivering the sting in the tail and you're doing it with a really sort of harsh teacher-type voice, they often turn off before you've even started.

The need for strictness tempered with kindness was mentioned in particular by those used to working in difficult conditions. In really challenging situations, toughness would prevail over kindness, in order for the teacher to survive:

> There's one particular class down at——where they're really tough — or they can be. They really 'monkey' about and I know they're like this, so I go right in, and as soon as some poor kid moves, that's it, because otherwise they would just make your life a misery. So I suppose the image I would project there would be as somebody tough.

In these circumstances, establishing dominance was seen to be paramount by others. One explained that there were clear rules she expected the pupils to adhere to and they should know that 'if they didn't, learning couldn't go on, and there was a nastier side to my nature.' The four supply teachers who said they did not consciously try to project any particular image felt it was unnecessary to be anything other than natural.

Establishing Relationships and Rules

Establishing positive relationships was seen by nineteen out of the twenty teachers as an important first step, or second step once dominance had been established, where this was thought to be a necessary first step. Time was mentioned as one major constraint working against the establishment of good relationships, as a supply teacher might only take a class for as little as a single afternoon.

Great emphasis was placed on the process of establishment. Most respondents used a deliberate settling-down period on first meeting the class, sometimes with the children sitting on the carpet, on other occasions with them sitting at their tables, during which a dialogue would take place, what one teacher described as a half-hour of 'pure conversation.' The physical proximity of having children grouped closely around the new adult in their lives was mentioned by several as a deliberate and precisely managed parent-like bonding ritual:

> perhaps it's about body language and things like that, really. I just feel I can relate more to them by being.... to have a bit more physical nearness. I suppose it's the closeness, and it's also having a hart with them, isn't it? And the talking and really getting to know them and how they are as a group as well.

Some reinforced the parental nature of the bonding by talking about their own role as parent, one teacher saying, 'I usually talk about my own children, particularly with young children, so that they know I've got children and I'm used to children.' Perhaps supply teachers, given that many stated in interview that they had chosen this option because of the flexibility it offered them to fit in with their own children's lives, can adopt this parental style of bonding ritual more easily than others.

Conscious of the need to do more than merely establish a relationship, some teachers described strategies they had developed for assessing which children might cause them problems, because they have learning or behaviour difficulties. One described how she would talk to each of the pupils individually in her very first lesson so she could appraise them:

> They all have silent reading book and they all know how to do that, so I get them very settled with their silent reading book and then I will just talk to them and, depending on their age or the mood or whatever, I'll just talk to them about something that will interest them, so that we will just feel the relationship together, so that I am somebody there today to help them and I would like them to work with me. At the same time, I am doing quite a lot of assessments..... I am sifting out..... where the difficult children are, the disruptives. You can spot them within the first minute, they stand out. So I do my survey first of all looking for those children, and then I look for the needy children who might be quiet but are slow learners. Once I've got those two groups charted the rest of the children just fall in, really.

There was a distinct division of opinion and practice on the matter of classroom rules of behaviour and procedure. Eleven out of twenty teachers made a conscious effort to apply rules from the outset, either their own or those they detected to be customary within the school. The others preferred to be reactive, to wait until circumstances required a rule to be stated or restated. This could, however, be at the very beginning of the first minute of contact. One of the common rules identified in the research literature (Wragg and Wood 1984) is 'No talking while I'm talking' in public situations. It was quite clear, in talking to one teacher, that this was, for her, an implicit classroom rule, and she revealed, in this account of a well rehearsed introduction, how she would establish it via a formal centre-stage, publicly enacted display of authority, emphasising the use of her eyes:

> I do not go in and say 'These are the rules.' I might, but not to every class. It all depends on how I sense the situation. If I think it's a really bubbly sort of class, if I sense danger to the health of the lesson, to the on-going of the lesson, if I think I detect some elements that might hinder the development of the lesson, I will say, 'Good morning, everybody. Will you pay attention, please, I wish to speak to the class. Now, I don't think everybody is looking this way.' And I look. 'Would you please not fiddle with your ruler? That's right, just put it to one side. Thank you.' And I look. I don't know how I appear, but I wait until everybody's hands are free and they are looking. I do not proceed until that applies.

Procedural rules could cause some difficulty, especially if the supply teacher's practice was different from that of the class's regular teacher. Some simply imposed their own conventions from the beginning. One teacher always established her own rule abut queuing at the teacher's desk. She set up a 'fast' side for spellings and a 'slow' side for problems needing a longer explanation. Another teacher, however, stressed the need to follow existing rules, commenting that 'it would be pointless trying to make out that it was *my* classroom.'

Handling Disruption

Skilful teachers prevent disruption wherever possible, but all teachers have to manage deviant behaviour at some time during their teaching, so we decided to use, as a stimulus, colour photographs of classroom misbehaviour in order to elicit what the supply teachers would do in the circumstances. The responses to two of these photographs are described here.

Incident 1

The photograph shows children pushing each other as they run into the classroom. Each respondent was shown the picture and asked, 'It is time for the second half of the morning on your first day with this class. They come running back into the room, pushing each other squealing, laughing. What, if anything, do you do?' There was little hesitation from any of the teachers, as they were well used to this happening in real life. All agreed that some kind of action would have to be taken, and no-one suggested ignoring what happened. Most (thirteen out of twenty) would send the children out and make them re-enter in an orderly fashion, some stressing that they would become very authoritarian using both voice and eyes:

> I would wait until they were all in the classroom, then I would use my assertive, cross voice and explain that in my class nobody comes into the classroom behaving like that; that we don't run into any classroom, that we walk into a classroom. And I would send them all outside and make them line up until there was absolute silence and then I would make them walk in, in an orderly manner, and sit down on the chairs properly.

The territorial aspect (*my* classroom) was echoed by

another teacher, who would also use voice and eye contact to establish authority, saying:

> Your behaviour was disgraceful, disgraceful. Never again shall you enter my class like that—*my* class, by the way: I am your teacher today. Never again enter a class like that. Oh, and by the way, look at my face—I'm not smiling, I'm dead serious.

Those who would not send children outside talked about some activity that would settle the class, preferring to look ahead to the lesson in hand, commenting only briefly on the poor behaviour. One teacher of infants was used to the boisterous entry and was also well prepared for it:

> They've obviously come in really high and excited from playtime and I would have quietening—down [activity], either a story or else a little game or something on the easel, either a number or a language thing. You can put up things like 'What can you tell me about the number 10?' And they have to think of sums about the number 10 or rhyming '-ing' words. But I think I would do something all together and say that they hadn't come in very nicely and perhaps next time to see how nicely they came in, without jostling each other because somebody's going to get hurt.

Incident 2

In the second photograph a girl is seen standing in front of the class, a boy sitting near by is laughing. Teachers were told, 'In the afternoon you catch this girl scribbling on someone else's book. You tell her off in front of the rest of the class and, much to your surprise, she mutters, 'Old cow,' under her breath. You do not think the majority of the class heard it, but those sitting near by start to snigger. What, if anything, do you do?

All the respondents found this challenge to their authority much more difficult to handle. First reactions revealed this. 'Oh dear,' 'My God, how am I going to cope?' 'Panic!' 'That's difficult.' Most decided that their reaction would be determined by the kind of child involved, and fifteen teachers emphasised the importance of being seen to take action by the rest of the class. Some distinguished between the way they would respond as a class teacher, taking the child to one side, because they would know her, and how, as a supply teacher, they would react in a much more peremptory manner:

> in a supply situation where she might have just done it and that's it -she's said a comment and somebody's heard and they snigger—the whole thing could escalate. I think I would ask her to repeat what she had said and say, 'I thought that's what you said. Go out of my classroom, because I'm not having somebody talk to me in that tone of voice.' I'd send her outside the door and I'd ask her to come in when she felt she could apologise to me.

A number of teachers expressed the view that supply teachers were more likely to be the subject of a 'try-on' than regular teachers, and some gave examples of what they had done in real-life situations when subjected to verbal abuse:

> I said 'Do you use that .... sort of language at home?' and he said. 'Yes', I said, 'Who to?' He said, 'My mum.' I know what it was — he said

> to me. 'Stuff it.' I said, 'I beg your pardon?' He didn't repeat it, and said, 'Don't you ever say that to me again.' I said, 'When did you say that to her?' He said. 'Well, she wouldn't let me go swimming the other night, so I said it to her.' I said, 'What did you mum say?' He said, 'Nothing,' and I said, 'Well, I'm saying something. You say that once more and you'll be in trouble, because I shall take you straight down to [the head teacher] and sort you out.....

Some teachers sought to defuse the event by taking the girl outside, away from her audience, talking to her quietly later, but only the one inexperienced teacher in the sample, in her first year, said she would ignore it completely, though four others said they would play down it importance.

Supply Teachers' Strategies

That much of what supply teachers said about their preparation, rules, relationships and handling of misbehaviour was not unlike responses from teachers in other studies is understandable. They were, after all, experienced teachers in every case but one. What distinguished them, however, was their lack of knowledge of the particular school and classroom conventions and of individual children. In order to compensate for this, they had developed coping strategies, preparing for several eventualities, like the 'infants' bag and the 'juniors' bag, usually arriving early to find out about routines and set up their class, and even to rehearse their opening.

They tended to see their role as the maintenance of someone else's system, but could quickly become territorial and take about '*my* classroom' or '*my* rules' to the impress on the class that though they might be transient, they were real teachers who were in charge. Most had developed routines that they could transplant, such as the 'fast' queue for spellings and the 'slow' queue for bigger problems. All were aware of the importance of their very first encounter, during which most tried consistently to project an image of being firm but fair. Many established a parent-like bonding ritual, mentioning their own children, asking pupils about brothers and sisters, sitting in close proximity on the carpet. Alongside this friendliness was a strong need to establish dominance should the occasion arise, by reacting quickly to misbehaviour, taking a more authoritarian stance than they might they might if they were the class's regular teacher. They were, in most cases, acutely aware of rules, routines and standards of behaviour, reflecting the observation of Brophy (1987) that teachers are like those circus performers who keep plates spinning at the top of sticks, managing, monitoring events continually and responding quickly when breakdowns threaten.

With their ability to be pro-active inhibited or curtailed by their lack of detailed knowledge of the children in their classes, supply teachers tended to make quick appraisals and treat some children as exemplars of certain stereotypes of behaviour or ability. Lacking the fully developed mental maps and file cards that would provide the knowledge available to the class's regular teacher, they often have to resort to typificatory knowledge (Brophy 1987), that is, intelligence about children at large, acquired in different circumstances, which then has to be used to meet particular events and incidents.

Expediency decrees that supply teachers should be able to respond quickly, behaving as experienced rather than novice teachers. This can involve a degree of stereotyping, of labelling certain types of child behaviour in terms of parallel experience elsewhere, assuming that what is encountered is illustrative of a whole genus of comparable events elsewhere. Most supply teachers tempered this pressure to respond instantly on the basis of generalisations with a genuine desire to get to know children as individuals, but this was only possible when they had a longer period of time with a class, rather than the single day or half-day which some experienced. In the circumstances, it seems regrettable that those supply teachers who needed most support, in return for lubricating the school' system, were often given least support and were, in most cases, unable to attend any training courses or even obtain copies of national curriculum documents.

Thus there are some aspects which make supply teaching a typical. On the other hand, there is much to be learned from those who cope well in sometimes unenviable circumstances, especially about preparation, presence, and the quick establishment of fair and effective rules and of positive relationship.

7

Pupils Views of Management

Relatively little research into teaching has solicited pupils' views. Yet they will spend several thousand hours sitting in primary school classes, and the German social psychologist Kurt Lewin (1943) claimed that children as young as 3 or 4 could be even more sensitive than adults to certain situations. One early survey of 672 studies of teacher effectiveness by Domas and Tiedeman (1950) reported that only seven of these had used some form of pupil rating. Only in higher education, particularly in the United States, has the student's evaluation been given any prominence (Marsh 1985).

The reluctance to use pupil perceptions is understandable. Most primary pupils have only experienced one school in one particular social setting, and they have a restricted view of teaching and of what adult life or the secondary phase of schooling may hold for them, so they will often favour the familiar. Were one to base a school or classroom system entirely on pupil opinion it would probably be ultra-conservative. On the other hand, even with limited experience from their interactions with and perceptions of others, from their reading, conversations, and viewing of television, children are capable of asking questions or making observations about classroom practice. Whilst few would advocate basing teaching entirely on pupil opinion, it is difficult to justify ignoring it completely, especially when such research as exists reports certain consistent findings.

It has commonly been found that pupils, when given a list of teacher behaviour or characteristics, will rate competence in key professional skills most highly. In one of the earliest studies Hollis (1935) gave over 8,000 pupils seven statements about teacher behaviour. Highest ranking was given to the teacher's ability to explain difficulties patiently, though the format of that particular study does not allow one to infer whether it was the explanation or the patience that was most valued. Nearly fifty years later Wragg and Wood (1984) analysed the responses of 200 pupils aged 11 to 16 on a checklist of thirty two items using a five-point Likert scale on their concept of 'the best teacher in the world.' The most highly rated statement was. 'This teacher would explain things clearly.'

Research into pupils' perceptions has been summarised by several writers. Evans (1962) concluded that pupils seemed to prefer personal characteristic such as kindness, friendliness, patience, fairness and a sense of humour. They disliked sarcasm, favouritism, domineering and excessive punishment. Nash (1976) used a repertory-grid technique to elicit constructs from young secondary pupils and found almost exactly the same characteristics: good discipline, explaining skills, interest in pupils, fairness and friendliness. Summaries by Meighan (1977), Cohen and Manion (1981) and Wragg and Wood (1984) reported a similar picture. The empirical study by Wragg and Wood also found that teachers were expected to be firm but fair. Teachers who were bossy or punitive were not esteemed, but neither were those who were too permissive. 'This teacher would let you mark your own tests' and 'This teacher would do something else if that's what the class wanted' were both statements which received very low ratings on the 'best teacher' schedule.

Despite the paucity of research into the pupil perspective on classroom life, there is, nonetheless, a tenable view that teachers ought to know what pupils think about teaching, not so that they can abdicate their own responsibility for setting and maintaining an agenda, but so that pupils' concepts of teaching can be a legitimate part of classroom teaching and learning. Weinstein (1983) argued the case strongly: 'Being award of students as active interpreters of classroom events forces teachers to examine more closely the effects of their own behaviour on the recipients of these interventions.' It was decided, therefore, that we would interview pupils as part of the Leverhulme Primary Project, so that there would be a pupil perspective from children in the very same classes of teachers we had observed and interviewed, rather than from a separate sample. In all, 460 primary pupils were interviewed, thirty as part of a pilot project and 430 in the main study.

Primary Pupils' View—The Pilot Study

Interviews with young children about teachers and teaching can be difficult, as some find it hard to be specific, tending to offer vague generalisations like 'It's all right,' so we decided to use photographs and a semi-structured interview schedule. A pilot study was conducted in a school which recruited pupils mainly from a large council estate. Thirty pupils from the two oldest classes were interviewed individually. Five photographs, some of them the same as had been used in the interviews with experienced supply and student teachers reported in other chapters of this book, were shown to each child and the interviewer recorded answers to set questions, which were similar in wording to those asked of the teachers.

Photograph 1 shows two pupils pushing each other at the end of a classroom. The interviewer said. 'A teacher is sitting with her back to this group when she hears a noise. She turns round and sees two children who are not working. She has already told them off once that day for not getting on with their work. What do you think the teacher will do?'

The most common response was that the teacher would move the children, ten saying they would be sent out of the room, nine suggesting that the pupils would be separated from each other and made to sit elsewhere. Four pupils thought a telling-off would suffice, but only one child suggested further action: 'Probably, after school, she'd have a talk with them and ask what they were doing and who started it and that, and then she might send a letter back to their parents.'

Photograph 2 shows children rushing into a classroom. The story line was: 'After playtime this class go running into their classroom pushing each other, squealing and laughing. What do you think the teacher will do?'

Almost all respondents suggested the children would be sent outside and made to re-enter in an orderly manner, usually with a reprimand, one saying 'Do it again and again until they get it right.' Two pupils embroidered their explanation of 'telling off' by suggesting the teacher would give a reason for it, one girl saying 'The teacher would get angry and I think she'd tell them to sit down and give them a good talking to and explain why they shouldn't be doing it, because someone could get hurt, or work could get knocked off the table and get damaged, or anything like that.'

Photograph 3 shows a girl standing at the front of the

class looking sullen and resentful. The interviewer said, 'The interviewer caught this girl scribbling on someone else's book. When the teacher tells the girl off in front of the class, the girl says something rude about the teacher. Not everyone in the class could hear what the girl had said, but the teacher and those sitting near by certainly did. What do you think the teacher will do?'

Such an insult to the teacher was seen as a major school offence by virtually every pupil, and eighteen thought she would be sent to the head. The others thought the teacher would deal with it herself and administer a punishment, like writing out a hundred lines 'I will not say rude words again' or even suspension from school, a power not actually vested in individual teachers.

Photograph 4 depicts the tail end of queue of children waiting to enter the hall. The children were told, 'A class is going into the half for a PE lesson and this is the back of the queue. The class teacher is at the front. When they arrive at the hall Bobby, the boy in blue, is crying. When the teacher asks him what is wrong he says that Jason, the boy in yellow, had thumped him in the back. The teacher had not seen what had happened this time, but she has been Jason thumping and nipping other children before. All the class are watching the teacher what do you think she will do?'

What was interesting about many of the responses to this picture was that several pupils assumed that Jason would lie abut the event, denying he had done anything, and thus causing difficulties for the teacher. Their responses, therefore, included suggestions about how the teacher might need to keep him in after school until he confessed. If he did confess, then, it was believed by respondents, it might be easier for him, but the teacher would almost certainly shout at him. There was great insistence on the teacher sorting out the problem properly, pupils clearly identifying with 'victim' in such circumstances and wanting protection, as this girl indicated: '(The teacher should find out the truth) because Jason keeps on going round hitting people and he should stop it and the teacher ought to find out if he's still doing it.

This notion of terminating aggressive behaviour to protect the rest, bringing in parents if necessary, was echoed by others:

> They'd just have to try and think of a way of trying to get it out of them [Jason and any friends who cover up for him] because.... If he keeps on doing it to other children and they won't admit it, he's just going to get worse and keep on doing it to other children. If he does keep doing it, they'll just have to get hold of his parents and tell them to come down because it's bad behaviour.

Few doubted Jason's guilt and some went so far as to suggest that both pupils would be kept in after school, on the grounds that such events are often two-sided, rather than isolated acts of aggression by unprovoked individuals.

Photograph 5 was of two pupils making paper aeroplanes instead of getting on with their work. The story line was: 'Just before home time the teacher is called out of the classroom to deal with a problem. When she comes back there is quite a lot of noise, two children are making paper aeroplanes and others are watching them. What do you think she will do?'

Half the respondents thought this was likely to be punished with a detention after school, and most ignored the role played by the observers. Eight children suspected that the paper aeroplane would be thrown in the waste bin, and one boy said that the teacher would reprimand them for wasting paper. This incident was probably the mildest of the five in the eyes of most pupils, and would have earned little more than a reprimand.

What was striking about these responses by thirty children to five picture situations, 150 replies in all, was that only one pupil said, 'Don't know,' to one picture, and the other 149 were usually clear and gave immediate replies to the stimulus of the picture, even though the interviewer had made it clear to the pupils that they could have as much time as they needed. The rudeness to the teacher in photograph 3 was clearly a major school offence in the eyes of most pupils and required higher authority. Few children suggested teachers would give reasons for their reactions, most assumed it would be instant and self-justifying. Leniency and humour were almost never mentioned, the common assumption being that teachers would react immediately and severely.

The Main Study

It was decided that the main study would not use all five pictures, as interviews would become extremely time-consuming. Instead we concentrated on the first three pictures, showing the two pupils pushing each other, the class rushing into the room, and the child insulting the teacher, as these had provoked an interesting mixture of responses and had been used with their teachers. We also decided to interview children across the whole primary age range, from 5 up to 12, and to add further questions about class management.

A sample of 430 pupils aged 5-12 in twenty classes in eight different schools was selected. The schools were in the North-west and the South-west of England and in

London. They represented a mix between inner-city and rural schools, were all in schools where we were studying teachers, and were almost equally divided between boys and girls, with 52 per cent and 48 per cent respectively. The additional interview questions asked, after an explanation of the purposes and nature of the interview, were: 'Can you tell me what things you are not allowed to do?' Do you think children should be allowed to talk to each other during lessons?' (Why?/Why not?) 'Imagine the best teacher in the whole world, someone who is absolutely brilliant at teaching. What do you think this very good teacher would be like?' (Followed by 'Imagine the worst teacher in the whole world,' etc.) 'What sort of things do children do in class when they are naughty?' 'What do you do?' and 'What happens?' These were designed to allow children to give their own perceptions of effective teaching, of inappropriate behaviour, and their own accounts of what they themselves do.

One important strategic decision about the interviewer's wording when introducing the three photographs was to substitute 'What do you think happens next?' for the previous final sentence, 'What do you think the teacher will do?' This was in order to permit a wider range of possibilities than just action by the teacher. As in the pilot study all children interviewed were told that there were no 'right' or 'wrong' answers, that they were to say what they really felt, and that no teachers or fellow pupils would be told what they had replied.

An interesting feature of the pupil perspective is that, because pupils related to the children in the picture, whereas the teacher respondents reacted as a teacher, they would often give replies that were focused on what pupils do. For example, no teacher in our sample aid. 'I would not notice (or would ignore) what happened, and, as a consequence, the pupils would continue to mess abut because I had taken no action.' Yet this kind of outcome was seen in classrooms, and pupils do offer suggestions like 'The pupils will fight' or that they would carry on fooling around, as table 7.1 giving the responses of the 430 pupils to photograph 1, reveals.

Children use their own neutral language when asked about classroom events. 'Telling off,' the most common response, was often unspecific, as children assumed that everyone must know what a telling-off means. Youngest respondents, particularly 5 year olds, simply used the expression 'get told off,' whereas older pupils were often more specific: 'The teacher would tell that one off,' said one 12 year old, pointing to one of the pupils he judged to be more at fault. Some pupils were aware of a choice of possible outcomes: 'They get sent to wait outside and they go to the headmistress, and they get told off, and the headmistress gets their mum to come in and speak to the teacher.'

TABLE 7.1

Percentage of Responses in Ten Most Frequently Occurring Categories to Photograph 1 (Two Pupils Pushing Each Other)

	Predicted outcome	*Percentage of Pupils*
1.	Teacher will tell them off	30.4
2.	They will be sent to the head	25.3
3.	They will be sent outside	7.9
4.	They will be sent elsewhere	7.4
5.	They carry on messing about	6.7
6.	They get into trouble	6.7
7.	The teacher will split them up	6.3
8.	They will fight	4.4
9.	They will get on with their work	4.2
10.	They will be kept in after school	4.0

Experienced teachers tended to give as their most common response that the children would be moved, but only 6 or 7 per cent of pupil respondents mentioned this. 'She'll put them in a corner' and 'She'll stand them at the wall' were two suggestions from 6 year olds, but it was usually older pupils who offered variations of the reply of the 10 year old who said, 'She'll be very angry with them and she might move them apart from each other so they'll get on with their work.'

Amongst responses from pupils which were not present in teachers' replies are several suggestions that the teacher would be ineffective: 'They fight again,' 'They didn't get on with their work,' 'When the teacher turns her back again, they start messing about again.' 'They start having a fight and messing about again. They get told off and go to the office.' These kinds of replies mirror quite accurately what we sometimes saw during observations of lessons. On most occasions teachers did respond with reprimands and orders to cease, the 'telling off' reported by pupils, and on some occasions they failed to respond before the misbehaviour had escalated or even, rarely, failed to respond at all. Pupil responses confirm this mixed pattern. Four 5 year olds said the children would be smacked by the teacher but we witnessed no corporal punishment in schools, and these young children probably based their surmise on home rather than school experience.

Photograph 2, of the children rushing into the room after break, also produced 'telling off' as the most likely response, but external authority was rarely cited on this occasion. Pushing and shoving were deemed to be part of everyday school life, and the teacher was most likely to shout and scold rather than involve higher authority, an option only mentioned by one per cent of respondents. Table 7.2 gives the breakdown of most common responses.

Some of the minor categories, too small to figure in Table 7.2, are of interest here. About 2 per cent of pupils suggested the teacher would give reasons why the behaviour was unacceptable, and 2 per cent also suggested that the bad behaviour would continue.

TABLE 7.2

Percentage of Responses in Ten Most Frequently Occurring Categories to Photograph 2 (Children Rushing into Classroom)

	Predicted Outcome	*Percentage of pupils*
1.	Teacher will tell them off	29.5
2.	Teacher will shout at them	17.7
3.	Teacher tells them to sit down	12.6
4.	Teacher makes them come in again	11.9
5.	Teacher tells them to be quiet	10.9
6.	Children will fall over	9.8
7.	Someone will get hurt	9.1
8.	Children get on with their work	7.9
9.	Children will sit down	2.8
10.	Teacher will tell children to stop	2.3

There was huge difference in the responses of teachers and pupils on the matter of re-entry. The most frequent response from teachers, at 77 per cent, was that pupils would be made to re-enter in an orderly fashion, but for pupils it was about 12 per cent. This may mirror actual practice, and we found numerous examples of close fit between practice we had observed and children's responses. There was one teacher in our sample who, both in her observed behaviour and in her interview response, was very keen on orderly entry, saying in her interview, 'Get them to do it again quietly. I feel you can do that preventively.' In her class nineteen out of the twenty-six pupils gave the re-entry outcome as their own reply, a much higher proportion than for the whole sample.

Children readily emphathised with other children seen in the pictures, and the pupil responses showed quite an awareness of safety and the possibility of injury:

> One of them falls over and everybody's going to run over him.
>
> (Ten year old)

> One of them gets hurt. There'd be a bundle. They wouldn't be able to get through the door. They'd have to back out and come back in one at a time.
>
> (Seven year old)

> Somebody might get hurt or somebody might fall over or they might bang their head on one of the tables if they do fall over.
>
> (Nine year old)

In their replies to the third photograph, of the girl who has scribbled on children's books and called the teacher an 'old cow' (the children were told that the child would say something rude'). There was an interesting focus not just on the girl, but on the rest of the class, which was not so noticeable in the teachers' responses. Table 7.3 shows the distribution of replies over the ten most commonly occurring categories. The pupils were well aware of the notion of 'audience' in their replies, for they are, after all, sometimes the audience for such events themselves. There was quite a deal of talk, therefore, about other pupils being reprimanded, not just the girl. For example, a boy is visible in the picture smiling at what is happening, and many respondents commented that he would be told off for laughing. Also about 10 per cent of children said that a pupil would tell the teacher what the girl had said. This was regarded as a serious offence with 17 per cent of pupils saying the girl would be sent to the head, yet this is lower than the 25 per cent who thought the two boys pushing each other in picture 1 would be sent to the head. The interviewer did not raise this specifically, so as not to put ideas into the children's heads, but it may be that higher authority was thought to be necessary for two aggressive boys, less so for one rude girl pupil. A further study would be needed to elicit this.

TABLE 7.3

Percentage of Responses in Ten Most Frequently Occurring Categories for Photograph 3 (Girl Calls Teacher 'Old Cow')

	Predicted outcome	*Percentage of pupils*
1.	Teacher will tell off girl and/or other pupil(s)	37.7
2.	Girl will be sent to the head	17.2
3.	Teacher asks pupil(s) why they are laughing	9.5
4.	Pupils tell teacher what girl said	9.5
5.	Girl will get into trouble	6.7
6.	Girl will be sent into corner	5.3
7.	Girl will be sent out of room	4.0
8.	Teacher will shout/show anger	4.0
9.	Teacher will speak to girl/others	3.7
10.	Teacher will give reasons why behaviour wrong	3.5

The pupils' response are not exactly comparable to the teachers' replies, as the former were asked what would happen next and the latter what they themselves would do. However, it is clear that pupils expect to be told off for misbehaviour, to be sent to the head of more serious misconduct, and to be moved, sent outside or shouted at if they act anti-socially with others. They are also aware that teachers' best intentions to curb misbehaviour are not always fulfilled and that deviance can and will escalate if unchecked. There were numerous other close matches between what we observed in a particular teacher's classroom and what the pupils responded. Five classes whose teachers tended to shout when they misbehaved showed a higher incidence of 'teacher shouts' responses and four classes showed a higher than average tendency to use the 'teacher tells to sit down' category, which was consistent with the teacher's normal behaviour.

In addition to the photograph response, pupils were asked a series of questions about behaviour in the classroom and about what teachers do, and a sub-sample of 105 of these detailed responses, consisting of one class each of 5-6, 6-7, 7-8, 9-11 and 11-12 year olds, are reported here. The intention of the first question, asking what pupils are allowed to do, was to generate positive rather than negative responses. The five most common responses were (1) work, (2) talk to each other, (3) play when we've finished our work, (4) choose something we want to do and (5) walk freely in the classroom (with a reason). This mixture of work an choice came out clearly in several responses, some respecting the freedom, others not:

> We've got to do our work, then sometimes, in the afternoon, if we do all our work 'we're allowed to play with the Lego and we're allowed to write letters over there (pointing) to people when it's their birthday or something.
>
> (Seven year old)

> We're allowed to get on with our work, sort of on our own. We don't have to do everything, we don't have to do the same things all the time.
>
> (Eleven year old)

> You're allowed to talk quietly, but you're not allowed to shout, which is what everyone usually does instead of getting on with their work.
>
> (Eight year old)

> We're allowed to choose. We're allowed to play in the house, we can play in the big sandpit or the little sandpit, which is out there, or we can play outside or do some writing or drawing.
>
> (Six year old)

Play was principally mentioned by the 5-6 and 6-7 year olds. It was perceived as play by pupils, but teachers saw it as school work with choice.

When it came to asking children what they were not allowed to do the list of responses was much longer. In first five places were (1) shout, (2) be silly/mess about, (3) fight, (4) through things, (5) run. Even younger pupils had a well shaped sense of what the teacher's rules were:

> We're not allowed to muck about, we're not allowed to fight and we're not allowed to yell at the top of our voices, and a few other things which I can't remember. We've got quite a lot of rules—loads.
>
> (Eight year old)
>
> We're not allowed to scream, we're not allowed to shout, we're not allowed to throw things around the classrooms, not allowed to be naughty, we're not allowed to do mean things to people like scratch and punch and kick, and that's it really.
>
> (Seven year old)
>
> You're not really allowed to copy, you've got to do your own work. When you [are] working with someone, you're to discuss it with them and not shout at them. If you haven't finished and you've had a long time to do a certain piece of work then you've got to stay in at break and

> finish it, and if it's like near the end of the day, then you've got to take it home and finish it for homework.
>
> (Ten year old)

The concern with shouting reflects the category of misbehaviour we observed most frequently, namely noisy chatter. Pupils were clearly divided by age on the matter of whether talking in the classroom should be permitted at all. Table 7.4 shows how they responded, and the older pupils took a more sophisticated view of classroom talk than the younger pupils, who usually assumed it must be wrong. Of the thirty-six 9-12 year olds who replied 'Yes', 16 qualified it by adding that it was legitimate only if related to work or if done quietly. The reasons for replies were mainly, for those who replied 'Yes,' because it helped you with your work, stopped you getting bored, helped concentration and allowed you to check your answers. Those who saw it negatively said it interfered with work, you got told off, you wouldn't hear the teacher and it interrupted others. Some of the more aware pupils in the 'it depends' category gave a balanced view of the pros and cons:

> If it's about work, then yes, and they're not making too much noise, but if they're mucking about or talking about what they did at the weekend, then no, because they're not getting on with their work properly and they'll probably get told off and get extra work.
>
> (Ten year old)

The question about the best and worst teacher in the world produced responses not unlike those reported in other studies described earlier in this chapter. The best teacher in the world would, according to this sample, do interesting activities and also let you choose, be 'nice,' kind and 'good at teaching, which was variously interpreted as a combination of subject knowledge ('brainy,' 'understands a lot') and professional skill (explains,' 'good at teaching you about computers' (seven pupils, all in the same class)). The best teacher in the world would be quite strict, 'not let you get away with things,' but not too bossy, and would have a sense of humour. This general picture of pupils' perceptions obtained from these interviews is almost exactly what other studies have found, confirming that the pupil perception literature is astonishingly consistent across time and age groups.

TABLE 7.4

Replies to Question, 'Should Children be Allowed to Talk to Each Other in Lessons?'

	Age group					
Response	*5-6*	*6-7*	*7-8*	*9-10*	*11-12*	*Total*
Yes	4	2	8	19	17	50
No	13	15	12	2	0	42
Sometimes	1	1	1	2	2	7
It depends	0	2	0	3	1	6
Total	18	20	21	26	20	105

Younger pupils tended to name a teacher quite naturally, often their current 'teacher, assuming she must be the best. Some twenty seven out of thirty eight 5-7 year olds named a teacher, and eleven of these were their current teacher, whereas only five of the sixty seven older pupils named a teacher, of which three were their own. When it came to the 'worst teacher in he world' stereotype only thirteen pupils named a teacher, again mainly younger ones, and only one of these was the child's current teacher. The responses here were often the obverse of the good teacher stereotype, and the most dislike characteristics were shouting and yelling at children, not allowing you to talk, telling people off all the time, often unfairly, not knowing how to teach, being 'nasty' and over-bossy, not letting you do things you like, being rude to children, setting work that is too hard and using excessive punishments. The greater sophistication and more abstract discernment of the older pupil and the more concrete, specific world view of the younger pupil are well illustrated by these two responses expressing a similar view:

> They'd get cross at the slightest thing and they'd go round not really noticing, they'd go round teaching people and they'd get cross if you got things wrong, instead of seeing how you got it wrong and making sure you understand. They wouldn't talk to you about it, so they'd just snap at you.
>
> (Eleven year old)

> The lady who's in there (pointing to a teacher in another room) she kept on shouting at us and we couldn't get on with our work. But I done it good, so I didn't get told off.
>
> (Six year old)

The questions about what naughty children do in class and how the teacher responds reflected and reinforced answers we had received to earlier questions. There were clear views on what constitutes naughty behaviour, and, as previously, these reflected violence to another person and noise. Kicking, pushing, fighting, shouting, screaming, throwing or flicking things, messing about and damage to property were all mentioned frequently, closely followed by illicit talking, swearing, not working, fidgeting and running. The most reported responses from the teacher were a telling-off, being sent to the head or sent outside, told to get on with your work, punishing with extra work, shouting, getting cross and warning about future conduct. In classes where teachers actually dealt with misbehaviour in a positive manner this was greatly appreciated by children, who often spoke spontaneously in approving terms, like this 7 year old:

> *What naughty pupils do* '..... punishing other people. Like Miss Brown [class teacher] says, if they swear at people they're getting bitchy. That's what Miss Brown says.'
>
> *What happens* 'We have a circle time [when the pupils and teacher sit around in a circle] and ask people what they do to people. Then Miss Brown tries to sort it out and mostly she gets it all sorted out and she's really good at it. She's good at sorting it out.'

About half (fifty two out of 105) the children admitted to being naughty in class, with older pupils showing few inhibitions about admitting it and younger pupils responding more warily. Only three out of the eighteen 5-6 year olds in the sample replied 'Yes,' whereas seventeen of the oldest twenty children replied in the affirmative. The contrast is revealed by these two responses from a younger and older pupil:

> *Are you ever naughty?*
> No. I get on with my work and I don't talk.
>
> (Five year old)
>
> *Are you ever naughty?*
> Sometimes.
> *What do you do?*
> Throw rubbers and paper.
> *What happens?*

> I don't know, I've never been caught
>
> (Twelve year old)

Most pupils were well aware of the consequences of misbehaviour and could describe them in great detail, appreciating such matters as confidentiality or the significance of status, even when the teacher or the school had intricate rituals, often involving the school hierarchy in an elaborate chain of events:

> I got a yellow card. It's just a warning. You get one when you get told off. The first card you get is normal, and then if you do it again you go into a corner or another class, and then you go to the headmistress and then you get a letter home to the parents.
>
> (Eight year old)

> Even very young children had a clear understanding of the borderline between what the teacher would regard as acceptable and what would be regarded as deviant. Fighting was the third most frequently mentioned 'naughty' behaviour, but there was a clear distinction between the real thing and rough-and-tumble role-played versions:

> I just plays on my own with my cousin and some of my friends. We plays a little fight, it's a play fight. You just pretended to punch like that (demonstrates mock blow), and that's pretending. You won't stand near the wall. I don't be naughty outside.
>
> (Six year old)

This part of our enquiry showed that children have a perspective on misbehaviour that is often different from that of the teacher, though they can repeat the school's official policies on discipline with clarity and apparent consent. Spending up to thirty five hours a week in school ensures that they experience their teachers management rituals and routines numerous times. There is little ambiguity in the minds of even the youngest pupils about what is expected, and what will ensue if they transgress. Yet their vantage point is different from that of teachers. They see shouting and telling off as a normal part of classroom life, to be expected even, whereas teachers tend to be more embarrassed at mentioning these, from their point of view, cruder responses.

Not surprisingly aggression features high on their list of concerns, as they are well aware that a fellow belligerent pupil can easily knock them over in a rush, hit them, or cause them some other mischief, and they appreciate teachers who, without themselves being over-domineering, are clearly in charge when it comes to dealing with over-aggressive behaviour. It confirms the popular child stereotype of successful teaching reported in other enquiries — in charge, firm but fair, knowing their craft, able to explain clearly, pleasant to be with, good-humoured and good-natured— and loath to shout.

8

Explaining and Explanations

Explaining is not only a professional skill which is highly esteemed by children. It is an aspect of communication which lies at the centre of human discourse in many fields: parents explain things to their children; radio and television presenters explain what lies behind news stories to listeners and viewers: pilots explain the cause of delay to air travellers. In the case of doctors and patients there can be, as in teaching, reciprocal explanations: the patient first explains symptoms to the doctor, and the doctor then explains causes and treatments to the patient. Explaining is not, however, a unidimensional activity, and the words 'explain' and 'explanation' are used in many different ways. For the purposes of this research we took as an operational definition the statement: 'explaining is giving understanding to another.' This interpretation allows the notion to embrace strategies other than imparting information directly, as it can include, for example, asking questions which encourage pupils to reach their own conclusions, engaging in practical work or giving a demonstration.

Explanations can help some to understand a concept like 'density' or 'prejudice,' and the notion may be new to the learner, or already partly familiar. They can also illuminate cause and effect, for example that rain is produced by the cooling of air. There are many other possibilities, such as the explanation of procedures, including both those within the subject domain, like how to convert a fraction to a decimal, and those to do with the management of the lesson, such as ways of ensuring that no one has an accident in a gymnastics lesson. There can be explanations of purposes and objectives, when a teacher explains why children are going to embark on a study of their own village, or what they will have learned at the conclusion of some activity; of relationships between people, events or the different parts of something, like why bees and flies are insects but spiders are not, or what religious festivals like Christmas and Easter have in common; of the processes involved in the working of a piece of machinery or the behaviour of people or animals. Explanations often answer real or imaginary questions based on common interrogatives like Who? What? How? Why?

Numerous investigations have sought to assemble a typology of explanations, and Brown and Armstrong (1984) have summarised work by Swift (1961), Bellack *et al.*, (1966), Ennis (1969), Smith and Meux (1970) and Brown (1978). They produced a chart (Table 8.1) which compares three views of the process of explaining. Research into explanations in the classroom has been summarised by Crowhurst (1988). Such research is sparse compare with enquiry into other teaching strategies. Smith and Meux analysed transcripts of eighty five lessons given by seventeen teachers in five high schools. They split the lessons into a series of 'episodes' and found that describing, designating and explaining were the three operations that occurred most frequently. Tisher (1970) used the classification scheme developed by Smith and Meux to analyse the relationship between teachers' strategies in nine science classes and children's understanding in science. Explaining ranked as fourth most frequently used strategy after designating, describing and stating.

Brown and Armstrong (1984) used their own system for analysing discourse to elicit which features distinguished the lessons of twelve student teachers explaining biological topics to children. They used independent ratings of videotapes of the lessons and pupil learning as measured by post-tests to identify the more 'effective' explanations. These were shown on analysis to be characterised by more 'keys,' that is, central principles or generalisations which help to unlock understanding. The more successful explanations also had more framing statements which showed the beginnings and endings of sub-topics, more focusing statements emphasising the key points, and used the rule—example—rule structure—e.g. an insect has, among other characteristics, six legs (rule), a fly is an insect (example), so insects have six legs (rule)—which had also been identified by Gage *et al.* (1972) as effective. However, the rule—example—rule pattern seemed to work best in interpretive explanations, when technical terms were being explored. In reason-giving and descriptive explanations, when processes were being explored, the example—rule—example model seemed to be effective.

The mater of cognitive level is also relevant to research into explaining, and this topic will be dealt with again in the report of the research on questioning. The level of thinking involved in classroom teaching and learning has been discussed by Bloom (1956), whose taxonomy of educational objectives in the cognitive domain has frequently been used or modified. Bloom formulated a hierarchical view of learning at six levels, starting with knowledge and then going on to comprehension, application, analysis, synthesis and finally evaluation. The assumption was that one needed the lower levels in order to achieve the higher levels: you need to have knowledge in order to comprehend, and you must comprehend in order to be able to analyse, synthesise or evaluate. Taba (1966) devised a similar set of thought levels in her work at San Francisco State College helping teachers move children up to higher levels of thought, though there is no constructive research evidence that operating at higher levels is inevitably associated with 'better learning,'.

TABLE 8.1

Three Typologies of Explaining

After Hyman (1974)	*After Smith and Meux (1970)*	*After Brown (1978)*
Type 1 Generalisation—Specific Instance		
Empirical The effects of pressure on the volume of gas	*Empirical-subsumptive* Seasonal changes on mammals	Reason-giving, answering the *question 'Why?'* Why does the volume of a gas decrease as pressure increases? Why do certain mammals hibernate in winter?
Probabilistic Relation between lung cancer and smoking	Judgmental Causes of higher crime rate in urban areas	Why do heavy smokers have a greater risk of contracting cancer? Why is there more crime in inter-city areas?
Non-empirical A verb agrees with its subject	*Normative* The proper use of knives and forks	Why do we say, 'He runs,' but 'They run'? Why do we hold a fork in the left hand?
Type II Functional		
Purpose The motives behind Lord Jim's actions	*Teleological* Birds of prey as efficient hunters	Interpretive, answering *the question 'What?'* What led Lord Jim to become the strange character he was? What uses do talons and curved beaks serve in birds of prey?
Function Unions and their members	*Consequence* Inflation and our money	What can unions do in an industrial dispute? What are the effects of a high inflation rate on the currency?

cont...

Type III Serial

		Descriptive answering *the question 'How?'*
Sequential Making a sponge cake	*Sequential* Constructing a perpendicular to a given line	How do you make a light sponge? How can a perpendicular be constructed using compass and ruler?
Genetic Differences between cats and dogs	*Mechanical* The operation of a car engine	As animals, how do cats differ from dogs? How does the internal combustion engine work?
Chronological Events leading to the war in Vietnam	*Procedural* Conducting a formal meeting	How did colonial history lead to the Vietnamese war? How does the chairman lead a meeting?

The Present Study of Teachers' Explanations

It was decided to study teachers explaining new subject matter to primary pupils in two major domains of the school curriculum, science and English, as this would enable us to investigate the field in two distinctive and contrasting subject areas. Preliminary informal observations in the classrooms of five teachers in three different schools were made, and lessons whose subject matter ranged from mathematics to country dancing were studied. Examples of explaining episodes were collected. There were also extensive interviews with the teachers concerned. The pilot study involved asking teachers to explain a variety of topics, such as 'the water cycle,' 'erosion,' the difference between 'their' and 'there,' mathematical concepts such as 'parallel' and 'perpendicular,' to small groups of children of different ability.

The pilot study confirmed that explaining took place regularly in lessons, that teachers appeared to use a variety of strategies, that explaining to individual pupils caused some management problems, like children waiting with hand in the air, or standing in a queue if the teacher was explaining at her desk, and that it would be worthwhile studying explanations to children of different levels of ability. The pilot also revealed that several explanatory episodes were related to misbehaviour and class management, like 'why we need to wipe our feet when we come in on a wet day'; that it was not too difficult to test more able children and those of average ability, but that testing low-ability children, particularly in younger age groups, caused great difficulty, as written forms of assessment were often not appropriate and oral forms were extremely time-consuming. Indeed, teachers in the pilot commented on the difficulty of explaining basic concepts to lower-ability pupils generally, about the time taken and the disappointment when little seemed to be understood.

Following the pilot it was decided to concentrate on two topics, one in English, one in science; to study in particular high and medium-ability pupils, as lower-ability pupils would really need a separate study; to give a post-test of learning; to limit the time available for the 'explanation' to ten minutes, as this had been shown to be the sort of time teachers devoted to public discussion of a new topic; and to give teachers a completely free hand in the strategies they used. It was also decided to confine the study to 8 and 9 year old pupils, on the grounds that they wee old enough to be able to write and were in the middle years of primary education, and to have four children in each group, as these could be monitored effectively and four was a size of group to which teachers had often been seen explaining something.

Thus the research was part experimental and part naturalistic. It was experimental, in the sense that the researchers controlled the amount of time available for the exploration (up to ten minutes maximum), the amount of time the children had to complete the post-test (up to fifteen minutes maximum), the two topics in English and science, the ability levels of the children and the number of children in each group (four). Furthermore there was a control group of children who took the post-test but had not been given the teacher's explanation first, as we wanted to see what differences having an explanation appeared to make. The research was also, in part, naturalistic, in that the children were from the teacher's regular class, the explaining took place in a location near the normal class with which children were familiar, say the library, or another classroom, and teachers had a completely free hand in deciding how they explained the topics.

A total of thirty-two teachers from sixteen schools in both urban and rural areas took part in the research. The sample was virtually random as only two schools approached did not wish to take part. Every teacher gave four explanations, two to groups of four children each consisting of two boys and two girls (1) of above average ability (IQ range 110 to 120) and (2) four children of average ability (IQ range 95 to 105). The control group consisted of four children of average ability, so that their test scores could be compared with the experimental average-ability group. It would not always have been possible to have a control group of above average ability, owing to small numbers in some classes. Two topics were selected-firstly a factual scientific topic, 'Insects,' and teachers were told that children should, at the end of the explanation, be able to identify insects and know the parts of an insect; secondly, there was an explanation of an imaginary island (figure 8.1) called the Island of Zarg, which was to be followed by children writing a story entitled 'My Adventure on the Island of Zarg.' The design was thus a very balanced one and the other of teaching was randomised, so that the topic and the ability range were not always taught in the same order by different teachers, otherwise artefacts might have been produced that were relevant to the order in which groups were taught. A summary of the design is given below.

No. of schools: sixteen.

No. of teachers; thirty two (sixteen of 8 year olds, sixteen of 9 years olds).

No. of topics: two, 'Insects' and 'Island of Zarg.'

No. of pupils:

Experimental groups : 128 above-average, 128 average ability.

Control groups 128 average ability.

Total : 384 pupils.

Total number of explanations: four for each teacher (two on 'insects,' two on 'Zarg'), 128 in all.

Order of teaching groups and topics randomised.

The Research Instruments

A great deal of data was generated in the study and several forms of analysis for both process and product data were used (Crowhurst 1988). In the case of the process data, that is, the actual analysis of the classroom explanation, all the explanations were observed live by one of the research team, and an observation schedule, Teacher Explanation Observation Schedule (TEXOS), was developed, which was first piloted in schools and then used in the main study. The TEXOS schedule was a category and sign system derived from observations made at the pilot stage and from ideas in other observation instruments such as those used by Galton (1978) and Brown and Armstrong (1984). All explanations were recorded on sound cassette for further analysis and corroboration.

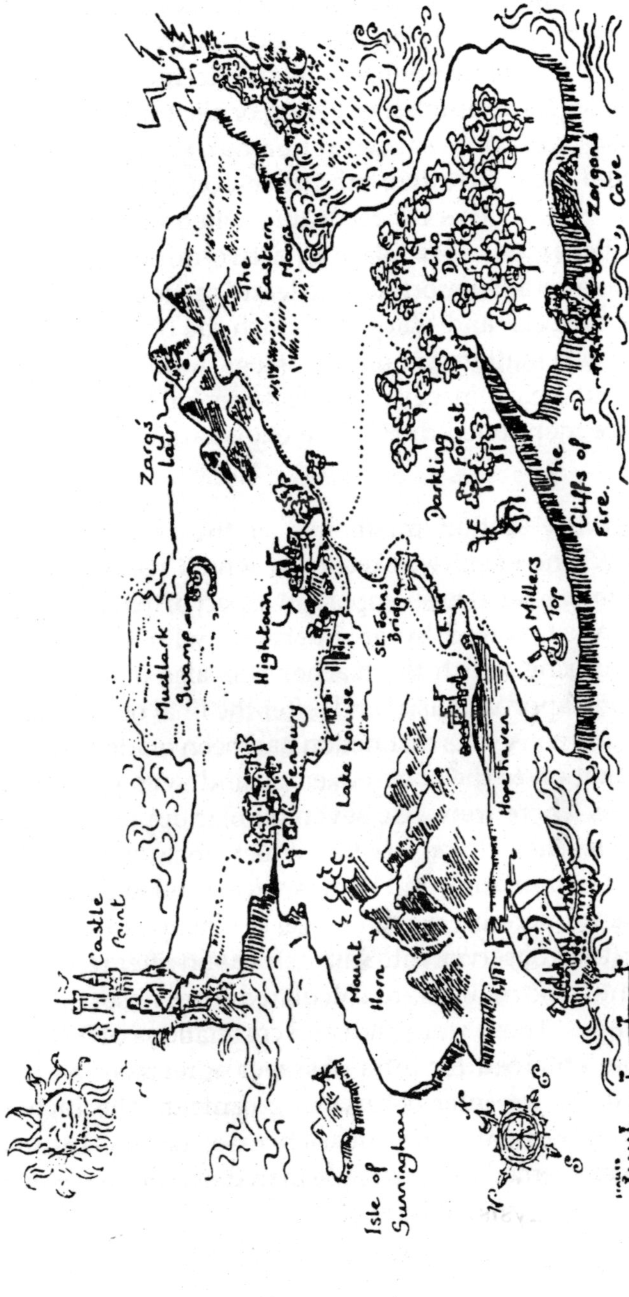

Figure 8.1 The Island of Zarg

Fig. 8.1. The Island of Zarg

The first section summarised background information about the teacher and the class, the second part was a coding system for tallying the nature of questions, pupil responses, teacher responses, linguistic moves, such as using analogies, examples, or giving or eliciting summaries and pauses, social moves such as humour, praise or chiding, and visual aids. Five two-minute lesson segments were coded, with the observer recording whether or not each form of behaviour took place in a two-minute segment. There was also an 'opportunity to learn' section, in separate form for 'Insects' and 'Zarg,' in which the observer noted whether such matters as number of legs, number of wings, spiders not being insects, and features of the Island of Zarg were mentioned during the explanation by pupil or teacher.

The third section made use of the critical events technique. One event was recorded which seemed to the observer to be related to an important aspect of that particular explanation, followed by an interview with the teacher about it, during which the teacher was also asked about the teaching approach used and, after the final observation, whether any conscious distinction had been made between the explanation to the above-average and average groups of children. There were also seven bipolar opposite rating scales of teacher characteristics which included warm/aloof, dull/stimulating and items which rated eye contract and fluency. Inter-observer (between two people) and intra-observer (each observer with self, before and after research) agreement coefficients were calculated from observations of videotapes. These were high and correlations of 0.779 to 0.934 were obtained for intra-observer agreement and of 0.674 to 0.723 for inter-observer agreement. The higher levels of agreement were, in each case, on the Insects topic, which seemed easier to code than the more discursive Island of Zarg explanations.

The product data were of two kinds. First of all there was a test of insect recognition, which involved pictures of several real insects and other creatures, like arachnids and crustaceans. There were also question about insects and an invitation to describe them freehand. Secondly, for the Island of Zarg, children had to write a free composition entitled, 'My Adventure on the Island of Zarg.' The insects questions were scored according to a scheme devised during the pilot study, giving a maximum score of thirty points. The correlation between two independent markers was a very high 0.941.

The creative writing piece scoring system was influenced by the work of Wilkinson *et al.* (1980) and Bennett (1984). It consisted of a series of five-point scales covering imaginativeness, mention of island features, coherence, sentence complexity and story length. Correlations between independent markers were 0.778 (island features mentioned), 0.784 (sentence complexity), 0.789 (coherence), 0.791 (imaginativeness), 0.841 (overall impression) and 0.90 (length).

Research Findings

Lesson Observation

Analysis of the strategies used by teachers revealed a fascination range of tactics, with short questions, short responses and teacher repetition of pupils replies lying at the heart of many explanations. Table 8.2 shows the most frequently occurring features of all explanations recorded using TEXOS. In each case, the range is from a minimum of 0 if the behaviour had not occurred at all, to an absolute maximum of 5 if it had occurred in very single one of the five lesson segments observed in each explanation. The pattern confirms that questioning is a frequently used strategy which leads to shorter or longer pupils answers. Table 8.3 shows, by contrast, the ten least frequently recorded categories.

The common pattern of teacher question, short answer, teacher repeats, teacher probes was observed in both science and English explanations. For example:

Insects

Teacher What sort of things does an insect have on its head?

Pupil Big round eyes.

Teacher Big round eyes, yes—and why do you think an insect needs big round eyes?

Island of Zarg

Teacher What is a Zarg?

Pupil He's a big, black, furry monster.

Teacher A big, black, furry monster. And what sort of monster is he? Is he friendly? Or fierce, perhaps?

TABLE 8.2

Ten Most Frequently Occurring Categories for all Explanations (n = 128)

	TEXOS category	*Frequency (max. = 5)*
1.	Short pupil responses	4.4
2.	Teacher repeats pupil answer	3.8
3.	Teacher open question	3.7
4.	Spontaneous pupil response	3.7
5.	Teacher probes	3.4
6.	Teacher closed question	2.9
7.	Long pupil response	2.9
8.	Teacher pauses	2.6
9.	Teacher rephrases	2.6
10.	Teacher summarises	2.5

TABLE 8.3

Ten Least Frequently Occurring Categories for All Explanations (n = 128)

	TEXOS category	*Frequency (max. = 5)*
1.	Teacher rejects pupil response	0.2
2.	Use of analogy	0.4
3.	No pupil response	0.5
4.	Teacher elicits summary from pupils	0.7
5.	Teacher chides	0.8
6.	Teacher explains links	0.9
7.	Teacher elicits example from pupils	1.1
8.	Teacher corrects pupil	1.4
9.	Teacher gives example	1.4
10.	Teacher gives verbal cue	1.4

The results of the analysis of the processes of explaining show that teachers tended to control the interaction quite carefully, making many of the significant moves themselves, like summing up, questioning, repeating answers, probing. At the same time, there was considerable interaction, and rarely was there no response from pupils, even though their answers were likely to be short. Relatively little use was made of analogies and examples. Analogies occurred mainly in the insect explanations, when referring to the exo-skeleton as being like a suit of armour, or when talking about the eye:

> The surface of the eye looks like lots of marbles packed together in a plastic bag.
>
> It looks like lots of TV screens put together side by side.

The patterns of interaction were further analysed to see what predominant moves occurred. The most highly significant product—moment correlations between the more frequently occurring categories of the TEXOS data are given in Table 8.4. All are significant at beyond the 0.001 level of probability, that is, they would have occurred by chance less than once in a thousand times. There were high correlations between some of the less frequently occurring categories, but these have been omitted as there can often be spurious correlations between frequently occurring pieces of behaviour. This analysis confirms the predominant question-and-answer pattern of interaction, with a variety of questions, some occurring in sequences, followed by short rather than long responses from the pupil (though spontaneous contributions from pupils were more likely to be long, rather than short). The following exchange was typical of this common pattern:

Teacher Is a woodlouse an insect?

Pupil 1 Yes.

Teacher Does it look like an insect?

Pupil 1 Sort of.

Teacher What about its three body parts? Can you find the head, thorax and abdomen?

Pupil 1 I can't find the thorax and abdomen.

Pupil 2 It looks like it's got lots of little body parts.

Teacher Ah! How many legs has it got?

Pupil 2 More than six.

Teacher More than six, and lots of body parts. Is it an insect?

Pupil 1 It can't be.

It was hypothesised hat science and English lessons would be different in explanatory styles adopted by the teacher, but this might not have been the case. Analysis showed that there were notable differences, however, Tables 8.2, 8.3 and 8.4 above show the mean category scores for

TABLE 8.4

Highest Correlations between Most Frequently Occurring Process Variables (All Significant Beyond the 0.001 Level).

	TEXOS features correlated	*Correlation*
1.	Long pupil responses and spontaneous pupil responses	+0.65
2.	Teacher repeats pupil responses and short responses	+ 0.62
3.	Teacher probes and sequenced questions	+ 0.60
4.	Teacher probes and open questions	+ 0.56
5.	Sequenced questions and teacher repeats pupil responses	+ 0.56
6.	Open questions and short pupil responses	+ 0.53
7.	Teacher corrects and short pupil responses	0.50
8.	Sequenced questions and short pupil responses	+ 0.50
9.	Open questions and teacher repeats responses	+ 0.49
10.	Closed questions and teacher repeats responses	+ 0.44
11.	Sequenced questions and closed questions	+ 0.43
12.	Closed questions and short pupil responses	+ 0.43

Comparisons between Science and English Lessons

both topics combined, but when we compared the type of explaining categories used by teachers for the two topics separately, some quite spectacular differences emerged. In order to investigate what differences there were between explanations in the two topic areas of Insects and the Island of Zarg, as well as between explanations to older (9 year old) and younger (8 year old) pupils, and to above-average and average pupils, we used analysis of variance. The F ratios for these comparisons are shown in the tables below. The higher the F ratio, the more significant the difference between the groups.

One of the most spectacular differences was in the category 'Teacher engages pupils' imagination.' Although it was not unknown in the Insects topic, for example, when a teacher occasionally asked children to imagine what it must be like to be an insect, the science topic was usually dealt with in a much more factual manner. Almost all the examples of engagement of the imagination, therefore, occurred in the English lessons on the 'Island of Zarg' map. The F ratio was a massive 531.4, the most significant of any obtained, well beyond the 0.001 level of significance.

Most highly significant differences of this kind, however, occurred in the opposite direction. Table 8.5 shows the greatest differences where there was a much higher incidence in the category of behaviour concerned in the Insects lesson. 'Use of visual aids' figures prominently, because teachers rarely used additional visual aids in the 'Zarg' lesson, as the map of the island was provided, though a few did occasionally amplify the map with additional visual aids. All the categories in Table 8.5 occurred more frequently in the Insects lessons at a degree of statistical significance beyond the 0.001 level.

The two differences where the incidence was higher in the English lessons on the Island of Zarg are worthy of comment. Table 8.6 shows the hugely significant difference in the category 'teacher engages pupil imagination,' but also the higher occurrence of verbal cues, where the teacher 'nudged' the pupils along with a helpful word. Though the F ratio is much lower, it too is significant at beyond the 0.001 level.

These quantitative data confirm other observations made above. The format of many explanations of insects was essentially that of programmed learning, with a short 'frame' of information, a closed question, a short answer, a rainforcement (usually praise) or repetition, and sometimes a summary from the teacher. There was also much more eye contact, organisation and conceptual clarity on the rating scales. The English lessons, by contrast, were more discursive, with a challenge to the imagination being central and longer answers also featuring.

TABLE 8.5

Most Significant Differences between Insects and Zarg Explanations in Each Case Higher Frequency of Occurrence Being in the (In Sect Lessons, All Differences Significant Beyond the 0.001 Level)

	TEXOS category	*F ratio*
1.	Teacher gives example	239.9
2.	Teacher elicits example	158.6
3.	Teacher gives summary	85.1
4.	Teacher elicits summary	64.0
5.	Eye contact	34.8
6.	Closed questions	16.9
7.	Teacher praises	15.3
8.	Organisation	13.4
9.	Clarity	12.5
10.	Teacher explains links	7.3

TABLE 8.6

Most Significant Differences between Insects and Zarg Lesson (Both are Significant Beyond the 0.001 Level)

	TEXOS category	*F ratio*
1.	Teacher engages imagination	531.4
2.	Verbal cue	7.5

Some of these and other more qualitative aspects of explaining the two topics can be illustrated from transcripts of lessons. The programmed learning format is implemented in the following rapid-fire exchange. The children were looking at a centipede:

Teacher What makes this different from insects? What id we say an insect has?

Pupil 1 Six legs.

Teacher Right, how many legs has that one got?

Pupil 2 Forty-two, I've counted.

Teacher So, is it an insect?

Pupil 3 Well, I think it looks like one.

Teacher Have a look. Is its body arranged like that? (Shows pupils diagram of an insect body.)

Pupil 3 Not at all.

Teacher So is it an insect?

Pupil 4 No. But spiders have eight legs, so they're insects.

Teacher Are they?

Pupil 4 I think so.

Teacher Well, are we gong to say spiders are insects and spiders have six legs?

Pupil 4 No, silly me. I always thought they were, though.

Despite the apparently neat programmed learning format, there is still some conceptual confusion. Pupil I has confirmed the prerequisite that insects should have six legs, but in the eyes of pupils 3 and 4 it is still a matter of intuitive 'feel' rather than criteria or 'must have' characteristics. Having what looks to be a tightly controlled 'information-question-pupil answer-teacher response' pattern does not of itself ensure clear structure or universal understanding.

Another teacher used a similar clipped rapid-fire dialogue approach, but in a different manner, this time to probe and challenge, starting with a 'not' analogy (a camel not being an insect):

Teacher A camel is not an insect. Why?

Pupil 1 It hasn't got antennae.

Teacher A snail has got antennae.

Pupil 2 Insects have wings.

Teacher So do nightingales.

Pupil 1 Insects collect pollen.

Teacher So do humming birds.

This challenging, slightly adversarial style raises interesting possibilities about teachers' reflections on teaching. Such is the speed of the exchange that there can be little time for reflection. Intelligent action by teachers may be based on deep and surface structures, the deep ones, laid down by reflection and experience over a period of time, determining the surface structures which are also influenced by rapidly processed context clues.

The features of high-scoring lessons will be discussed below, but here is an example of a teacher whose pupils performed particularly well on post-tests who used the same programmed short frame approach in her summary when she was revising the main points children would need to remember:

Teacher So then, let's go back to my little friend here (pointing to a model of an insect she has made an used earlier). Who's going to tell me the names of the parts?

Pupil 1 Head.

Teacher Head, yes.

Pupil 2 Thorax and abdomen.

Teacher Well done. What are these?

Pupil 3 Feelers.

Teacher And what are they for?

Pupil 3 'Testing' the air.

Teacher Yes, tasting the air, that's a good description.

In the case of the lessons on the Island of Zarg there were numerous examples of attempts to invoke the imagination. Some responses were elicited through open but focused questions, such as:

> If there was something terribly dangerous on this island, where do you think would be a good place to hide?
>
> Let's say that ship down there is a pirate ship. Imagine you are on that ship, arriving in Hopehaven. What's going to happen to you when you land?
>
> Tell me where the best place on this island would be for me to have my holiday?
>
> What does he name 'Darkling Forest' conjure up n your minds?

Verbal cues were more frequent in the Zarg explanations because teachers ended to give clues about what pupils might do just before they began writing. It should be pointed out, incidentally, that the two differing patterns described above were predominant tendencies, not exclusive patterns. Imagination was sometimes evoked in Insect explanations:

> What must it be like to be an insect?'

Do you know that butterflies can taste with their feet? (Laughter.) Yes, when they land on things they can taste them using their feet. Wouldn't it be funny if we could taste with our feet?

Age and Ability of Pupils

The issue of matching tasks to pupils has been investigated by a number of researchers (Bennett *et al.* 1984). The task is, however, but one part of the matching process, for the other important element must be teaching strategies. One might expect that, just as there were significant differences between the strategies used for the factual Insects topic and the discursive Island of Zarg creative writing assignment, so too there might be differences in patterns of teaching average and above-average pupils and 8 and 9 year olds.

Analysis of variance was again used to elicit whether significant differences did occur between the TEXOS categories obtained for the various groups. In the case of age of pupils the most striking finding is that not one single element of the observation schedule reached even the 5 per cent level of significance. Given that there are more than twenty categories in the schedule, at least one difference at the 5 per cent, one in twenty, level would have been expected to occur by chance, but no such differences emerged. Furthermore the teachers of 8 year olds were not the same people as the teachers of 9 year olds, another reason why some significant differences might have occurred, yet none did. Perhaps the slight difference in the ages of pupils, only one year, may account for this similarity of approach. Had the study involved a wider age difference, say, 7 year olds and 11 year olds, the differences might have been more marked. The lack of contrast found in the quantitative reports was analysed. No differences of any note emerged here either. The inescapable conclusion, on the matter of the age of pupils, in this study, therefore, is that a small difference in age, like one year, appears not to be associated with different strategic approaches.

Whereas the non-significance of pupil age as a factor was not too surprising, the findings on pupil ability level were perhaps more noteworthy. Analysis of variance on the process data from the explanation given to average ability and those given to above-average ability showed astonishingly little difference, even though, in this case, it was the *same* teachers who were involved in both cases. Table 8.7 shows that only four elements of classroom process showed any significant difference at all. In each case all the differences were in the direction of more of the behaviour concerned occurring in the classes of the average ability group, and only one was highly significant at the 0.001 level, the other three being significant at the 0.05 level.

TABLE 8.7

Four Process Measures Found to be Most Significant in the Comparison between Explanations to Average and Above-Average Pupils, in Each Case More Occurring in the Lesson with Average Ability Pupils

	TEXOS category	*F ratio*
1.	Teacher corrects	7.7 ***
2.	Teacher rephrases	6.4 *
3.	Teacher explains links	4.5 *
4.	Teacher gives summary	4.5 *

Analysis of both interviews with teachers and lesson observation field notes confirmed that the differences in process were slight, confined mainly to the consequences of incorrect or partially correct responses in the Insects lesson, when teachers corrected, rephrased, explained links and gave summaries. Most teachers, however, confirmed in interview, when asked specifically, after the explanation had been given to both groups. 'Were you conscious of any differences in the way you explained to high and average-ability children?' That they had not consciously sought to vary their approach.

Only two teachers outlined different strategies for the two ability groups for the Insects topic, and only six for the Island of Zarg. Only one teacher said he used different strategies on *both* topics. One style changer was the teacher whose pupils obtained the highest scores of any in the sample on the test following the Insects explanation. He was a biology graduate teaching in a small village school in a not especially privileged area, where the ability of the children in the two groups was no different from that of children observed in other schools. He explained how he had deliberately made the explanation to the average ability group 'more concrete.' Whereas, with the more able pupils, he had discussed the characteristics of insects and then looked at specific examples, with the average ability pupils he began with a 'not analogy,' an approach favoured by other teachers, which involves inviting pupils to compare an insect with a non-insect, like an elephant, a cow or, in this case, a bird.

> *Teacher* Is a bird an insect?
>
> *Pupil 1* No, that's silly.
>
> *Teacher* Why?
>
> *Pupil 1* Well, it's too small. A bird's bigger.
>
> *Teacher* So all insects are small, then, and all birds are big?
>
> *Pupil 2* No, you can have little birds..... and big insects.
>
> *Pupil 3* It's got the wrong number of legs.
>
> *Teacher* Why, how many does an insect have?
>
> *Pupil 3* Six.
>
> *Pupil 1* No it doesn't. It's eight. A spider's got eight legs..
>
> *Pupil 3* A spider's not an insect.
>
> *Teacher* Well, let's clear that one up first.

The children went on to consider each part of the insect and then looked at actual insects. The matter of strategies used by teachers in higher and lower-scoring explanations is discussed below, but the most important issue here is that so few teachers did consciously opt for a change of approach. Even those that did sometimes found that circumstances brought about the change, rather than pre-planning. For example, one teacher who had obtained several responses from the above average group about the castle on the Island of Zarg found little response when he asked the same questions to the average ability group.

> *Teacher* Who do you think lived in that castle?
>
> *Pupil* (No response).
>
> *Teacher* No ideas at all?
>
> *Pupil* (No response).
>
> *Teacher* James, what about you?
>
> *Pupil* (No response).
>
> *Teacher* Anybody? Well, I think perhaps it could be some important dignitary, either a king or a queen.

He then continued with an extended monologue, but in interview said that this was as a result of the poor response of the pupils, not through pre-planning. This finding that so few teachers opted for different styles of approach with pupils of different abilities could be explained by two factors. One is that the explanations were undertaken back to back, with the second group coming in about an hour after the first group, though the order of topic and ability group was randomised, so that some teachers explained first to higher ability pupils, others first to average pupils, and similarly with the order of the two topics. Given the slight artificiality of covering the same topic on the same day with two different groups, perhaps this imposed constraints which might not apply in a more naturalistic setting. Secondly it might be argued that the difference between the two groups was relatively small-man IQ 100 in the average group, mean IQ 115 in the above-average group—and that, had two groups of mean IQ 85 and 115, or 80 and 120, been compared, the differences might have been spectacular.

Styles of Explaining

One further analysis was undertaken on the classroom observation process data. In order to reduce a large set of data (640 lesson segments) to something more parsimonious and easier to interpret, as well as to corroborate or refute other forms of analysis, a principal components factor analysis and non-hierarchical cluster analysis were performed. A principal components factor analysis and non hierarchical cluster analysis were performed. A principal components factor analysis puts together those measures which correlate most highly and produces a smaller set of factors. Three factors were obtained which had latent roots above 1.0, with latent roots of 5.3, 4.5 and 2.1 respectively. These accounted for 20.3, 17.3 and 8.3 per cent of the variance.

Factor 1 (20.3 per cent of variance): a programmed learning factor: This factor loaded most heavily on all categories of questions, open, closed and sequenced, and on short pupil responses, teacher corrects, repeats, rephrases, praises, and on teacher summary. It was confirmation of the question—answer—reinforcement pattern described earlier, reminiscent of programmed learning principles.

Factor 2 (17.3 per cent of variance): a topic dissemination factor: The second factor had both positive and negative loadings. The factor loaded *positively* on visual aids, teacher and pupil giving examples, summaries from teacher and pupils, and explaining links, and *negatively* on open questions, long pupils' imagination. It reflects the essential differences between the more high structured Insects explanation and the more discursive Island of Zarg lesson.

Factor 3 (8.3 per cent of variance): a pupil response factor: The third factor also showed both negative and positive loading, and pupil responses figured in both. The factor loaded *positively* on no pupil response, pauses, sequenced teacher questions and probes, and *negatively* on long and spontaneous pupil responses. It confirms that a higher frequency of teacher behaviour, like sequencing questions and probing, was associated with a lower frequency of long and spontaneous responses, from pupils. It does not mean that there is a *causal* link, however, As was shown above, teachers sometimes resort to reserve strategies as a result of poor pupil response, so it cannot be said that sequencing questions and probing *cause* a zero pupil response or low occurrence of longer, spontaneous pupil contributions, merely that the two go together. It cold equally be argued that low pupil response might be a cause of the teacher using sequences of questions and probes, not the result of it.

The non-hierarchical cluster analysis took the whole explanation as the unit of analysis, so all 128 explanations were used to assemble a taxonomy of teaching styles. Whereas factor analysis puts together the various *measures* to form a smaller number of factors, cluster analysis puts together individual profiles of explanations to form a smaller set of groups or clusters. The procedure begins with 128 clusters and ends with one, when all have been combined. The four, five and six cluster solutions were inspected, and the four cluster solutions displayed the clearest, least diffuse model. The clusters, from now on called 'styles,' were as follows:

Step 1 (containing thirty-nine explanations) This involved a higher incidence of pupil response, especially long and spontaneous ones, more open questions, much more engaging of the imagination, more teacher rephrasing and much less use of visual aids. The emphasis is on pupil contributions to discussion. Not surprisingly the thirty-nine explanations in this style contained thirty-five from the Island of Zarg creative writing lessons and only four from the Insects lesson.

Style 2 (containing sixty explanations) The style here was as described earlier in the description of the Insects topic, for all sixty were about insects, with greatest emphasis on teachers giving and eliciting examples and summaries. It was the more tightly structured factual topic approach, with far lower engaging of the imagination.

Style 3 (containing twelve explanations) All of these were Island of Zarg lessons and most of the differences between this style and the rest are because of much lower occurrence of short pupil responses, summaries, praise teacher repeats, asks closed question and makes personal references.

Style 4 (containing seventeen explanations) These were also exclusively Island of Zarg lessons, and the distinguishing characteristics were both in a positive and in a negative direction, with much higher occurrence of engagement of the imagination and verbal cues, but much lower use of visual aids, sequenced questions, giving and eliciting examples and praise.

In general these multivariate analyses, like factor and cluster analysis, gave a similar picture to that described above, and certainly confirmed the significance of the relationship between type of topic and strategies adopted.

Pupil Achievement and Learning

At the conclusion of each explanation, tests of insect

identification, knowledge of insect characteristics and ability to explain insects to others were given, as described above, and after each Island Zarg lesson pupils were asked to write a story entitled 'My Adventure on the Island of Zarg.' The post-tests were scored by two independent markers whose scoring correlated highly, as was described earlier in the chapter.

There were three aspects of these outcome measures that were a particular interest. The first was the effectiveness of having had a teacher explanation at all. That would be resolved by inspecting the score of the sixty-four children in the sixteen average ability 9-year old groups to whom the teachers had explained, and the sixty-four in the sixteen control groups of similar ability from the same classes, who had received no explanations. The scorers did not know which pupils were in which groups. In order to test the significance of any difference in scores a null hypothesis was adopted, that is, it was assumed that teaching would make on difference and the scores of the experimental and control group would be the same. A two-tailed t test of all outcome measures was then undertaken.

The second element of interest was whether having an 'opportunity to learn' made any difference. For example, if a teacher does not mention or elicit the fact that insects, have six legs, then there has been no 'opportunity to learn' it, in that lesson at any rate. Pre-tests were not used, as the research design was quite complex and time-consuming, and adding extensive pre-testing might have alienated children and teachers, so conclusions are based on post-test assumptions only and must have some reservations attached to them.

The third area of interest was what distinguished high-scoring and low-scoring lessons. This is as near as one usually gets to measures of 'effectiveness' in research on teaching, but, given hat the tests are short-term measures of learning, or may reflect prior knowledge and experience, again a caveat must be applied. The epithet 'effective' would have to be used purely within the limitations and constraints of this particular price of research.

Did 'Teaching' Make a Difference?

Table 8.8 shows the results of the t test on the scores obtained by the experimental and control groups of average ability children. Although in general the experimental groups outperformed the control groups, this was not always the case. Some teachers had merely 'toured' the Island of Zarg in their explanations. This produced 'listing' responses which did not score high on the 'imaginativeness' dimension:

TABLE 8.8

Mean Scores of Experimental and Control Groups of Average Ability Pupils on Tests-about Insects and Creative Writing (Sub-scores and Total Scores)

Test	*Experimental*	*Control*	*t value*
Insects	22.9	15.8	4.69 ***
Creative writing			
Length	2.8	2.0	2.5 *
Sentence structure	2.6	1.9	0.56 (n.s.)
Coherence	2.9	2.2	2.6 *
Features	2.9	2.4	1.4 (n.s.)
Imaginativeness	3.3	2.2	2.8 *
Overall impression	2.9	2.1	1.8 (n.s.)
Total score	17.8	12.7	2.4 *

*** Significant at <0.001 level, *Significant at < 0.05 level, n.s. not significant.

I started at Mount Horn and then I went to the castle and fell in the swamp and met Zarg outside his lair and he sent me to visit Zorgon in his cave. After that I went to Miller's Top, Fenbury, Hopehaven and sailed home.

On the other hand there were pupils in the control group clearly capable of writing imaginative stories with nothing more than the map of the island, as this extract from a high-scoring story shows:

> Deeper and deeper we plunged into cave. CRUMP! We hit the bottom. In the distance we heard a strange rumble as if someone was snoring very loud....

In general, however, the experimental groups did better than the control groups on each of the sub-measures of creative writing, though not all the differences reached statistical significance.

The scores in Table 8.8 show that having received an explanation was associated with hither achievement on every single measure in the whole set of post-tests and that in the tests of knowledge about insects the superiority of the experimental over the control groups was significant at beyond the 0.001 level. There was no statistical significance in the difference on sub-scores of creative writing, like sentence structure, mention of the island's features and overall impression, but in sentence length, coherence, imaginativeness and total score the differences in favour of the taught groups were significant at the 0.05 level. Having had an explanation did, therefore, seem to make a significant impact on pupils' learning and achievement in several important respects.

Opportunity to Learn

An analysis above shows that having some sort of explanation appears, in general, to be better than not, but we wanted to see whether specific mention of certain aspects of insects' characteristics did appear to be related to their ability to recognise them accurately. The creative writing exercise was not scrutinised in the same way, as it would have been difficult to relate specific and discrete pieces of process data to such outcome measures as 'imaginativeness.' It was easier to inspect the analyses of he Insects explanations to elicit whether, for example, the teacher had mentioned that spiders were not insects, and whether this was related to pupils answering that question correctly.

A correlation analysis was undertaken, therefore, relating frequency of factually correct mentions of feelers, thorax, abdomen, number of legs, number of wings, and spiders not being insects, to number of pupils in the groups correctly identifying each of these in the post-test. Analysis of observation data showed that over 90 per cent of teachers made at least one mention of feelers, thorax, abdomen and number of legs during one of their explanations, whereas the figures for number of wings and spiders were 78.4 per cent and 64 per cent respectively. Table 8.9 shows the correlations obtained for all sixty-four lessons to 256.8 and 9 year old pupils receiving Insect explanations.

These results must be interpreted with caution. For example, if teachers feel that most children already know that insects have six legs, they may mention this feature less frequently than, say, 'thorax' or 'abdomen,' which are likely to be new to 8 and 9 year olds. Also since correlations are of frequency of mention, not intensity or context, these quantitative measures do not distinguish on qualitative grounds, and are thus relatively crude, needing to be set alongside other kinds of information, like that in the section on high and low-scoring lessons below. Within these limitations it is of some interest to note that the correlations between frequency of mention of thorax, abdomen and spiders not being insects were significant beyond the 0.001 level.

TABLE 8.9

Correlations between Frequency of Mention of Insect Features and Number of Pupils Correctly Answering Relevant Item on Post-Test

Feature mentioned	*Correlation with test item*
Feelers	0.29 **
Thorax	0.46 ***
Abdomen	0.46 ***
Number of legs	0.05 (n.s.)
Number of wings	0.04 (n.s.)
Spiders not insects	0.38 ***

*** Significant at <0.001 level, ** Significant at < 0.01 level, n.s. = not significant.

High- and Low-Scoring Lessons

A qualitative analysis was performed on the lessons of the teachers whose pupils obtained the highest and lowest post-test scores on both topics. The following cases show the flavour of some of these high-scoring lessons:

Mrs. Archer (high-scoring Insect explanation) The explanation began with Mrs. Archer producing two larger display cases full of insects.

> *Teacher* Do you know what these are?
>
> *Pupil 1* Bees and wasps.
>
> *Teacher* Yes, that's right and what are these?
>
> *Pupil 2* Bluebottles
>
> *Teacher* Yes, bluebottles, greenbottles. They're all flies.... What about this beautiful creature?
>
> *Pupil 3* He's a dragonfly.

At this stage one of the pupils wanted to talk about frogs, which also live by ponds. The teacher listened and then skilfully redirected and refocused.

One of the most notable features of her explanation was her use of voice intonation and emphasis, and pauses. At the end of the first phase of the explanation, she recapped with some vigour:

> All of these creatures (pointing to the display cases) are all so different, *but* (emphasis) (pause) they do have *one* (emphasis) thing in common (pause). They *all* (emphasis) belong to the family called (pause) insects (pause) — insects.

The main body of the explanation was devoted to covering each of the features of the insect body. When talking about the insect's feelers she used an analogy:

> The feelers are rather like radio aerials, they pick up all sorts of messages in the air around the insect.

Much of the explanation involved question-and-answer and reference to the insect display cases, but she also had a model of an insect she had made herself, and this featured frequently in the exchanges.

A high degree of learning in Mrs. Archer's explanations appeared to be related to clear structure and explanation of key points through question-and-answer, skilful use of different types of visual aid, both simplified home-made insect shapes and cases of actual insects, refocusing discussion when it strayed off the point, eliciting a summary from pupils in which the main characteristics of insects were again illuminated, and effective modulation of voice, with emphasis and pausing for effect.

Mr. Barlow (low-scoring Insects explanation) By contrast with Mrs. Archer, the explanations in Mr. Barlow's lessons lacked clarity from the beginning. What is more, they were also factually incorrect and confusing from the very outset.

Teacher I'm going to give you the little word 'insect.' Immediately in your mind there's a picture of something, I expect. There is in mine. What sort of picture have you got, Cassandra?

Pupil 1 A spider.

Teacher OK, you think of a spider. You keep the spider there. Peter, what about you?

Pupil 2 (No response).

Teacher When I say 'insect' what do you immediately think of — an insect?

Pupil 3 A ladybrid.

Teacher Yes, that's right.

Pupil 4 A worm.

Teacher Yes —anything else?

Pupil 3 A snail.

Teacher How do insects move around, Peter?

Pupil 2 Legs.

Teacher How many legs has an insect got?

Pupil 2 Six.

Teacher Yes, six; but do insects get around any other way?

Pupil 2 Some insects fly.

Teacher Yes, some insects use wings. Can you think of an insect that flies?

Pupil 2 An eagle.

Teacher An eagle? Is that an insect? No, it's bird. A bird is definitely not an insect.

The factual inaccuracies and lack of conceptual clarity, with shape, movement and example confused and blurred, were compounded at the end of the lesson whn Mr. Barlow summed up for the pupils what had supposedly been learned.

> *Teacher* So we've thought about a whole set of different insects today: snails, centipedes, ladybirds, caterpillars and wood lice, and we've also found a lot of ways in which these insects move about-crawling, walking, sliding, swimming, flying and hopping.

The low degree of learning during Mr Barlow's explanation appears to be related to a lack of distinct key points which would have given conceptual clarity, and factual inaccuracy, a topic which will be discussed further in chapter 10. He establishes that insects have six legs, but never returns to the spider mentioned by Cassandra, nor explains why such creatures as worms, centipedes or snails are allowed into the genus when they do not have six legs. It was not surprising, therefore, that the concept 'insect' in the children's minds wrongly included gastropods, arachnids and other unlikely members. The pupils' test responses showed that their conceot of an insect was anything smallish that crawls, swims, flies or hops around and is not a bird.

Mrs Charles (high-scoring Island and Zarg explanation): In the interview following this lesson Mrs. Charles modestly said. 'I reckon they could have managed quite well without me.' Yet this explanation was located in Style 4 in the cluster analysis, emphasising the stimulation of pupils' imagination and verbal cues. She concentrated in her exposition on encouraging children to use their imagination about the features of the island and on extending or exploring their vocabulary, as this exchange shows:

Teacher Can you see anything that attracts you about the island? Anywhere you'd like to visit, David?

Pupil 1 Castle Point.

Teacher Why would you like to go there?

Pupil 1 It's exciting.

Teacher Yes, it's exciting. Have you found anywhere you'd like to go, Emma?

Pupil 2 I think ....

Teacher No, it's Emma's turn. I'd like to hear what Emma has to say.

Pupil 3 Eastern Moors. There's creature.... it's .... it's......

Teacher There's something up there that Emma's found. What has she found coming out of the sea?

Pupil 4 A monster.

Teacher Yes, it could be. What's coming out of his hand?

Pupil 3 Lightning.

Teacher What else has he got coming out of him?

Pupil 2 Rain.

Teacher Rain and thunder, so it's almost as if he's in control of the....?

Pupil 2 Weather.

Teacher The weather, yes, I think so..... What would be a good word to describe Darkling Forest?

Pupil 2 Spooky and creepy.

Teacher Beter than 'spooky and creepy'?

Pupil 1 Strange and weird.

Teacher Yes, strange and weird. How about a word beginning with two e's? Do you know it?

Pupil 1 Eerie.

Teacher Yes. What does 'eerie' mean?

Pupil 3 Scary.

What the transcript does not show is the high degree of pleasure, signalled through voice, intonation and facial expression, at the pupils' responses. The exchanges were fairly rapid, the responses brief; however, the management was benignly but tightly controlled. The level of excitement was high, like the pace. This enthusiasm, pace, regular involvement of pupils, albeit with short replies and discriminating response to their answers, which were not automatically accepted, may all be related to the quality of the children's written work, which was scored very highly by the markers. If these explanations were snapshots of what had happened over a longer period of time, it would appear that the effect of these strategies may well be cumulative. Children do not become skilful writers overnight, or after one such lesson. In interview Mrs. Charles stressed the importnace of the initial stimulus: 'They need a starting point. Once they have that, their story can take them anywhere.'

Miss Dogger (low-scoring Island of Zarg explanation): It soon become clear in Miss Dogger's lesson that the storv the pupils were to write was one she would provide, not one that they would invent. The transcript shows that her explanation was a mixture of 'Guess my story' and 'Here's what you're going to do.' This was evident from her opening.

Teacher In a minute I'm going to ask you to writ a story. Do you think your story is going to be about modern days or olden days?

Pupil 1 About olden days 'cos there's a castle on the island.

Teacher Oh, well, you see lots of castles around today.

No, there was one thing I thought gave it away. Can't you see it?

Pupil 2 The windmill.

Teacher No.

Pupil 3 The ship.

Teacher Yes, that's right—the ship.

She gave more information about the ship, and then the first and only spontaneous response came from a pupil:

Pupil 2 Hey, there's a monster there.

Teacher Yes, I don't think he's a monster though, I thiink he's supposed to be some sort of rain god. Look — there's rain coming from his hands.

No further spontaneous responses occurred, and the children listened patiently as she elaborated more detail of what was essentially her own story that they were to attempt to reproduce:

Teacher You're on that ship, and it's called *Gull*. You're sailign over to the island, when there's a storm and you're washed overboard. You get washed up here at Mudlark Swamp. Now, the inhabitants of Hightown are unfriendly, but up in the hills you'll see a cave—Zarg's lair. Now, Zarg is a fearsome creature, a bit frightening, but he's friendly.

The approach was a contrast to that of Mrs. Charles, who often sought precise vocabulary but was open minded about story lines. The children's low scores in Miss Dogger's group seem to be related to restrictions on their imagination imposed by this more prescriptive approach and the lack of enthusiasm and drive which was a feature of the lesson of Mrs. Charles.

Summary of Features of High-Scoring Explanations

The main points that emerged when two separate analysts went through the explanation tapes and transcripts are a little different for the two topics. The highest-scoring Insects explanations were, in general, clearly structured, with the 'keys' or central ideas made distinct and linked to one another in a logical sequence and shape, often with a teacher or pupil review at the end of the section or the whole explanation, and the teacher's subject knowledge was factually correct. Language choices were sensible, neither too banal nor at too high a level of abstraction, an appropriate register being employed. Voice was clear and well modulated, with effective movement, facial expression and animation, and there was fluency and pace. Good visual aids to learning were employed and the occasional illuminating example or analogy was given or, more likely, elicited. There was an overall simplicity of structur which gave clearity. Indeed, one high scoring teacher, who began with a simple line drawn on the blackboard, said in interview. 'You just need the very basics in an explanation like this, other pictures would have confused the children.' Anther, who started by establishing why insects were a distinct group, stated in interview, 'I thought it would be a good way to go from the general to the particular. I wanted the children to be sure that "insects" is the name of a group of animals early on.'

In the creative writing lessons on the Island of Zarg, some of he above applied, but personal characteristics like enthusiasm and voice being used to create or evoke an atmosphere of mystery or curiosity figure prominently. Questions and statements that provoked thought and stimulated the imagination were notable ('A thick fog comes down,' said one teacher), but both prescriptive and exploratory approaches could be successful. The effectiveness of this single lesson was probably a reflection of the cumulative effect of strategies whch led to skilful writing being employed over a period of time.

Other features of high-scoring lessons were the occasional use of humour which was relevant to the topic, as opposed to gratuitous humour. The use of the 'advance orgnaiser' (Ausubel *et al.*, 1978) sometimes occurred, when the teacher employed wht broadcasters call a 'tease' at the beginning of their explanation, to give shape or to arouse curiosity:

> *Teacher* If I told you in, say, a bucket of earth there were hundreds of them. They're in the air, they're even in ponds and rivers. There are millions of them in a tree. They live all over the world, except at the North and South Poles. There are over a million different types of them. There are 200,000 different types in this country alone. Some of them can fly. Some can swim, some make holes in the ground, and some make holes in wood. What do you think I would be talking about?

As is often the case, however, despite some communalities, high-scoring explanations were also different from each other, with their own unique qualities. The general conclusions above are not universal prescriptions, but rather interesting illuminations from one intensive study.

9

Teachers' Questions

In daily adult life, if we were to ask one another questions to which we clearly new the answer, this kind of behaviour would be regarded with suspicion. It would be extremely odd, for example, if one person were to say to another, 'What's the weather like today? When both could clearly see it was pouring with rain. Equally, if one adult were to ask another a series of probing questions, it would be regarded as socially rude and in sensitive, invading the other's privacy, the sort of behaviour only permitted when the person interrogated is suspected of having committed some criminal act.

Yet in classrooms questioning is one of the most regularly employed teaching strategies. Questions are asked to individual pupils, to the whole class, to small groups. In some parts of lessons there may be five or even ten questions in a single minute, and most teachers will ask hundreds of questions within a few days. Even as early as 1912, Romiett Stevens found that two-thirds of questions being asked required children to recall the sort of information that could be verified from textbooks. Other early studies reported similar findings. Haines (1925) analysed the demands made on twelve 13 year old pupils by teachers' questions and concluded that 70 per cent required factual recall, whereas only 17 per cent made demands on pupils' thinking that went beyond pure recall.

When Gall (1970) reviewed research on questioning, three seemed to be a 3:1:1, split between different types of questioning, with 60 per cent asking for the recall of facts 20 percent demanding a higher mode of thinking, and 20 per cent dealing with the management of classes or individuals. The ORACLE study of primary schools (Galton *et al.* 1980) found that 12 per cent of time in class was devoted to questioning, and the ratio was rather different, more like 2:1:1 but this time most questions came into the category of management, with 47 per cent. The figures for factual recall and questions about ideas were 29 per cent and 23 per cent respectively.

The reasons why teachers ask questions are varied. Turney (1973) produced a list of twelve, covering such purposes as to arouse curiosity, focus attention, develop an active approach , stimulate pupils, structure the task, diagnose difficulties, communicate expectation, help children reflect, develop thinking skills, help group reflection, provoke discussion and show interest in pupils' ideas and feelings. Brown and Edmondson (1984) asked forty secondary teachers to state their reasons for asking questions. The five most common responses, in order of frequency, were: 10 encourage thought and understanding; to check what pupils knew and could do; to gain pupils' attention to the task in hand; to review, revise or reinforce what had been learned; to help with class management.

As was described in the previous chapter on explaining, with which this chapter has a great deal in common conceptually, some researchers have concentrated on levels of thought and related their study of questioning to these. Sadker and Sadker (1982) built much of their training programme in questioning skills on Bloom's taxonomy (Bloom 1956). Trainees were encouraged to ask questions in each of the categories of the taxonomy in the cognitive domain. A question at the first level, 'knowledge,' might be 'Who wrote Hamlet?' At the second level, 'comprehension,' the teacher might ask, 'What is the main idea that this chart presents? This continued up the levels until level six, 'evaluation,' was reached, where an appropriate question might be 'Which picture do you like best and why?'

The problem with this approach is that it often presupposes that higher order questions are in some way qualitatively 'better' than lower order questions, yet the research evidence on this is divided. Even those who have summarised research in questioning have disagreed about whether there is a causal link between the asking of higher order questions and pupil learning. Two reviews of similar studies came to opposite conclusions, partly because they used different methods for aggregating findings. Whereas Winne (1979), who analysed experimental studies of questioning where teachers deliberately asked certain types of question, concluded that there was no causal link, Redifield and Rousseau (1981), who did a meta-analysis of most of the same studies, decided that there was a positive association between higher order cognitive questioning and pupil learning.

The findings from research may not always be consistent, but some features of it are. There does seem to be evidence that questioning is an important strategy which teachers usually employ; that it can occur with some frequency; that teachers' questions are of several kinds—some to do with the management of the lesson, others dealing with the substance of it, that questions serve different purposes and demand different levels of response, though what is arguably 'higher' and what is 'lower' order is a matter of some disagreement.

There is little work on pupils' questions, though Barnes and Todd (1977) studied children working in small groups and found that they generated more exploratory questions, hypotheses and explanations when a teacher was not present than when one was. Other aspects of pupil perspective have also been studied, and Tobin's (1987) review of 'wait time,' that, is, the effect of a teacher pausing for longer to allow pupils to respond, shows that pausing can elicit longer answers, encourage more pupils to take part in answering questions and produce more questions from pupils. Much of this work goes back to the seminal studies of Rowe (1978), who found that teachers frequently allowed less than a second before breaking the silence by asking another question, giving more information or redirecting, restating or rephrasing the original question.

The finding by Adams and Biddle (1970), who analysed several hours of videotaped lessons, that most of the action was directed at children sitting in a V-shaped ledge in front of the teacher's favoured position in front of the class, also has relevance to work on questioning, in that it suggests that children on the periphery, or those siting outside that V-shaped wedge, could be out of the action. Given the degree of self-selection of seating in many classes, there might be a tendency therefore for those pupils most keen to answer questions to select those 'busy' central seats, and for quieter pupils to choose seats in areas of the classroom where they are less likely to be called on during whole-class teaching, thereby reinforcing the predominant behaviour patterns of both the eloquent and the silent.

The Present Studies of Questioning

During the Leverhulme Primary Project we undertook four studies of questioning. In the first we asked a group of twenty-eight primary teachers in twelve primary schools to keep a log of some of the questions they asked during their teaching. Fourteen schools were randomly selected, of which all but two agreed to co-operate. Each school was asked to find either two or three teachers to volunteer to take part. Six schools provided three teachers, for found two volunteers and two produced one teacher. All the studies of questioning in this chapter are of teachers who agreed to take part and, as with all cases in this kind of research, they may not be typical of teachers at large. Nonetheless, the view of observers was that the teachers in the sample did not appear to be different in any perceivable way from other teachers, except that they chose to volunteer to participate.

The second study described below is of over 1, 000 questions asked by a group of seven teachers who were observed during the study of class management described in chapter 4 and 5. They agreed that the observer could return to do a further study of their classroom, in which all question asked during several half-hour periods would be logged. Again this is an opportunity sample of teachers willing to be observed taken from a large sample of teachers in another study. The third enquiry into questioning involved the observation of the classes of twenty teachers in ten schools which had been chosen randomly and which, in all cases, agreed to participate. In each school, two volunteer teachers were observed, their lessons recorded and transcribed, and the questioning episodes in them were analysed. In all three studies the use of questioning by a total of fifty-five primary teachers was studied. The fourth study was the analysis of the questions asked during explanations described in the previous chapter.

All analyses were undertaken by two members of the research team. Three tests of agreement on categorisation where questions were coded as 'managerial,' 'higher order' or 'lower order' showed a mean agreement of 95 per cent.

Three sets of 100 questions were selected randomly and agreement was 95.94 and 96 per cent respectively. All questions about which either coder had any doubt were rated until agreement was reached.

Study 1 The Teachers' Log of Questions Asked

The twenty-eight teachers who agreed to take part in this study were asked to keep a log of questions they asked under several headings. Each was given a structured diary in which to record, as soon as possible after the event, what kinds of questions they asked and what the responses were. In the first section, teachers were asked to record three question asked to the whole class, a small group, or an individual child on one particular day. They wrote down the actual wording of the question, the context in which it occurred, the main purpose of the question, and the response and outcomes. The second section asked them to record a sequence of questions, consisting of at least two and not more than five questions asked one after another. Again, they had to record the essential features of wording, context, purpose and outcome. Thirdly, they answered attitude and frequency questions on five-point scales, and these are reported in tables 9.1 and 9.2. Finally, they were asked what tips they would give to student teachers about questioning. Some teachers recorded several lessons and took the diary entries down from the cassette, some recorded just one lesson, about half did not record at all but wrote their report from memory.

The overall total of 187 questions recorded by the twenty-eight teachers were different kinds, and those asked in sequence followed various patterns. Questions were coded as 'managerial' if they were to do with the organisation and management of the lesson, 'lower order' if recall of information was predominantly what was required, and 'higher order' if more than remembering facts was needed.

Teacher recorded a far lower level of managerial questions than is normally witnessed in classrooms, as well as far more higher order questions. This is because they found it more interesting to record and comment on the questions which provoked thought or activity, as is to be expected if one asks a teacher to select and analyse in some depth particular questions asked during a day. The 187 questions logged and analysed consisted of ten managerial, seventy-eight higher order questions. This study certainly does not, therefore portray a random sample of questions, but rather a set of questions teachers themselves selected for further analysis.

There was, as one would expect, considerable variety according to the age of the children. Half of the teachers taught infant age children from 5 to 7, and the other half taught juniors from 7 to 11. Teachers of reception class and early years pupils often said in interview that they believed in keeping their questions simple, and one, talking about her own philosophy of questioning, said, 'Always use-simple, understandable words. Try not to embarrass the child by asking to difficult a question.' Her own questions were indeed simply phrased, her chosen sequence of five questions being entirely about colours: (1) 'What are the names of these colours [of the rainbow] '(2) Which colour do you like best?' (3) 'How many people like red the child's answer] best?' (4) 'Can you think of anything else that is red?' (5) 'Can you see anything red in our classroom?' It was a funnelling style of sequence, based entirely on simple colour questions, not so much raising levels of thought as focusing them.

Some infant teachers asked simple questions, but used their sequence to extend and lift thought as advocated by Taba *et al.* (1971). Another teacher of 5-6 year olds again began with colours, but for a purpose. She showed a picture of baby birds in a nest and began with two lower order questions: 'What colour is this egg?' and 'How many more eggs are there in the nest?' Her main theme is about birds life and her next three questions became more demanding than just recall as children were asked to use their powers of reasoning and imagination: 'Does the mother bird look after her chicks?' 'Why didn't this egg hatch—what do you think?' 'How does the mother bird feed her chicks?'

The strategy of extending and lifting was seen with older pupils as well, and often pupils' responses helped determine the nature and level of each succeeding question. One class of 7 year olds was studying 'forces,' including magnetism and gravity. The children were looking at a paperclip attached by a thread to a block of wood on a table. By holding a magnet above it, the teacher appeared to make it float. Her questions grew in complexity and were highly responsive to children's replies:

> What force is making the magnet stay in the air? (Replis: 'The magnet,' 'It was trying to get the magnet,' 'No, the magnet was trying to get it,' 'The paperclip was metal and the magnet was pulling it.').
>
> Where there any other forces acting on the paperclip? (No coherent replies).
>
> When you moved the magnet a bit further away, what happened to the paperclip? ('It fell down,' 'Oh, gravity,' 'Gravity made it fall down').
>
> Was gravity pulling it all the time? (Reply: Yes').
>
> So why didn't the paperclip fall straight away? (Replies: 'It wanted to get to the magnet,' 'The

magnet was stronger,' 'It was strong when it was near').

Was there anything else stopping the paper clip doing what it wanted?

(Replies: 'The string wouldn't let it, 'It did stretch a bit,' 'The block,' 'The weight of the block').

The path of extending and lifting was not smooth here, as the teacher tried to lift the level too rapidly by asking about forces the children had not identified. However, by giving a specific concrete example, of moving the magnet away, she allowed the class to focus on gravity and the downward pull.

Some funnelling sequences were skilfully sculptured so that decisions could be made on the basis of shaped reasoning. A teacher of 10-11 year olds recorded a set of five questions in a musicless on which helped children learn to discriminate sounds. She began with two chords played on the piano, asking the class if the chords were the same as each other or different. The chords were a C major and a C minor. In response to the first question, four children thought they were the same, four were not sure and the rest all believed, correctly, that they were different. Her second question 'How do you think the chords are different?' was too diffuse and only one child could give any impression of a sound being 'lower.' She next played the chords as an arpeggio (as two sets of four separate notes) and asked, 'Tell me which note you think is lower. Is it the first note, the second, the third or the fourth?' and then checked out each with 'Is it the first?' which four children believed to be correct, and 'Is it the fourth?' also believed to be correct by four pupils. Finally, she checked out the middle notes, by which time the great majority of the class correctly identified the second note as being the one that was lower. This was an interesting example of a funnelling strategy that went from the diffuse to the precise in a small number of steps.

Sometime it was not until a later question that class discussion became animated and discussion flourished. Another teacher of infants aged 4-6 described her sequence with groups of children who were making a house from blocks. Her first question was a disguised command: 'Can you go and choose the boxes that you think you will need to make your house?' Early responses called most blocks 'cubes' and only distinguished 'big ones' from 'little ones.' Initially the children in the group wanted to stick the paper boxes together as whole blocks, but her fifth question, 'Do you need scissors?' focused their attention on the actual shapes and what the test really entailed. She reported:

> This resulted in much more interaction and discussion.... thoughts on size, angles of cutting and how easy/difficult it was to get surfaces to fit and stick together. The last question was in fact the one that really got the task underway and questions/answers flowing from the children with a sense of them working together, rather than individually, which I felt the activity was leading to before this point.

All twenty-eight teachers in the sample completed the structured questionnaire parts of the teachers' log. Each item was based on strategies observed by members of the team carrying out classroom observations, or from statements given by teachers in interview. The first set, shown in table 9.1, death with attitudes to questioning, and responses were on a five-point Likert scale ranging from 1 = strongly agree to 5 strongly disagree, with the mind-point 3 = neural. Thus the lower the score in table 9.1 the higher the agreement. Scores are shown in descending order of agreement, so statement 1, about putting the question back to the same pupil, attracted most agreement.

The responses in table 9.1 show a clear preference for allowing pupils to answer questions if they have failed at their first attempt and a degree of support for calling on non-volunteers to answer but ambivalence over the issue of involving other pupils in correcting many answers. There is an equally clear rejection of the notion that written questions are superior to oral ones and that teachers' questions should be confined to those to which they themselves know the answer.

Table 9.2 shows a different set of strategy statements designed to elicit frequency of behaviour. Again, a five-point scale was used, with 1 = always, 2 = frequently, 3 = about half the time, 4 = occasionally, 5 = never. The order in Table 9.2 is in descending order of frequency, so praising correct answers was thought to be the most frequent occurrence.

TABLE 9.1

Responses of all Twenty-eight Teachers to Attitude Statements in Descending Order of Agreement (on Five-point Likert Scale from 1 = Strongly Agree to 5 = Strongly Disagree)

	Statement	*Mean Score*
1.	If a pupil does not understand a question it is better to rephrase it for him rather than put the same question to another pupil	1.71
2.	During whole-class teaching the teacher should nominate pupils to answer, not just rely on volunteers	2.43
3.	If a pupil gives an incorrect answer it is best to ask someone else in the class to correct it	3.04
4.	Teachers should not ask a question unless they know the answer	4.04
5.	The important questions have to be set and answered in written form rather than discussed orally	4.68
	Overall mean score	3.18

TABLE 9.2

Frequency of Questioning Behaviour in Descending Order of Occurrence (On a Five-point Scale from 1 = Always to 5 = Never)

	Statement	*Mean Score*
1.	I praise correct answers	1.54
2.	I address questions to the whole	2.61
3.	I get children to ask each other questions	2.89
4.	I call on a pupil by name to answer a question	3.14
5.	I ask questions systematically around the class, calling on each pupil in turn	4.39
	Overall mean score	2.91

Statements in attitude questionnaires often produce paragon ideal assertions of good intent, rather than accurate portrayals of actual behaviour. A number of replies given by teachers in this study do not match what we actually observed in lessons in other parts of the Leverhulme project. For example, seventeen out of twenty-eight teachers gave the response 'always' to the item 'I praise correct answers,' yet none of the teachers we observed invariably praised answers that were right. Twelve teachers replied 'Always' or 'Frequently' to the statement 'I get children to ask each other questions,' yet this was something we rarely observed. There seems to be a strong tendency to reply in the affirmative to these two child-centred statements, in contrast with what we actually observed in live observation of classrooms. On the other hand, the endorsement of asking questions to the whole class was something which did conform to what we observed in lessons, where it was the second most frequent occurrence, after asking questions to individuals, which was in first place (see below).

On the matter of advice to student teachers on questioning, teachers responded in a disparate manner with relatively few communalities. Teachers of younger pupils stressed simplicity" 'Always use simple, understandable words—keep the question short. Try not to embarrass the child by asking too difficult a question,' 'If you only want one answer, then [your] question must be short and precise.' The most common advice, in descending order of frequency of mention, was:

1. Use a variety of both open and closed questions.
2. Get the language right and choose words carefully.
3. Listen carefully to children's answers.
4. Be prepared to rephrase questions and redirect them.
5. Keep questions brief and simple.
6. Start from what pupils know.
7. Admit when you don't know yourself, but then find out answers.
8. Hands up and one at a time to answer.
9. Give everyone a chance to answer at some time.
10. Watch for diversions or 'silly' answers and discourage them.

The main emphasis was on variety, and avoiding asking only one style of question and on empathising with the pupil, that is, choosing the most suitable language register, listening carefully to answers, as these give valuable information, and being flexible and responsive enough to rephrase or redirect a question which was not quite in its best form, or did not evoke a response in its initial form.

Study 2 Observations of Over 1, 000 Questions Asked in Teachers' Lessons

Whereas the study just described was of teachers' self-reports on questioning the other two studies of questioning reported in this chapter involved live observation and recording of teachers' lessons. The first of these was an analysis of 1,021 questions asked by seven teachers. It was based on an actuality log of questions asked during several half-hour periods of observation. A trained observer who was a member of the research team observed the teachers in the sample of several half-hour sessions, and wrote down in a sequential log all the questions asked by the teacher during the period of study, as well as information about the responses, whether the question was managerial, lower or higher order, as described earlier in this chapter, and whether it was addressed to an individual, a group or the whole class. Two raters coded all the questions separately, agreeing on 95 per cent of occasions, with the remaining 5 per cent discussed until agreement was reached.

Table 9.3 shows the overall categorisation of the whole sample of questions. The high incidence of managerial questions and the low occurrence of higher order questions is not unlike the study of transactions in secondary classes reported by Kerry (1984), which found 54 per cent, 42 per cent and 4 per cent respectively using a similar categorisation of 'managing,' 'informing' and 'stimulating.'

TABLE 9.3

Percentage of Questions (n = 1, 021) in Each of Three Categories

Type of question	*Percentage of questions*
Managerial questions (to do with running of lessons)	57
Lower order (information/data recall)	35
Higher order (more than data recall)	8
Total	100

Table 9.4 shows the distribution of questions to different targets. Two thirds of all questions were directed to individuals. Table 9.5 combines the two in a single 3 x 3

contingency able and shows the distribution of each type of question to each of the three targets.

TABLE 9.4

Percentage of Questions to Different Targets

Targets of question	*Percentage of questions*
Individual	66
Whole class	22
Small group	12
Total	100

TABLE 9.5

Percentage of Questions Over Categories and Targets

Type of question	*Individuals*	*Whole class*	*Small Group*	*Total*
Managerial	37	12	8	57
Lower order	24	8	3	35
Higher order	5	2	1	8
Total	66	22	12	100

There are numerous interesting inferences to be drawn from just these tables alone. Teachers asked relatively few higher order questions and addressed few questions to small groups. Questions related to the management of the lesson predominated, and most of these were addressed to individuals. The managerial questions were of different kinds, as the examples from the question logs given below reveal. Details of pupil and teacher responses are given in Table 9.6 and 9.7

1. *Managerial — Organisation — target whole class — acceptable pupil response — neutral teacher reply*
   'Has anyone got any book club money?'
2. *Managerial — Pupil behaviour — target individual — non-acceptable pupil response — neutral teacher*

reply 'Martin, how is it you manage to join in every conversation I'm having?'

3. *Managerial — disguised command/reprimand — target class, no pupil response, no teacher reply* 'Could you all please stop fussing?'
4. *Managerial — sequence — target class, acceptable pupil responses, positive teacher reply* OK, who gotten out often? 'Who got nine?' Who got eight?' 'Anybody less than five?'
5. *Managerial — threat — target group, acceptable pupil response, neutral teacher reply* 'Who else wants to stay with me?' (threatening to keep pupils in after school if they misbehave).
6. *Managerial — sarcasm — target individual, no pupil response, no teacher reply* 'Did I say go and do a quick scribble?' (to a pupil whose work is unsatisfactory).
7. *Managerial — miscellaneous* 'Are you a girl today or a boy?' (said with humour to a girl pupil who was supposed to have left the room with the rest of the girls, and now found herself the only girl left in the room). 'Are you a school dinner?' (sorting out who has a packed lunch and who goes to the dining room for a cooked meal). 'Have you hidden your tongues?' (asked with humour to a group of children who had not replied to a question).

The second largest category, involving the recall of information or data, was also of diverse kinds. Frequently such questions were closely related to the immediate subject matter and produced simple, often one-word, replies. Some involved number ('What number is it?), others the naming of people ('Who can remember what Jesus' mummy and daddy were called?)' or of properties such as colour ('What colour is the chimney?'), the articulating of words ('What does that say?'), and the repeat or recall of information just given ('What do you think an adverb does?' 'What did he find when he found the star?' 'Who was this big fat lady?').

There were several examples of sequences of questions that moved from lower order to the less frequently occurring higher order category. A group of children were observed measuring the distance travelled by various-sized toy car rolled down a ramp. The sequence began with a simple observation question, but went on to a higher, more complex reasoning and hypothesis-stating level:

1. 'Which one went the furthest this time?'
2. Which one might go the furthest next time?'
3. 'John, why do you think the green one might go furthest?'

Higher order questions occurred in various forms, the most frequent of which was introduced by the 'Why?' interrogative. ('Why do you think it would make her happy?' 'Why did he go to Wales?') Sometimes the interrogative 'Why?' was simply used on its own to extend a brief pupil answer to a previous question. A 'Why?' question was not always a precursor to higher order thinking, however, Management questions like 'Why are you siting there?' were disguised comments/reprimands and rarely an invitation to give reasons. Some higher order questions involved pupils' imagination, as in the case of a group of pupils learning about the Second World War, who were asked, 'What do you think you'd have to take into an air raid shelter?,' which required a great deal of thought about human needs, survival, what was available in the 1940s and the nature of war. In general, however, there were very few questions that required an imaginative leap.

There were a few examples of higher order questions within the management category, and this occasionally posed a coding problem, as personal and social education can be regarded as a legitimate 'subject' within primary education. There were very few disagreements between researchers about categories for coding, but two of the questions about which coders disagreed were of this kind, as both involved the teacher asking pupils to empathise with her: 'Can any one tell me why I get cross when I see people kneeling on their chairs?' and 'How do you think that makes me feel?' Eventually both were coded as management, as they produced very short answers and appeared to be principally admonition rather than an invitation to reflect.

This shows the importance of context in the analysis of questions. Questions cannot be understood in isolation, and because question logs and recordings were available and, as one of the analysts had observed the recordings were available and, as one of the analysts had observed the recordings were available and, as one of the analysts had observed the lessons live, the context was available to the investigators. A question like 'What is the question?' can only be understood when one knows that the class is studying number bonds and looking at the six-times table. The children have been asked 'What is three times six?' or 'What is five times six?' but now the teacher reverses the process, give an answer like 'Thirty-six,' and asks the children what the question must have been to produce this response.

The humorous question 'I'm not such an ogre, am I?' occurred when the teacher discovered, at the end of the lesson, that one child had not understood something but had not asked the teacher to explain. The question was preceded by the teacher encouraging the child to ask in future, and the good-natured suggestion that children had nothing to fear if they did not understand seemed to the observer to have been well received by the child concerned.

Children's and teachers' responses to questions also varied considerably. Table 9.6 shows the breakdown of pupil responses into three categories: (1) no verbal response, (2) correct or acceptable response, (3) incorrect or unacceptable response. The double categories correct/ acceptable and their obverse are necessary because an answer can be deemed to be factually 'correct' ('What colour is this?' 'White.' 'That's right.') or 'acceptable,' like when the teacher said to her class, 'What do we say to Mrs. Smith?' (Mrs. Smith was a classroom assistant who had just helped a group of children make some buns for one boy's birthday) and the pupils replied, 'Thank you,' which the teacher felt was an acceptable response.

TABLE 9.6

Types of Pupil Response

Type of pupil response	*Percentage of occurrences*
No verbal response	36.5
Correct/acceptable response	56.5
Incorrect/unacceptable response	6.9
Inaudible response	0.1
Total	100.0

The category 'non-verbal response' does not indicate no response at all by the pupils, though this might be the case, it merely shows that no one spoke in reply. When one teacher, on showing the class a picture, said, 'Can you see?' no one replied verbally, but body posture showed that she needed to turn the book round to face some of he pupils, which she did.

Once pupils had responded (or not done so, as the case might be), the very next act by the teacher was what we called the 'teacher reply framework.' This can be a very important part of the whole questioning process, as it sets the climate and offers important signals to pupils about the accuracy of their replies, or how they have been received by the teacher. The teacher's responses to pupils' answers were coded under 'neutral framework' (which includes no responses, giving further information, changing to another activity, but not giving an evaluative reply to the pupil's response): 'positive framework' (e.g. praise, assent); 'negative framework' (e.g. criticism, dismay); 'immediately asks another question' (including repeated and rephrased questions), and 'inaudible.' Table 9.7 shows the distribution obtained. About half the teacher replies were within a positive framework and relatively few unacceptable pupil responses and negative teacher replies were recorded, but then, as stated earlier in this chapter, most questions asked were simple and straightforward, and only a few involved complex levels of reasoning.

TABLE 9.7

Teacher Reply Frameworks Following Pupils Response

Type of teacher reply framework	*Percentage of occurrences*
Neutral framework	20.2
Positive framework	49.4
Negative framework	12.8
Immediately asks another question	17.4
Inaudible	0.2
Total	100.0

Study 3 Questions in Factual and Discursive Lessons

The second live observation study, of twenty teachers, involved recording a sample of two of their lessons, one on a largely factual topic, the other on a more discursive one such as creative arts or writing a story. Each teacher observed was asked to give the observer a time when such lessons could be observed. Analysis of lesson transcripts confirms many of the points made about questioning in this chapter and in chapter 8 on explaining. Several dimensions of questioning were identifiable, not dissimilar to some of the points made in the analysis of explanations, as one would expect, since the two are related. These included:

Narrow/board

Most questions asked were narrow or closed, though in the more discursive topics broader or more open-ended questions were more common. Most of the narrow questions produced very short answers. A discussion on fruits with 5-6 year olds, for example, where the teacher asked children the names of fruits produced the following twenty successive answers, only one of which is longer than three words: 'No,' 'Lemon.' 'A melon,' 'A big fruit,' 'Yellow,' 'Lemon,' 'Bruised,' 'Gone off,' 'There's white stuff in the middle,' 'A lemon,' 'Duck,' 'No, duck,' 'A duck,' 'Yeah' 'Orange,' 'Apple,' 'Apple,' 'Tomato,' 'Cut them up,' 'Eat them.' Often page after page of transcript showed a similar pattern of short, clipped responses. Word counts of several segments of lessons revealed that on some occasions 90 per cent or more were uttered by the teacher, though more commonly it was about three-quarters.

Yet even in these factual episodes some teachers' questions and reactions to responses could elicit longer responses. This teacher used a broader question followed by enthusiastic reinforcement of good longer responses and an acceptance and enhancement of pupils' ideas, which together produced considered replies from 8 year olds talking about air pressure:

Teacher Where's the pressure?

Pupil Inside the cup, and then there's pressure in the balloon. It's kind of like a piece of steel and a magnet going together, and there's a bit of something in the middle that they can't get through and that means that they keep on sticking together.

Teacher What a wonderful explanation, what a wonderful idea.. What about the air around here, what about the air pressure around here, because you mentioned the air pressure in the balloon and the cup—do you think there's any air pressure round here?

Pupil Well, if it's air pressure and it's pushing down, it's..... helping it to not let any air out, because it's trying to get in and all the air is trying to get out of the side of the cup. The air pressure is trying to push it in.

Teacher Isn't that a good idea!

Observation / Recall / Thought

There is a close relationship between observation and recall in education. When children are asked to observe, they are also, by implication, asked to recall facts and constructs within which to place their observation. While it is possible to ask children to recall facts without using their senses to make an observation, the two acts are often combined. Indeed lessons often begin with recall and observation and then progress to thought and reflection:

Teacher Let's just recap a little bit what we've been doing. We started off.... making what?

Pupil Gliders.

Teacher Gliders first of all, right? ..... Can anyone remember what we learned about that?

Pupil 2 If it had a pointed nose it was aerodynamic.

Teacher Right ..... what does aerodynamic mean, then?

Pupil 3 The wind can pass through.

Teacher Is that right?

Pupil 4 Cut over it.

Teacher (holding up paper dart) Cut over it, yes. Do you mean the dart itself will cut through the air, right? We'll move on from there .... Now, there's something else I want you to do. When air gets hot it moves up.

Pupil 5 Like steam.

Teacher Right. Well, we won't talk about water just for now .... Do you remember a moment when something went 'click' in your mind and you thought, 'Ah, that's it'?

Pupil 6 I didn't think that these spirals would spin round in hot air. I thought they'd just kind of bounce up and down.

Teacher Was that a surprise? Why did they spin round?

Pupil 6 It was kind of catching on it so it took up ... kind of goes up and makes it spin round.

After the lesson the teacher said in interview how he had deliberately checked out what pupils remembered, then encouraged them to engage in analytical and imaginative thought, though he felt disappointed at some of the responses, and finally had gone on to creative practical activity:

'I was quite pleased at how much they'd remembered, and they came out with words like 'streamlining' and then understood about parachutes and gravity and weight.... The disappointing bit was, having primed them all and brought them carefully on to the idea that hot air rises, when I came on to say, 'OK, what could we devise?', the children had no idea at all, so.... I had to start to spoon-feed them a bit.... [but] the practical work that followed up was quite inventive.

Confused/clear

Sometimes questions wee very clear, phrased in language which the children understood and which seemed appropriate for the context. On other occasions questions were embedded in an envelope of extra information, or even in other questions, with the result that confusion would almost invariably follow, or the teacher would need to rephrase what had been asked. This confused sequence emerged from an unclear question about two eggs asked of a group of 6 year olds. Unsure of the purpose or focus of the question, the pupils eventually became distracted:

> *Teacher* That was the first egg. What is the same about this one?
>
> *Pupil 1* It's smaller.
>
> *Teacher* No, what's the same?
>
> *Pupil 1* Bigger.
>
> *Pupil 2* Shell.
>
> *Teacher* They've got the same shall. What do you mean by the same shell?
>
> *Pupil 2* Same colour.
>
> *Pupil 3* It's outside.
>
> *Teacher* And it's outside?
>
> *Pupil 3* Out of the egg.
>
> *Teacher* 'Cos it's a shell it's outside, that's right.
>
> *Pupil 4* A peacock might come out.

> *Teacher* Shh! Alex, Alex ... Let's see what happens when we open it ..... Let's try not to shout, and that means Alex and Royston.

The key point the teacher was trying to elicit, that one egg was cooked and the other egg was raw, only emerged later, when the two eggs were cracked.

By contrast the same teacher skilfully constructed a painting activity by encouraging children to mix paints and then asking them questions about each colour choice. The concepts of how to make a colour lighter or darker, how to name the new colour and how to mix paint were all developed by clearly focused questioning and practical activity:

> *Teacher* Let's see how many lovely colours you can make. What happens to your colour [blue] when you add yellow to it?
>
> *Pupil 1* It goes dark green.
>
> *Teacher* How many colours have you got here? They're all green, but they're different, aren't they?
>
> *Pupil 2* I've got two greens now.
>
> *Teacher* So you have. What did you add to it? Blue or white? .... What happens when you add white to it?
>
> *Pupil 2* Light.
>
> *Teacher* It's a light green, that's right. (To another pupil) That's a super green, how did you make that one?
>
> *Pupil 3* Yellow and dark green.
>
> *Teacher* That's like a spring green, isn't it, very bright.... Lovely .... Dip your brush in there, make it clean and then take some more powder. Wipe it on the side, then pick up more powder.

These three studies of questioning strategies have produced a set of interesting conclusions which will be discussed again in chapter 12. Certainly primary teachers might like to reflect on the large number of managerial and lower order questions we noted and the relatively low incidence of higher questioning that required analytical, evaluative or imaginative answers. Equally the skilful way in which the more skilful communicators can raise the level of thinking, reflection and practical activity, the place of clearly structured sequences of questions and the large number of very short answers sometimes recorded, provide patterns for consideration which will be discussed further in chapter 12.

10

Teachers' Subject Knowledge

The Two National Surveys

In chapter 8 it was shown how, when teaching a topic like 'Insects,' which requires teachers to have a secure foundation of knowledge themselves, children's own conceptions could be unclear when the teacher was not himself sure what characteristics distinguished insects from such creatures as arachnids and gastropods. During the Leverhulme Primary Project we undertook two national surveys of 901 and 433 primary teachers respectively. In the companion book to this one, *Learning to Teach* (Bennett and Carre 1993), there is a full description of the research undertaken by Neville Bennett and his team into student teacher's subject knowledge. This chapter describes the research conducted as part of the class management enquires into how primary teachers cope with teaching a fresh topic for the first time, when their own subject knowledge is insecurely founded.

In the first stage of a two-part national survey of primary teachers in England, following the 1988 Education Act, which introduced a structured national curriculum for the first time, a stratified random sample of 901 teachers in 152 schools replied to a lengthy questionnaire which sought information about how competent teachers felt to teach the ten subjects in the primary curriculum with their existing subject knowledge (Wragg *et al.* 1989). The response rate was 72 per cent (152 out of 212 schools approached). Teachers were asked about the nine subjects in the national curriculum—art, design and technology, English, geography, history, mathematics, music, physical education and science, as well as religious education, which had been a compulsory subject since the 1944 Education Act. Two years later, follow-up questionnaires were sent to many of the same schools, though not to all, as some had indicated that they did not wish to take part in a second survey. Sample loss was inevitable, as some teachers had moved schools, and fresh schools had to be drawn randomly from the *Primary Education Directory.* Of the 131 schools which participated in the second survey in 1991, there were fifty-six which had also taken part in the first. The second survey produced replies from 433 teachers, of whom 223 had taken part in both surveys. A separate analysis of teachers who had participated in both surveys revealed that there were no significant differences in the patterns of response compared with the total sample, and this applied in terms of both statistical significance and direction of change (Bennett *et al.* 1992).

The questionnaire not only asked teachers to respond to the subject overall, but also invited self-ratings of competence on specific topics within maths, science and English. In each case, respondents were asked to use a four-point rating scale:

1. Yes, I feel I am competent with my existing knowledge and skills.
2. Yes, I feel competent, with some help from colleagues.
3. Maybe, I'd feel competent with in-service help from colleagues.

4. No. I feel I would not be competent without substantial in-service support.

This kind of response allowed analysis either as categoric data, for example, how many readers needed substantial in-service support, or as continuous data, permitting mean scores to be compared.

TABLE 10.1

Percentage of Teachers Feeling Competent with Existing Knowledge and Skills in Each of Ten Subjects in 1989 National Survey and 1991 Follow-up

	1989 survey (n = 901)		*1991 follow-up (n = 433)*	
Subject	*Cat. 1*	*Rank*	*Cat. 1*	*Rank*
English	81	1	77	1
Mathematics	68	2	62	2
History	54	3	38	5
Geography	48	4	36	7
Art	48	5	40	4
Physical education	47	6	37	6
Religious education	45	7	33	8
Science	34	8	41	3
Music	27	9	23	9
Technology	14	10	14	10

The results of the two surveys on the question about each of the ten subjects primary teachers are required to teach are show in Table 10.1. Only Category 1 responses are shown, that is, those believing they are competent to teach the subject with their existing knowledge. Relatively little movement was noted in half the subjects, the rank order of English and maths (first and second), physical education (sixth) and music and technology (ninth and tenth) remaining the same. Science moved up from eighth position to third in the two-year period, explained to some extent by the fact that many teachers had spent tow years teaching the new science curriculum, but technology remained rooted firmly at the bottom of the list at 14 per cent. The percentage of teachers feeling competent dropped, in all the other eight subjects, and this was especially noticeable in history (54 per cent down to 38 per cent) and geography (48 per cent down to 36 per cent), where the final subject syllabuses, both of which were wide-ranging and full of subject knowledge demands, were published just before teachers filled in the follow-up questionnaire.

It was not surprising that teachers demonstrated such low confidence in their own knowledge in subjects such as science, music and technology. Analysis of the main subject specialisms of teachers in the first sample had revealed that only 8 per cent had majored in science, only 7 per cent in music, and a tiny 0.3 per cent in technology. Over half had an arts/humanities background. Study of responses to specific topics in science and technology showed a wide range, from about 75 per cent feeling able to teach the 'water cycle' or 'looking after living things' with their existing knowledge down to 10 to 20 per cent for topics such as 'adding to a database' or 'using graphics to develop new ideas' or 'using microelectronic kits.' Under half felt competent to teach electrical circuits or the use of power sources.

Comparisons between groups of respondents showed that male teachers expressed greater feelings of competence than female teachers in science and technology, and women felt more competent than men at art, English, music and religious education. All these differences, in t tests, were significant at the 0.01 or 0.001 level. When we scrutinised the responses of teachers of different ages, ratings declined with age in subjects like science and technology. Teachers with over thirty years of experience rated themselves much lower than those with under five years. In technology, only 6 per cent felt competent, compared with 13 per cent of the youngest teachers, and in science it was 27 per cent compared with 37 per cent. Teachers in medium-size schools (101-300 pupils) rated themselves as more competent in science and technology than those in large or small schools, both differences being significant at the 0.05 level. Junior school teachers also rated themselves more competent than infant school teachers in science, technology, geography and history, all significant on t tests at the 0.001 level, except science, which was significant at the 0.05 level.

In view of the special problems in science and technology, we decided to study a sample of teachers who were teaching certain topics in these fields for the very first time. There were two separate studies. The first involved teachers who had little or no experience of teaching a topic like electricity. Twelve schools in one region, randomly chosen from lists of schools in each of four categories, were approached. The four categories were large urban, small urban, large rural and small rural. Ten teacher of 7-11 year olds who had never, or only rarely, taught physical science topics such as magnetism and electricity agreed to be observed and interviewed about their experiences teaching the topic 'electricity.' In addition we studied two teachers teaching technology to 6-8 years olds for the first time. In the second piece of research there was a four-strand study of teachers using the BBC videos on primary science, which involved such topics as 'levers,' 'stiff shapes' and 'floating and sinking,' most of which were new to the participants.

Study 1: Teaching Science and Technology

Most of the twelve teachers in the sample were apprehensive about teaching physical science and technology topics they had not taught before. As few primary schools had all the necessary equipment we decided to provide sets of circuit broads and components. Only two of the teachers felt they would have been able to make a start on the teaching of electricity with their school's existing equipment. Four basic kits were provided, consisting of circuit boards, batteries, bulbs, switches and wires. Written notes for sets of activities, which covered fur of the attainment statements of the national curriculum, were also offered. Teachers had a free choice about how they taught, some choosing to teach the topic as a self-contained set of activities, others incorporating it into a project on 'energy.' The two teachers who were observed teaching technology had a completely free hand in their choice of topic or activity.

Interviews were held before the teaching began and after the observation of lessons. Teachers were asked how they decided on their approach, how effectively they felt they had handled the lessons, what difficulties they had encountered, how the pupils had responded, how they handled children's questions and what support they had found or felt they would have needed. Classroom observation, in this case, was not structured, except that trained observers made extensive field notes and looked for, and recorded, 'illustrative events,' that is, incidents or aspects of practice that seemed worthy of further scrutiny and questioning in interview. The observation was non-participant, except in the case of one of the teachers of technology, who was a member of the research team.

There was considerable apprehension before the teaching began. Comments included: 'Horror! I haven't taught it before,' and 'It's a challenge. Everything in education is a challenge. Children...... They've got to meet it, so why not the staff?' Most teachers turned to other people for help, rather than to books. Few found the children's books available in their library to be adequate for the pupils, let alone themselves, but in any case their greatest need was for a *person,* usually the school's science co-ordinator, but it could also be any fellow adult who was knowledgeable, so a spouse, a pupil's parent, a school governor who was a science graduate, and a teacher from a nearby secondary school who came in to answer questions once a month, were all cited as sources of information.

Some teachers confessed their ignorance to the class immediately. One began, 'Look, I've got to be honest with you. I know nothing about electricity. I can just about change a fuse.' Classes of up to thirty six were observed and teachers established groups of from two pupils up to six to work on the units. It soon became clear that most teachers had to spend a great deal of time on preparation, except for one who said, 'It's dreadful' (laugh). 'It's dreadful for two reasons. One, I haven't spent a lot of time preparing for it. It's one of the many things that are going on.... um, what else? ...... I just feel so lacking in confidence about the whole thing..... I don't know what I would do without David' (a former school governor who had offered to help).

The two most perplexing problems faced by these teachers were first of all not knowing the relevant scientific principles, and secondly inability to cope with pupils' questions. "Why is this happening?" "Why isn't this working?" Mostly to do with the practical and lots of questions about the actual theory of it.' One teacher simply referred children back to the written notes when any query came up and asked them to see if they could find the answer themselves. Others were perplexed and bemused by the mysteries of electricity: `I can't understand why, when one battery [of three] is put in backwards, the lamp still light up.'

Despite their anxieties some teachers were quite prepared to take on adventurous-looking projects which took them and their class way beyond their own subject competence. The routes through the specified attainment statements were varied, but some classes went on to make a burglar alarm or doll's house lights, and one teacher even strayed, unwittingly, into topics normally covered by much older pupils, like series and parallel circuits, electricity generation and distribution to domestic and industrial premises.

The actual attainment statements which teachers had to cover included eight mentions of specific cognitive skills, such as knowing, understanding, describing and recording. There were also the practical skills of constructing a simple electrical circuit, varying the follow of the current, and observing what was happening. Most teachers gave emphasis to the actual practical activities, but little systematic checking of understanding was observed. On the other hand teachers' own observations influenced their judgement about how effective the lessons had been, some commenting specifically on children's enthusiasm, or the value to lower-attaining pupils: 'James did *very* well the first time. He's not a high achiever usually, but I presume that was previous knowledge that he'd had. He set up a circuit very, very quickly and got the switch in, and a light-emitting diode.' Less able children performing well on a practical activity where the teacher herself was not secure was a great surprise to some teachers. One commented on the case of a boy with special educational needs who showed such manipulative skill he was appointed 'leader' by the rest of his group, an event that had not occurred previously. Another low-achieving pupil asked if she could take away bulbs and batteries so she could work on them at home.

Aware of the many demands on them once the lesson started, most teachers prepared in far greater detail than for other activities in their day. One teacher described how she stayed up until past midnight practising with the electricity kits until she felt confident enough to supervise their use by others. Even then she simply omitted reference to topics or concepts she did not herself understand: 'amps, volts, wattage, atomic structure...... Perhaps I should have I would have gone to the *Oxford English Dictionary* if I'd had to teach it.'

Experiments in technology were similar. One teacher was observed working with children who were designing an egg holder. When one pupil decided to use the centre of a kitchen roll to hold his egg and then had to pack enormous amounts of plasticine around its base to hold it firm, eventually having to give up and even tape the egg on the top to prevent it falling off, she never discussed design principles or such notions as 'centre of gravity. Yet in other subject areas she was competent and proficient.

Another technology lesson involved the making of kites, where children first designed and then made kites out of wood veneer and tissue paper. Seven year old children were not, in this school, allowed to use sharp scissors, so there was considerable frustration amongst them as they found the delicate paper tearing when they cut it with blunt round scissors. The teacher had little idea whether to intervene and cut out the shapes for each child, or to give them extra paper so they could try again. Nor were explanations forthcoming about why some kites flew well and others did not.

Despite the difficulties most teachers claimed afterwards they had enjoyed the experience:

We're all so excited. We've loved doing this.

> It the main (it has gone) quite well. But, left to their own devices, we got some very complicated circuits. Everyone enjoyed it.'

> I'm quite excited about it now, because you can see their results ..... what they can discuss with you. So now I say to colleagues, 'Well, now look at me. I'm a prime example of someone who panicked. I'll look forward to doing it again.'

The picture in this story is a clear one. Most teachers were enthusiastic, if still apprehensive, about their experiences teaching a new topic for the first time, but their own lack of knowledge raised problems. Outside the classroom these were resolved through lengthy preparation and recourse to people such as the science co-ordinator, governors, parents even, who possessed the knowledge they lacked. Inside the classroom most were perplexed by not knowing the relevant scientific principles and by pupils' questions, many of which were unanticipated or unpredictable. The most common coping strategies were evasion, that is, avoiding altogether subject matter not properly known, and turning children back on their own devices, asking them to improvise a solution themselves, or offering to find out for a future lesson. Particularly bewildering, if gratifying, to some teachers was the unexpected competence of certain of their pupils, thought to be slower learners, when faced with a practical activity in which the teacher herself was not well schooled. These findings raise several issues which will be addressed again in chapter 12.

Study 2: Teaching and Learning with Science Videos

During interview teachers sometimes said that they would like high-quality video material to help them teach topics that were new to them, so we decided to investigate how teachers used videos, what they themselves learned from them and what they then did with the pupils. The BBC had produced a set of primary science videos for teachers on topics like 'levers,' 'floating and sinking' and 'stiff shapes.' It was decided to conduct a four-strand investigation of the first two of these topics. A questionnaire survey of users constituted the first strand. Case studies of four schools, a large and a small urban, a large and a small rural, which had ordered the videos was the second strand. The third strand was of four different schools, selected, as in the second strand, but this time from schools which had not ordered the videos. In this case the four schools were given the videos. It was decided to adopt this particular strategy as teachers in schools that send away for videos might be especially competent or keen. The fourth strand involved a study of student teachers to elicit what they themselves learned from watching the videos.

The questionnaire survey was of seventy three schools throughout the country which were, according to the BBC, the first set of schools to order the videos. It became clear that many schools reported they were under such pressure they had not yet had time to use the videos at all, in some cases not even to look at them. These constraints of time and over-demand are real at a time of rapid curricular change in primary schools. Heads and science co-ordinators had usually placed the order for the videos, and the main target for them was said to be 8-9 year olds or upper juniors. Fewer than a third of respondents had had time to use them properly. Most teachers had watched them at home or as a group after school. Many felt that preliminary viewing had helped clarify scientific principles in their own mind. What they most wanted, they reported, was three things: an enhancement of their own scientific knowledge, practical ideas for classroom work and high-quality out-of-studio visual material, showing, for example, why lifeboats do not sink, or examples of levers in everyday life.

The case studies of four randomly chosen user schools involved interviews with teachers and observation of lessons. Semi-structured interviews were held and these were tape-recorded. Observation, as in the earlier study in this chapter, was freehand, with collection of 'illustrative events.' Most difficulties caused for teachers, as in the earlier study, arose from pupils' questions, especially those involving a request for information about underlying scientific principles, usually 'why?' Questions. Why, for example, was it easier to raise two people close to the centre of a ladder than two sitting at the extremes; why a whole apple floated, but when the same apple was cut into pieces they sank; why most grains of sand fell to the bottom of a water tank, but some stayed floating on the surface. Teachers readily confessed their ignorance of 'density,' 'surface tension' or 'Archimedes' principle' which were central to an understanding of these phenomena. Several said they had not themselves realised, for example, that scissors were levers, so they welcomed a video which gave a wider set of illustrations than they would have selected themselves: 'We needed the videos for the principles. Bill [top juniors] knows a lot about science, and even he found them helpful. We need the scientific principles. The videos pinpoint the principles.'

Some teachers felt having greater security on principles, as well as powerful visual ideas about science in the world surrounding their pupils, had given them confidence they might not otherwise have had. One group visited a lifeboat station after seeing a scene in which a lifeboat is shown being submerged and then righting itself. Another group had visited a canal and been on a boat. Like other groups they had taken the topic 'floating and sinking' as part of a larger project on 'water,' which had involved studying the water cycle, the use of waterways, water in our daily lives as well as floating, sinking and other scientific aspects. Other teachers incorporated 'levers' into their project on 'toys.'

Once more, teachers spoke appreciatively of people who helped them. One science co-ordinator produced a booklet of ideas to go with the videos. Another had been through the videos noting down the tape counter references for each science and offering suggestions for use within the school's pattern of project and topic work. Teachers insecure with their own subject knowledge welcomed this sort of practical help, which left them more able to concentrate on classroom process, especially as most expressed problems about using videos, ranging from the difficulty of having to more learning equipment to their own classroom, when the television area was not free, to coping with children's questions about the video scenes. One teacher in a large rural school, winding forward to a particular scene, suddenly found Wimbledon tennis being transmitted on the regular channel as the video recorder was locked on fast forward. It ruined the concentration of the 8-9 year olds in the class: 'You see, it's all right for the first bit' (showing the first scene). 'When you set it up, hat's fine and it's ready to go, but if you want to use the effective bits afterwards—particularly if they're short snippets—well, you saw what happened.' When teachers are teaching unfamiliar material, logistical or equipment problems merely compound their difficulties.

In the third strand, when four schools were selected which had not brought the videos, similar observations were made, but there were also additional ones. These schools were not especially enthusiastic about science, unlike the strand two schools, where some key person had been keen and knowledgeable enough to tract down and order science videos. One of the schools, in the London area, contained several teachers who had been on primary science 'booster' courses in the previous two or three years, so those teachers felt more confident than the teachers in the other urban school and the two rural schools who had had no such courses. Indeed, most teachers confessed in interview, to being especially worried about physical science topics and abut scientific processes in general, like testing hypotheses, or conducting a 'fair' experiment. The relationship between 'density' and 'flotation' was one that was mentioned as a source of mystery by many of those interviewed and observed.

Some teachers said they needed help with absolutely basic ideas. 'I have no idea at all how a buzzer works,' one teacher confessed, 'yet my children are supposed to use one.' One teacher found a problem when the class tried to imitate a scene from the video in which a balloon floated. The class found the balloon also floated when it was empty and the teacher was lost for an explanation, admitting that she even had no idea which principles to investigate, let alone explain.

In one of the rural schools that had several new members of staff there was the advantage of fresh teachers who were keen and willing to experiment. A number of them felt the videos had made them realise there was much more to topics like 'flotation' and 'levers' than they had realised on their own. Video materials can help solve problems by giving teachers and children a firm foundation of scientific fact, high-quality visual images, illustrating principles in action, and practical ideas for classroom practice, but they can also create problems by exposing teachers in areas where they are insecure and by provoking questions from pupils that teachers cannot answer. The more self-confident teachers cope with this and use words like 'challenge' in interview, whereas ones less confident see it as yet another potential pitfall in an already hazardous occupation.

If teachers are themselves still learners in some subjects, then it is important to know what hey might learn from the same video materials seen by their pupils. In the fourth and final strand of this study we decided to study a group of twenty-one primary trainees. All were near the end of a one-year postgraduate teacher training course, and only one of them was a science specialist. They were given tests of scientific knowledge and teaching ideas immediately before and after watching the videos. Some fascinating differences emerged, not all predictable.

Levers

Respondents were asked, before and after, to identify levers commonly found in the home. All were able to give at least one example beforehand. The trainees were able to cite on average 2.85 more examples after watching the videos, usually though not always examples shown in one film, like nut-crackers, doors and scissors. When asked to define the purpose of a lever the results were more mixed. Six were able to give a correct definition before and after about half the group produced a more correct response after viewing. Four, however, still gave the same or a different incorrect response after viewing the film.

The most difficult question for respondents was about a gate which was closed, and students were asked the position one would pull the gate open to which would need he least force. This topic was not covered directly in the video, and most peoples gave the same answer before and after, about half being correct and the others being incorrect. Only two people changed their thinking from incorrect to correct. Finally, there were two questions about the fulcrum. Students were asked to identify where, in a bottle opener, the fulcrum was located. Most identified it incorrectly before and after, four were correct before and after. Of the remaining four students, one moved from incorrect before and after. Of the remaining four students, one moved from incorrect to correct, but the other three gave a wrong answer after the film, having given the correct answer beforehand. When asked to explain the relationship between force applied and distance from fulcrum when using a lever, half were able to give a better definition after the viewing, the others did not improve.

Flotation

All students were able to name correctly objects which floated and sank before and after viewing. More objects were named afterwards, but also previous answers were refined: for example, 'bottles' became 'empty bottles,' 'cups' became 'empty cups placed the right way up,' and 'plastic bags became 'plastic bags filled with air.' When asked to explain why a polystyrene brick floats, but a brick sinks, most students compared the densities of the two objects, but did not refer to the density of water. Only four students referred to the importance of air in flotation.

In the next section, students were asked to comment on the correctness or incorrectness of four statements. The results of the twenty students who were not science graduates were as follows:

1. 'Light objects float, heavy objects sink' (false). Sixteen correct before and after, remaining four correct after.
2. 'Large objects sink, small objects float' (false). All twenty correct before and after.

3. 'The shape of an object can make it float or sink' (true). Seventeen correct before and after, two incorrect before and after, one incorrect before but correct after.
4. 'Metal objects always sink' (false). Eighteen correct before and after, one correct before, incorrect after, one incorrect before, correct after.

A high degree of prior knowledge clearly affected these responses, as was the case in a question which showed four different balls floating in a tank of water, some sitting higher than others. When asked which balls were the most and least dense, all responded correctly, but in response to the question asking which ball had a density nearest to that of water, eight incorrectly chose a ball which was half in and half out of the water. This did not change after viewing the video on floating and sinking. Finally, when asked to explain why an empty bottle floats, but a full one sinks, eight improved their original definition after seeing the video, usually by mentioning the importance of air, eight gave equally good before and after responses, three gave poorer replies after the video and one did not give a second explanation.

When asked about teaching ideas, most felt they had gained a much wider understanding of levers and would be able to give pupils more examples of levers in everyday life, mentioning in particular bottle openers, traffic barriers, the beam engine, the mobile TV camera on a boom, scissors, a door opening and the human arm. About half mentioned an appreciation of the points made in the videos about children explaining to each other. Many were still not clear about the fulcrum. Observations on flotation involved a better awareness of high and low floaters, the acquisition of ideas for using parachutes, raising a sunken plastic bag by blowing air underneath it, doing tests with air in cans and testing children's hypotheses. There was still some admitted confusion about density, buoyancy and Archimedes' Principle.

These studies reveal aspects of a matter analysed in greater detail in the companion book of research findings from the Leverhulme Primary Project (Bennett and Carre 1993), that teachers' subject knowledge can be an important constituent of effective or ineffective teaching. It is clear, both from our national surveys and from our case studies, that large numbers of primary teachers admit their own subject knowledge in science and technology is insecurely founded. This research has shown that most teachers manage this deficit by extensive preparation outside the classroom, by recourse recourse to people rather than books, and occasionally by evasion and pressing pupils to fall back on their own resources inside the classroom. It has also revealed that teachers can themselves learn from good-quality video material, in terms of both understanding the scientific principles (though film can also occasionally generate confusion) and acquiring practical teaching ideas, but that these may be limited. Sometimes this will be as a result of the failure to apply a scientific principle learned in one context to a novel or unpredicted situation, like a pupil's question, but on other occasions it can be simple constraints to do with logistics and equipment. If teachers working for the first time in unfamiliar territory are to become more effective, then several messages can be drawn by those responsible for policy and practice, and matter which will again be addresed in the final chapter of this book.

11

Student Teachers' Professional Skills

As is the case in virtually all professional and vocational training, student teachers must complete periods of field experience in which they work in conditions close to those surrounding full-time practitioners. These may vary from opportunities to teach individuals or small groups on an occasional half-day or whole-day basis, up to block practices lasting a term or longer, usually on a reduced timetable. Novices on teaching practice have often been studied by researchers. Wragg (1972) documented 578 lessons given by 102 student teachers during a ten-week practice and found that many students had fairly fixed patterns of interaction which hardly altered during the practice. Fink (1976) used diaries, questionnaires and lesson observations in her study of twenty-five student teachers, showing that they became more custodial towards their pupils as the practice progressed. Preece (1979) found that students' anxiety fell during teaching practice when he studied 100 students on a postgraduate secondary course.

Partington and Hinchliffe (1979) conducted fifty six case studies of students thought to be especially good or poor at managing classes and reported that the establishment of good personal relationships, effective preparation, skilful organisation of group and individual work, clear questioning and explaining, and effective presentation of self were all associated with 'success' as perceived by tutors and supervising teachers. Wragg and Dooley (1984) observed 204 lessons given by thirty four secondary postgraduate students and found that most of the deviant behaviour which occurred was of a minor nature, most commonly noisy chatter punctuated by requests or commands to desist. Few students had serious discipline problems, though many lessons sank into minor chaos with prolonged mild deviance, which occurred most frequently during transitions from one activity to another. Wragg and Wood (1984) observed 210 lessons given by twenty eight undergraduate or postgraduate secondary students during their first encounters on teaching practice, and compared these with 103 lessons given by thirteen experienced teachers. The students were less likely to be rated 'confident', 'businesslike' or 'stimulating' and made less use of their eyes to sweep the room or engage individuals in eye contact. They were less certain about classroom rules and expectations and less deliberate about learning pupils names, though they identified themselves more closely with pupils than did the experienced teachers.

There have been several reviews of research on teacher education and student teachers, including some covering a wide field (Wragg 1982, Tickle 1987. Diamond 1991) and some dealing with specific aspects such as the supervision or mentoring of students (Little 1990). Much of the writing on teacher education is analytical, and a great deal is political or polemical, but relatively little is based on live observation of lessons given by students, though some has addressed closely related matters like attitudes or attitude change. We decided to base much of our Leverhulme Primary Project work on student teachers, in the strand of the project reported in this book, on studying their behaviour and experience in the classroom during teaching practice. Substantial research into cohorts of student teachers in the strand of the project directed by Neville Bennett is described in the companion volume to this one (Bennett and Carre 1993). This chapter describes three studies. The first is of undergraduate student teachers' first encounters on their final block teaching practice. The same procedures were used as for the study of experienced teachers' first encounters described in chapter 3. The second study is of students' teaching strategies during teaching practice and in particular their handling of disruption. The procedures used in this study are the same as those used in the observations of experienced teachers described in chapters 4 and 5. The third study is of student teachers' attitude change before and after their final block practice. The same set of photographs used in other research described in this book were used to elicit responses, and both freehand comment and answers to structured attitude statements were analysed.

Study 1: Students' first encounters

It was not as straightforward to observe the first encounters of student teachers as it was to study the first lessons of experienced teachers. At the beginning of the school year the new class teacher usually devotes her whole time to her new class from the very first moments of the first day. Student teachers tend to ease gradually into their role, perhaps observing for a few days, but also supervising a small group, working with individuals or taking the lead for part of a lesson shared with the class's regular teacher. It is much less likely that there will be a single clean 'moment of entry'; rather, first encounters will be diffuse, more phased than sudden.

A sample of undergraduate primary students on final teaching practice was selected largely at random, except that an effort was made to choose students in a mixture of small and large urban and small and large rural schools. A total of sixteen students were observed by trained observers, using procedures described in chapter 3. The observers spent the first three days in the students' classrooms, once the initial period of observation was over, but it was not always possible to ensure that the very first encounter of this blurred beginning was witnessed, for the reasons given above. Four students were not seen during their very first lesson, one because she had taught a lesson during her observation phase, one had taught several lessons during what was meant to be observation, a third had taught all the class but in separate groups, and the fourth was team teaching with the class's regular teacher from the beginning.

Preliminary interviews were held with each student during the last week of the term preceding teaching practice, the equivalent of the pre-observation interview with experienced teachers. All had had previous experience of eight weeks of block practice in two primary schools and several single days of school experience. All taught in the 7-11 age range, though two were in small village schools and so encountered occasionally a number of younger pupils.

Two said they had been given no preliminary advice by teachers, but others mentioned the sort of tips reported earlier in this book, most citing the 'firm but friendly' preliminary image favoured by experienced teachers in chapter 3. Students' description of hints and tips received included: 'Be firm but friendly; ignore unnecessary comments,' 'Be friendly, but be strict; better to be strict in the first few weeks.' 'Be firm from the very start, let the children know what you expect of them and what the rules are. Establish the rules with the help of the children,' and 'Be firm, don't smile too much. Best to establish that *you* are the boss and fully in control and they are thus to treat you as they would their regular teacher. Don't be an ogre, though.' Other commonly offered advice concerned getting to know names quickly, getting to know children as individuals, and starting with easy work that children can do.

Asked about their classroom environment, most expressed satisfaction at the space available for teaching but had reservations about shortage of storage space. Only one was very unhappy about this, as she had to teach thirty five children aged 9—10 in a cramped space. She had observed the class and was apprehensive about possible class management problems because so many children had to work in a corridor. Four of the students worked in open plan schools. Most had access to reasonable facilities, but fewer than half had classrooms or work bays with specialist areas for maths, science or reading. Five had no access to a sink for work with water or for washing up. In general the students were uncomplaining about lack of facilities, using terms like 'reasonable', 'adequate' or 'awkward'.

Interviewers asked students whether they would like to change the room in any way once they took over their teaching programme. Most said not, or expressed uncertainty, especially where teaching areas were shared with others. Two said they would like to create a carpet space for class discussion and one wanted to put up more posters, but the predominant reaction was non-territorial, a recognition that it was simply not their own territory, a complete contrast to those experienced teachers reflecting before the school year on 'my class', 'my classroom' or 'my rules'. This 'guest' status was further enhanced by the various other adults who, students' already knew, would share the classroom, including the class's regular teacher, the head occasionally, classroom assistants and parent helpers. Only six were told they would be on their own.

None of the students, however, seemed apprehensive about support and assistance. All spoke of the positive attitude towards them when they had visited, and words like 'friendly', 'supportive', 'helpful', 'welcoming', 'co-operative atmosphere' and 'family atmosphere' were used by respondents in all the interviews. The main possible constraint mentioned was lack of specialist space, particularly for practical activities, storage and display, rather than people. Two students were apprehensive about team teaching, especially one who would be working with sixty children and two teachers in an area she had found very noisy and confusing when she had visited the school. One student was worried about the head, who, she said, used very long words and seemed to have a strange manner. All felt they had learned valuable information from their preliminary visits, especially about pupils with difficulties, the wide spread of reading ages in the class, the work schemes and the general ethos of the school. Most students had come away with a positive view of the class they were to take, though one said she had not been able to form any picture of them, and two were aware of social problems that might cause concern.

Students were also asked how they thought their management style might differ from that of the class teacher. Half said they were not able to judge. Some of the others mentioned that they might need to be more strict, do more practical work or teach in a more structured environment. One said she might find it a problem working with two other teachers in a team, as they had different styles from each other, and she was not yet sure how best to fit in. Students tended to be more concerned about fitting in with the work schemes than with the management styles, however, and all were aware of the need to be well prepared for what was a wide variety of approaches to the curriculum, some based on 'subjects', others on often widely differing themes from school to school. Topics like 'Roman history' and 'The countryside' were sometimes given to students by the school, but in most cases students would be expected to improvise their own schemes to fit in with the school's general approach to the national curriculum.

Fewer than half were able to describe in preliminary interviews what their first lesson might be and the following were the only responses which gave any indication of content or style: 'I may tell a story,' 'A brainstorm session on the topic "Invaders" and an outline of how I see the topic will run,' 'Let the children know exactly what I expect of them,' 'Introduce the topic "water", words which describe water.' Their replies to questions about how they would feel an hour before their first lesson varied from the domestic 'Getting my own children to school,' 'What to have for breakfast. I will be very nervous, worrying,' 'Whether I have packed everything in my bag- sandwiches, pens, money, lesson notes, bus pass, and whether my contact lenses are going to stay in,' to dress rehearsals: 'I will be thinking about lesson materials - have 1 prepared enough?' 'I'll be looking forward to it I'll want to be enthusiastic, fun, likable, exciting, but also stand for no nonsense'.

The 'dress rehearsal' was particularly noticeable in the responses to the question about what they would be doing five minutes before their first lesson:

> How I am going to introduce myself. Talking to myself about what I'm going to say. Making sure I know how to organise the children. Re-read lesson plans and have them near by.

> Trying to remember the first couple of things I want them to do, so I don't have to look at my notes too much. Trying to relax and fed confident.

> Panic. Here goes. What to say at the beginning, how to make the lesson enjoyable.

Some of these comments reveal the kind of image the students hoped to project, but we had asked specifically about this. The same words recurred in the responses: 'Firm' (eight people) was the most frequently cited description, followed by 'confident' (five), 'friendly' and 'interesting' (four each). Some of this vocabulary recurred when questions were asked about relationships and rules. Most were eager to let children see that if they were firm, even severe, at the beginning they were also human:

> I want to get to know their names or characteristics as quickly as possible, by giving away information or impressions about myself and helping the children to see me as a person.

> I want to first establish my position as a teacher. When I have earned the children's respect then I can concentrate on building more of a friendship role.

There was a highly significant difference between students and experienced teachers on the matter of classroom rules. In chapter 3 there were nine categories of classroom rule, each with several examples of sub-categories, stated by teachers in interview, and, in the main, implemented in the classroom. The students in this sample were far less clear in their minds about their own classroom rules. Some mentioned generic headings, rather, than specific rules, such as 'respect for others' or 'ensure harmony in the classroom'. Three mentioned 'no talking when someone else is talking' and two talked about respect for property. The great majority, however, used variations of the notion that existing rules would be enforced or rules would be established when needed:

> At first I'll just observe to see what rales are already in force. I'll only establish my own if necessary.
>
> The rules will come up naturally as the lesson proceeds.
>
> Yes (I'll introduce rules) if I think I need them. I don't know what. I'll discuss it with the class, and I'll word them positively.

Altogether each of the sixteen students was observed for between six and eight sessions lasting up to 100 minutes, a total of 116 sessions altogether. Once the students began their teaching practice some of their intentions were overtaken by the pressure of events. One student who had expressed a relaxed view about the need for classroom rules found herself having to improvise them quickly in the very first lesson, when pupils rushed into the room noisily. There was not always a clean hand-over from the class teacher to the student, so it is not possible to make too many comparisons with the patterns observed in the classes of experienced teachers described in chapter 3. However, of the seventy three occasions when a clear beginning to a lesson could be observed, the student was already present on fifty seven occasions, the pupils entered the class first on twelve occasions, and in four cases the student and the pupils came into the room simultaneously. This is not too surprising, as, unlike the experienced teachers in the chapter 3 sample, the students did not have other responsibilities, such as playground duty, in these first few days.

In all cases the observer commented that the teacher seemed prepared for the start of the lesson. The one student, however, who spoke at greatest length in interview about the need for discipline and orderliness and how she would discuss rules in the very first lesson, actually did none of these, even though her class entered quite noisily. The first classroom entry of the children was quite varied, and, to some extent, in the very first encounter tended to reflect the pattern with the class's regular teacher rather than that of the newly arrived student. Only three classes were recorded as 'noisy' on entry to the first lesson. By the seventh and eighth sessions this had grown to five. One class which had been orderly on the first day had begun to rush in noisily from the playground. Another class had a group of boys who began to run into the room on the fourth session and were reprimanded by the teacher for noise and unruliness. This happened again in two of the following four entries. Three classes were described as noisy or disorganised after the lesson should have started, the others tended to settle down much as they had done for experienced teachers.

In almost all the lessons there was a task demand fairly soon after the pupils had settled down, and here was another big difference between students and experienced teachers. First of all there was no special emphasis in the school assembly on the new school year or on high expectations, none of those moral demands and exhortations that had characterised the first school day in September. Secondly the students felt able to move straight into lesson content. Few made any reference to rules or routines, for these had, by then, been established by the class's regular teacher. Most students secured a high degree of application to the task. Observers noted that in all except eleven sessions almost all the pupils applied themselves to the task in hand soon after the lesson had begun. One student only was recorded as needing more than ten minutes for the class to commence work. Only three students had sessions where a significant number did not become engaged in their work at the beginning of the lesson. One had three sessions when between six and ten pupils did not commence work, another had two sessions where six to ten and one session where eleven to fifteen pupils did not begin their task, and a third had one session with six to ten not occupied and two with eleven to fifteen not engaged in the task in hand.

Attention-getting behaviour by the students was a less confident, more shaky version of what had been observed for experienced teachers. 'Right' and 'Shhh' were common devices for opening, voice and position playing a prominent role. Some students lacked the conviction of the class's regular teacher, so they needed more than one attempt to get silence. One student even tried standing on a chair. Another confessed her learner status freely: 'I'm going to take the register now. It's my first time, so I'll need some help.' Others soon found resistance to their carefully planned lessons: 'Right, we're going to be doing aerobics' (groans from group of reluctant girls) 'so you might as well be enthusiastic' (more groans). 'You'll enjoy it. Right. Make two lines, please.'

It was not long before some students had to deal with misbehaviour. A student who said she would only establish rules if necessary began a session following a day when several pupils had misbehaved with a huge display of anger: 'Right!' (Slams file down on desk.) 'Yesterday was disgusting. Your behaviour was appalling. It will not happen today or else we'll not do anything interesting.' Another student who had expressed, in interview, a desire to make what she said worth listening to. so children would learn to accept her as their new teacher, found difficulty in commanding a hearing and was soon rilling out the imperious stereotype she was eager to avoid, as she sought to establish social control:

> Right, then. You're not going to do anything till you're quiet. If anyone's going to be silly they can go straight back to the classroom. Put your money away, Peter. (Angrily) Now! Jonathan! We're waiting for your group.

Whereas most students had no difficulty controlling the class, and those that did generally asserted themselves, albeit with difficulty, one student was too nervous to take action when challenges to her authority occurred. She had said in interview that she would be nervous and would feel panic, and in an early session one boy began to yawn ostentatiously, eventually lying across his desk pretending to snore. She ignored it and carried on addressing the rest of the class. By the second day the observer noted that children appeared to wander off to an adjacent area where their normal class teacher was working, the classroom was generally noisy, no procedure for attracting attention by pupils or teacher had been established and there was no feeling that the student had actually taken over the class. Though she wandered round the room looking at pupils' work in a perfunctory manner, this did not reduce the misbehaviour.

In such circumstances pupils will sometimes, in the absence of clearly defined rules, seek a definition by testing the limits of misbehaviour, so that case law can be established. This is exactly what happened in this student's lesson. One pupil set off the alarm of his watch; there was no reaction. Another repeatedly sharpened her pencil, saying she did not feel like working; the student told her to sit down. One girl played with a doll and talked to four others, another pushed her table backwards and forwards, one pupil played with a hand-held computer game, two girls talked incessantly for ten minutes about matters other than the task, two boys donned sunglasses, another boy banged on the table to gain attention, a pupil persistently annoyed another, two boys put their feet on the table and began whistling. Many of these were ignored, others were met by an order to cease, but not in a convincing or assertive manner. The limits were not being defined, so pupils kept seeking some consistent reaction to what was and was not permitted.

One particular difficulty for student teachers was the individual pupil who was particularly badly behaved. The class teacher had warned one student that Three-quarters of these children are from broken homes' and that one pupil in particular was very badly behaved and had been expelled from two other schools. She was largely unable to cope with a succession of anti-social acts from him which made a considerable impact on the other pupils. He was seen to kick a ball in a girl's face, stamp his hand with a rubber stamp at the teacher's desk, dance on a chair, grab a pupil by the neck and shake him, take a girl's pencil, throw things across the room and numerous other attention-seeking or disruptive acts. The student tried using a rough and angry voice, but to little effect, so she kept a distance from him. On one occasion when he refused to write, saying he could not do the task, she replied, 'I'm sure you could if you tried. That's your trouble, you just don't try.' She did not, however, sit with him to see what his problem was, nor was she given any advice on how to cope.

As the case in the classes of experienced teachers reported in this book, most inappropriate behaviour was noisy or illicit chatter. This arose for different reasons. In one student's class the children's task was to plant cress in trays. She had explained what was to be done, and the class had been attentive, but she had not prepared the trays. As soon as the transition from whole-class to group activity occurred the pupils, uncertain how to get a tray, began to talk to each other. The teacher eventually gave out the trays, but by then there was a noisier working atmosphere; she ignored it and concentrated on one group at a time. In a later physical education lesson the organisation was even more complex, but she had learned from her previous experience, had all the equipment available, explained clearly what the class would do, set up demonstrations to reinforce what the task involved and used her eyes to sweep over the whole room and control the activity. There were no incidents of disruption.

Analysis of those lessons which had high levels of activity and orderliness showed that the more effective students had prepared the activities adequately, explained clearly what was involved, answered pupils' questions, monitored the work of individuals or groups, but kept an overview of the whole class and were especially vigilant during transitions, curbing misbehaviour before it escalated. They also were more likely to devise lessons and tasks which engaged pupils' attention. Obversely the lessons with more disruption and inattention were usually well prepared in terms of content, but less so in organisation. Misbehaviour recurred most frequently at the beginning and end of lessons and during transitions from one activity to another. Younger pupils especially became restless at the end of the longer sessions, and one student had problems because she overestimated the ability of the class and devised work which only the more able would do, resulting in large queues of pupils at her desk with a succession of queries, and resultant obscuring of the rest of the class from her view. Another student put some sheets on the blackboard that were so small children had to get out of their seats to see them. The more robust students learned immediately from their organisational or procedural misjudgments, but the more nervous or less perceptive took little or no remedial action.

The primary differences between the students and the experienced teachers were principally lack of clarity about classroom rules and the limits of inappropriate behaviour, a less confident and convincing manner when dealing with disruption, a lower level of whole-class vigilance when working with individuals or whole-class groups, fewer coping strategies when organisation or relationships went wrong, and less attention to the rules of behaviour in the very first encounter. Student teachers gave almost all their planning time to subject matter, less to organisation and little to 'tone' or desired classroom atmosphere. They were especially keen to work with individuals and small groups and gave a great deal of attention to these. This close identity with the individual child before professional socialisation has taken place was also noted in the study by Wragg and Wood (1984) of secondary trainees.

Study 2: Students on teaching practice

Once student teachers have completed the first few days of their teaching practice they have to sustain and enhance their class management over several weeks, usually under the supervision of the class's regular teacher. In chapters 4 and 5 there was a description of the management strategies of a sample of experienced teachers in London, the North-west and the South-west. We also observed student teachers, using the same research procedures, and twelve out of the sixty teachers in the sample were second-year students on their first longer six-week block of teaching practice. They had already experienced one day a week in school followed by a three-week block practice in their first year. It would have been interesting to follow through the group of students observed during their first encounter, but researchers must nowadays be sensitive to the pressures on schools and not outstay their welcome. Intensive observation of lessons can be intrusive on a school when many novelties and rapid changes in curriculum consume the time and energy of teachers.

It was decided, therefore, to follow a different group of students, using exactly the same procedures as were employed for experienced teachers, except that, on the observation schedule, the category 'another teacher' was expanded to incorporate the 'intervention of the class teacher whilst her student was taking the class. We had intended that some of the class teachers would themselves agree to be observed as part of our study of experienced teachers, and only two of them declined, so in the case of ten students in the sample we had observation data in exactly the same classroom environment collected from their class teachers after they had left. In each case the same class management observation schedule was used during four visits. There are thus four sets of five structured two-minute observation blocks for each participant, four sets of deviance and on-task measures, four sets of freehand observation notes, critical events, as well as interview data for both student and experienced teachers. Altogether forty sessions were observed for both students and teachers, making 200 observation blocks in each case.

In quantitative terms, therefore, Table 11.1 shows comparisons between the two groups for exactly the same number of lessons observed using identical procedures, as the two students whose class teachers did not wish to be observed have been excluded. The figures in Table 11.1 show the principal activities in which students or teachers were engaged. These could either be teachers acting solo, for example addressing the class, teacher-pupil interaction, pupils working with the teacher, either monitoring what they were doing or not, and transitions from one activity to another, with or without movement. In each case the predominant type of activity was recorded. The most striking differences between the two groups lie in the greater amount of teacher-pupil interaction seen to students' lessons and the consequent lower incidence of pupils working with teacher monitoring. Student teachers feel more of a need to present themselves to rehearse their presentation skills on teaching practice, hence also the higher incidence of 'teacher solo' in which students often explained content or procedures to the whole class.

TABLE 11.1

Percentage of each activity during structured observation of 200 lesson segments in the classes of experienced and 200 in the classes of student teachers

Principal type of activity	*Experienced teachers*	*Student teachers*
Teacher solo	6	13
Teacher-pupil interaction	15	33
Pupils working, teacher monitors	69	51
Pupils working, teacher does not monitor	4	2
Transition with movement of class	1	1
Transition without movement of class	5	0

There were some notable differences in the occurrence of misbehaviour. Table 11.2 shows the frequency of deviant behaviour in lessons. It needs to he borne in mind, of course, that observers noted any mildly deviant act, including illicit chatter, and that having one or two such acts does not mean classroom mayhem.

TABLE 11.2

Percentage of lesson segments (out of 200 for each group) in which different numbers of pupils were observed misbehaving

Number of pupils misbehaving	*Experienced teachers*	*Student teachers*
0	55	40
1	19	12
2 to 4	10	18
5 or more	16	30

It was much more likely that students would have a small cluster of pupils not attending to the task, often the children at one table. There were also differences in the nature of misbehaviour, as Table 11.3, showing four of the commonly observed types of deviant behaviour, reveals. As one might expect, students have more occurrence of noisy chatter than the class's normal teacher, but the category of children moving when they were not supposed to is the same (twenty two). There was also a difference in responses to deviance. Student teachers responded in 98 per cent of cases, whereas experienced teachers did so in 90 per cent, preferring sometimes to ignore it. The responses to deviant behaviour shown in Table 11.4 are also based on percentages, to help comparison, as there were more responses from student teachers because there was more misbehaviour overall. In Table 11.4 A1 to A3 figures show the target of the responses, B1 and B2 the timing of the intervention, C1 to C12 actual strategies, and D1 and D2 the length of the response. There are several similarities between student and experienced teachers, but the most striking differences are to be found in the students' greater tendency to address their response to groups of pupils, issue an order to cease the misbehaviour and use facial expressions, whereas the experienced teachers were far more likely to address individuals, seek to re-involve pupils in their work, and use praise and to make sustained responses.

TABLE 11.3

Percentage of lesson segments (out of 200 for each group) When four categories of pupil misbehaviour occurred

Type of behaviour	*Experienced teachers*	*Student teachers*
Noisy or illicit pupil talk	22	45
Inappropriate movement	22	22
Inappropriate use of materials	8	11
Defiance to teacher	5	8

TABLE 11.4

Comparison of experienced and student teachers' responses to misbehaviour (figures show percentage of all responses to misbehaviour by each group)

Teachers' responses to misbehaviour	*Experienced teachers*	*Student teachers*
A1 To whole class	35	41
A2 To group	19	35
A3 To individuals	46	24
B1 Before escalation of misbehaviour	95	97
B2 After escalation of misbehaviour	5	3
C1 Order to cease	65	90
C2 Pupil named	64	64
C3 Reprimand	43	41
C4 Involve pupils in work	43	14
C5 Proximity (going over to pupil)	18	21
C6 Touch	10	12
C7 Praise	9	3
C8 Gesture	9	9
C9 Facial expression	8	21
C10 Pause	6	8
C11 Pupil moved	5	0
C12 Threat	5	3
D1 Teacher response brief	71	87
D2 Teacher response sustained	29	13

The outcomes of these interventions are shown in Table 11.5. Rows A1 to A3 give the pupils' reactions, B1 to B4 reveal whether the misbehaviour increased, decreased, remained the same or ended, and C1 to C3 show whether the teacher appeared calm, agitated or angry. There are few large differences, experienced teachers being slightly more likely to secure pupil acceptance of the action (e.g. 'Yes miss') and to see the misbehaviour ending, though, paradoxically. the were also slightly more likely to see it sustained. These differences, however are too small to be of any interest.

TABLE 11.5

Outcomes of experienced and student teachers' interventions (shown as percentages of all responses by each group)

Outcome of teacher intervention	*Experienced teachers*	*Student teachers*
A1 Pupil(s) silent	80	90
A2 Pupil(s) accept (s) teacher's action	16	6
A3 Pupil(s) altercate (s) or protest(s)	4	4
B1 Misbehaviour ends	76	71
B2 Misbehaviour lessens	15	24
B3 Misbehaviour is sustained	9	5
B4 Misbehaviour increases	0	0
C1 Teacher calm	92	90
C2 Teacher agitated	5	9
C3 Teacher angry	3	1

Two measures of on-task behaviour and deviance were computed, as described in chapter 4, by studying each pupil in the class separately, producing scores ranging from 0 to 100. In the case of the on-task index, a score of 0 would indicate that no one was on task at any time and a score of 100 would mean all pupils were on task all of the time. A deviance index score of 0 would mean no child ever misbehaved, whilst a score of 100 would indicate that every child misbehaved badly on every occasion. Table 11.6 shows for each class the comparable on-task and deviance scores for both students and teachers. All the comparisons are based on the full four sessions, except for class I, where the normal class teacher was seen teaching a different class for two of the visits. Class I figures are based on two lessons only, therefore.

In general experienced teachers showed higher on-task and lower misbehaviour scores in this individual pupil survey, but in class E the student experienced less misbehaviour and achieved more on-task pupil behaviour.

TABLE 11.6

Average on-task and deviance index scores for experienced and student teachers

	On-task scores					
Class	*Experie- nced*	*Student*	*difference*	*Student Experienced*	*Deviance Student*	*Student difference*
A	71	71	none	3	7	higher
B	91	65	lower	0	7	higher
C	87	76	lower	0	5	higher
D	81	75	lower	2	1	lower
E	64	76	higher	3	1	lower
F	75	72	lower	1	6	higher
G	57	63	higher	6	10	higher
H	77	69	lower	4	9	higher
I	72	60	lower	3	13	higher
J	53	62	higher	10	12	higher

Observers' field notes and analysis of initial events collected in both student and experienced teachers' lessons helped explain and illuminate some of the data collected using quantitative methods. Observers' notes, for example, showed that noise levels tended to. rise in students' lessons whenever the class teacher left the vicinity, and not all students reasserted the level they wished to have when on their own. Often it was a single group of children round one table who began to make more noise, hence the greater frequency of misbehaviour involving two to four or more than five pupils and the students' more frequent use of group reprimand or order to cease misbehaviour. Some students used the class teacher, who had often told pupils to behave in her absence, as an invisible surrogate authority. The following were all noted in various lessons given by one student:

> Richard, stop talking and get on with your work ... Richard, remember what Mrs Jenkins [class teacher] said.
>
> [Looking up suddenly at noise.] Er, remember what Mrs Jenkins said. [Pupils fall silent.]

This class is being so silly. Mrs Jenkins will not be pleased when I tell her.

Students were very conscious they were on another's territory. One student, when asked about an event involving two children who regularly misbehaved, said in interview after the lesson:

> They [the two children] are a constant problem. It's hard, because I don't want to split them up. Well, personally I'd probably split them up, but because it's Sally's classroom, she doesn't split them up very often.

Whereas in secondary schools students are frequently left to teach alone, in primary schools the class teacher is often near by, or even in the room. This awareness of the likely proximity of the class's normal teacher was thought to be inhibiting by some students, underlining in their own eyes and those of the pupils their novitiate status. Towards the end of one lesson the student told the class to put their work away. As she did so two pupils left the classroom. The class teacher had entered the room and another pupil told her about the two early leavers, whereupon the class teacher instructed her to go and recall them, asking them publicly, on their return, where they had been. The student explained she had told pupils they could leave when they had finished. The class teacher apologised. Afterwards in interview the student said:

> Well, I'd said they could go, but ... it's really hard, because Janet [the class teacher] is such a forceful person and when she says (something), it's hard for me to do anything.

Students were not always overawed by the class teacher's style and way of doing things. Some could act quite independently. There were occasions when we saw both student and teacher, in different contexts, dealing with children who had become 'target' pupils, that is, those in receipt of more reprimands, either because they appeared to misbehave more frequently, or because they had become typified by the teacher as illustrative of a whole genus of misbehaving pupils. One such pupil was Roger, who attracted the frequent attention of both student and class teacher. Two events illustrate this. In the first Roger asked if he could go to the toilet just after playtime, and the class teacher said, 'You seem to think break time's for you to play and class time's for you to go to the toilet.' In the second event she suddenly looked up from the group she was with and called across the class, 'Roger, you shouldn't have pens in your hand, you should have a book in your hand ... Put the pens down!' Roger complied. In interview the class teacher said about the first event:

> His mother's a bit odd. She came to see me and said, 'He gets embarrassed about going to the toilet during a break time,' and could I let him go when ever he wants to. But you just wonder how often he's just swinging the lead.

On the pens incident, she said:

> He was just messing around, basically, trying to avoid getting down to his work - you get to know which children to double-check - and he was busy just having a chat and just fiddling with his pens ... so it's just a point of letting him know you've noticed and remind him to get down to it.

The student teacher also had difficulties with Roger but actually achieved a higher on-task level in the lessons observed than the class teacher. On one occasion she reprimanded him for doing too many lines of writing when she had just congratulated another child for writing four extra lines. However, she often adopted a more positive strategy with him, reinforcing good behaviour when it occurred. On one occasion she said to the class:

> Everybody should be handling their work in to me, and then sitting down at a nice tidy table with their reading books out... (A minute later)... I can only see two children sitting down and reading, and that's Alan and Roger.

Soon afterwards she needed two children to fetch a piece of equipment, which was regarded as a privilege, and nominated Roger because he had been a good boy for reading his book as he had been asked. In interview she said:

> He [Roger] likes to be noticed. I think he likes playing around ... All of them love going off to get things . . . they all like helping and because they [Roger and Alan] had been sitting reading I chose them to go and get it.

Misbehaving children were often seen by the class teacher as the joint responsibility of herself and the student. Amanda was a girl who was often reprimanded by the class teacher. Once she became so exasperated she shouted:

> Amanda, where is your maths book? Don't you dare tell me you can't find it. . . I gave you your maths book.. .you go and find it quickly, young lady ... (prodding her) ... You've lost your playtime and your dinner time. You've just been idle, Amanda.

When the student teacher came she had similar problems to the class teacher:

Student What did you think of the cavemen?

Amanda It was boring. (Slight laughter from class.)

(later in lesson)

Student Amanda, go and sit over there by the door!

Pupil She's being stupid.

Amanda I promise I won't be.

Student I'll send you out if you're stupid, like I did yesterday.

Amanda I don't care.

Pupil (to student) You should split them up they're being stupid.

Student Amanda!

Pupil They keep on being stupid.

Student Amanda, if I tell you again you're going out.

The class teacher came in and later told the student to make sure Amanda was always seated next to her desk so she could keep an eye on her. In this instance, however, it was the pupils' running commentary on the student's lame attempts to control a disruptive child which reinforced the novitiate label. The class teacher took the line of offering to share responsibility away from the hearing of the class, but some primary age children are not so well socialised and offer their advice publicly.

Inevitably student teachers felt themselves under the tutelage of their class teacher supervisors, especially as these were second-year students on their first full teaching practice. Though many took on the procedures and ways of working of their mentors, the more independent-minded were not afraid of fashioning their own methods, even if these were different from usual practice, and in some cases what the students did seemed to be accompanied by lower deviance or higher involvement in the task, though in most instances the reverse was the case.

Study 3: Attitude change during teaching practice

Some of the research into student teachers' attitudes has suggested that their attitudes change and become less 'liberal' or 'child-centred' during teaching practice or in the early years of teaching (Wragg 1982), as if the realities of classroom life somehow hone down the novice's idealism. The close identification of students, usually nearer in age to the pupils they teach than the class's regular teacher, was pointed out in the 'first encounters' study earlier in this chapter. In order to see whether some of the students studied in the present research underwent such changes we took a sample of eighty-two trainees and showed them immediately before and immediately after teaching practice three of the photographs used in the research with children and experienced teachers in other studies during the

Leverhulme Primary Project. In each case they were asked to complete two response schedules, firstly a freehand response to the pictures, asking what they would do in the same circumstances, and secondly responses to eighteen strategy statements, six for each picture, on a five-point Likert scale, ranging from 'strongly agree' to 'strongly disagree' with the mid-point, 3, labelled 'neither agree nor disagree'.

In the freehand accounts the students were asked, 'What, if anything, would you do?' and 'Why would you do it?' It was explained that, if the student chose to take no action, the 'Why? question response should be used to explain why no action was taken. The freehand accounts were completed first so that the attitude statements in the second schedule would not affect the replies. In the second schedule six statements of attitude were given, all direct quotations from our interviews with experienced teachers, representing different strategies, namely delay, ignore, manipulate and engage in low, moderate or severe confrontation.

A total of sixty-four students completed both pre- and post-tests, and tables 11.7. 11.8 and 11.9 show the correlated t tests and degree of significance for each set of six statements. Students who did not complete both sets were dropped from the sample. In each case, since 'strongly agree' was coded 1 and 'strongly disagree' was coded 5, the higher the mean the higher the *disagreement* with the statement. A negative t value shows higher *disagreement* after teaching practice, and a positive t value higher *agreement* with the statement after teaching practice. Since no direction of difference was hypothesised, a two-tailed t test was used to test the null hypothesis, that is the assumption that there would be no change in attitude after practice. In each of the tables the asterisk system is used to indicate the0.05,

0.01 and 0.001 level of significance and n.s. means not significant.

TABLE 11.7

Means and correlated t tests of sixty-four students' attitude scores before and after teaching practice for photograph 1 (two children seen pushing each other)

		Mean score		
Statement	*Category*	*before*	*after*	*t value*
A I would simply move one of the children to another table	Confront (moderate)	2.28	2.36	-0.46 n.s.
B I would leave it until the end of the lesson then ask them to stay behind and talk to them about their behaviour	Delay	3.13	3.00	+0.88 n.s.
C I would pretend that I had not seen what was happening and hope they would eventually settle down to their work	Ignore	4.61	4.67	-0.73 n.s.
D I would go over to their table, look at their work and talk about how they could extend what they had already done	Manipulate	2.45	2.56	-0.87 n.s.
E I would punish them by making them stay behind when the bell went to finish the work they should have done during the lesson	Confront (severe)	3.09	2.88	1.44 n.s.
F I would sit down at the table with them and talk to them quietly about their behaviour	Confront (low)	1.84	2.22	-3.72***

What is interesting here is the direction of movement The most consistent categories of strategy are 'ignore', where in each picture the scores show greater *disagreement* after teaching practice, and 'severe confrontation', where the scores show greater *agreement* in each case after teaching practice. The greatest significant changes occur in the category 'low confrontation', where students reveal they would be less inclined at the end of teaching practice to give a child a talking to. The rank order shows that a low

TABLE 11.8

Means and correlated t tests of sixty-four students' attitude scores before and after teaching practice for photograph 2 (children rushing into classroom after playtime)

Statement		*Category*	*Mean score* before	*Mean score* after	*t value*
A	I would not say anything about it at the time, but just before lunchtime I would mention that I did not like the way they had entered after break and that I would expect them to enter in an orderly manner after lunch	Delay	3.30	3.64	-2.14*
B	I would get the children together and talk to them quietly about the way they had entered the room. I would point out the reasons why they should not enter classrooms in that way, stressing the danger of someone getting hurt	Confront (low)	1.81	2.13	-2.87**
C	I would not say anything about the way they had entered the room but I would immediately change the start of my lesson plan. I would get all the children together, around me, and do a 'quietening down' activity in which everyone would participate.	Manipulate	3.34	3.52	-1.37n.s.
D	I would raise my voice and tell them to stop and stand absolutely still. I would then tell them that such behaviour was disgraceful, that they should not enter my classroom in that manner, that they should sit down and get on with their work in silence and that I did not expect to see them ever entering the classroom in that way again	Confront (severe)	3.63	3.31	2.17*
E	I would not make a fuss about this incident. I would simply tell the children to sit down and get on with their work	Ignore	4.11	4.36	-2.65**
F	I would send the children outside, make them line up, wait until they were silent and then tell them to enter the classroom again in an orderly manner	Confront (moderate)	2.16	1.91	1.95n.s.

to moderate degree of confrontation is the most preferred approach, and ignoring the behaviour the least favoured. Such movement as there is over the teaching practice *it* largely in the direction of students supporting more severe degrees of confrontation than was thought likely before the practice.

TABLE 11.9

Means and correlated t tests of sixty-four students' attitude scores before and after teaching practice for photograph 3 (girl calls teacher 'old cow')

Statement	*Category*	*Mean score* before	after	*t value*
A I would deal with the situation then and there. I would raise my voice and reprimand her for being so rude. I would then give her a punishment - something she did not like doing which would put her in her place	Confront (severe)	3.78	3.62	0.94 n.s.
B I would pretend that I had not heard what she had said. I would avoid a confrontation by simply telling her to sit down and get on with her work	Ignore	4.03	4.17	-1.08n.s.
C I would immediately tell the others to on with their work, and take her to one side. I would talk to her about scribbling on other people's books and about the language she had used. I would tell her that I did not want to hear her using such language again	Confront (moderate)	1.98	2.03	-0.40n.s.
D I would see her later, at playtime, and talk to her about the comment she	Delay	2.37	2.35	0.11 n.s.

cont...

	had made and why she had made it				
E	I would tell the girl to sit down with the group at the table she was standing next to. I would talk to her calmly and quietly about why she had used such language and what she meant by it. I would hope to deflate her aggression and neutralise the abuse by asking such questions	Confront (low)	2.73	2.62	0.87 n.s.
F	I would tell her to bring her work to my desk and then look through it for something I could comment positively on	Manipulate	3.32	3.22	0.74 n.s.

Freehand comments written before responses to the structured attitude statements further illuminate these shifts. All written responses were read independently by two members of the research team who then merged their analyses by agreement and selected illustrative quotations. One very striking change was that there were more strategies after teaching practice than before. The second photograph, showing children bursting into the classroom, elicited most responses, followed by the third photograph, where the girl calls the teacher 'old cow'. Table 11.10 show this increase clearly.

TABLE 11.10

Mean number of strategies for each situation given before and after teaching practice

		Mean number of strategies	
	Photograph	*before*	*after*
1	Two pupils pushing each other	3.0	3.5
2	Children rushing into room	5.2	5.8
3	Girl calls teacher 'old cow'	4.3	4.8

The medium confrontation strategy involving warning or threat doubled from 16 per cent of responses before teaching practice to 32 per cent afterwards. The post-teaching practice replies were usually more specific and detailed, both in strategies and in reasons, as these extracts from one student's response to the two children misbehaving in photograph 1 reveal:

Strategy before teaching practice I would go across to the two children and remind them that I had already asked them to settle down. I would quietly point out that they were wasting my time and that I would waste theirs if they caused me to speak to them again.

Reason I would approach them rather than shout, because I would not wish to draw attention to them. I feel that, without an audience, they would feel defeated. I would give them a final chance with a threat because I wouldn't want to deal out a punishment unless I was pushed to it.

Strategy after teaching practice I would get up and go over to the two children, bend down so that I would be at their height level and very quietly remind them that this was the second time I had asked them to behave. I would say that if I needed to speak to them again they would be separated and stay behind at playtime to work.

Reason I would do this to (1) not draw vast attention to them by shouting in front of the whole class. (2) let them know that I did not intend to stop the other children from working whilst I saw to them. (3) warn them of the consequences of continued disruptive behaviour and carry out my intended threats if necessary.

The use of body language (stooping to child height), the threat to separate, rather than 'waste their time', and awareness of the impact of a disciplinary act by the teacher on other pupils; are amongst several additional dimensions to this student's and others' responses after teaching practice. With photograph 1 there was little change in other categories Of response like 'explain/ discuss behaviour with pupils' (57 per cent mentioned it before, 59 per cent after) and 'separate pupils' (59 per cent before, 57 per cent after).

In the case of the second photograph students had, in almost every case, encountered the incidence of children rushing into a room after break. Requiring children to repeat their entry in a more orderly manner went up from 58 per cent of respondents before teaching practice to 71 per cent afterwards, though 'explaining/discussing' was even more frequently cited (66 per cent before, 76 per cent after). After bruising first encounters early in the term students had often needed to become firmer at the very beginning of lessons, an awareness this post-practice response reveals:

> (I would) take the class back outside the classroom, tell them how I expect children to behave on entering a classroom, before making the class re-enter the classroom according to the code of conduct just established ... I would do this in order to make the class realise that I am not prepared to accept a poor standard of behaviour in the classroom. This allows myself as a new teacher to establish my own set of rules, possibly with the aid of the pupils themselves.

Three categories of response showed notable increases after teaching practice. The first was to stop the children before they were all in, the second to state that the behaviour was unacceptable, the third was to shout or raise the voice. Comments like these were much more frequent after teaching practice than before:

(I'd) say, 'Stop where you are!' wait for silence, tell them that their behaviour was unacceptable and point out the dangers of it... because of the danger hazard they were causing by pushing and shoving. I would have to stop them before they came into the classroom.

(I'd) ask them what they thought of the way they'd entered the classroom (if necessary ask the more boisterous individuals), stress points of safety (tripping up, etc.) . . . ask them how they *should* come into classrooms.

The personal threat to the teacher's authority of the girl in photograph 3 calling the teacher 'old cow' evoked a range of responses, but 65 per cent of teachers before and 74 per cent after teaching practice mentioned the need to discuss, or ask the girl to explain, her behaviour, some addressing the insulting language, others the scribbling on books, often both, but sometimes it was not clear which misbehaviour would be discussed. Before teaching, practice 48 per cent said they would want to see her alone, but this rose to 63 per cent afterwards. More students wanted an apology, either to the teacher or to fellow pupils, after teaching practice than before, though only ten students mentioned it at all. Reference to higher authority was one of the four categories to decline as 17 per cent mentioned bringing in another teacher, the head or the child's parents before teaching practice, but only 11 per cent afterwards. Giving extra work, asking the girl to reflect on what she had done, waiting for her to behave well so that praise could be administered, and trying to discount her motives, all increased in frequency after teaching practice. About ten per cent of students suggested some kind of humiliation, and this number did not change over the period of teaching practice.

These three studies of student teachers give fascinating insights into the professional socialisation of teachers as well as the development of their views and practices in class management. The 'first encounters' study showed how good intentions could evaporate under the pressure of actual teaching; how students did not have in support those collective moral exhortations that characterised the beginning of the school year for experienced teachers; how content, rather than negotiating rules and relationships, would dominate early lessons; and how early in the teaching practice classes and individuals might test the limits when rules were not clear. The second study, of students on teaching practice, revealed how most pupil misbehaviour consisted of excessive noise rather than severe deviance, and the third study of the responses to photographs showed how students after teaching practice became more detailed in their responses to misbehaviour, but also tougher, less likely to ignore inappropriate behaviour, more likely to take on and confront those who misbehaved.

Their final position was not unlike the responses of experienced teachers, but the apparent increased toughness was still overlaid with elements of concern for the individual, a desire to empathise, to reason rather than dictate and discuss instead of always command. It was not the vague, sometimes ill-focused good intentions of the period of liberality that precedes teaching practice, but it had certainly not become hard, cynical or indifferent, simply more specific, pragmatic and a little closer to the practice of experienced teachers.

12

Educational Problems

Situations such as these illustrate the problems faced by teachers in present-day schools. It is easy to express an opinion about them, but it is not nearly so easy to arrive at a sound professional solution. Every profession requires its membership to be equipped with techniques for solving new and complicated problems. The profession of education is no exception. From your first day in the classroom you will meet situation after situation for which there is no ready-made answer. Even if you are working in a school system where there is a detailed course of study, there will be countless day-by-day decisions in which only your professional judgment can determine what is best for your pupils. You have chosen a profession which demands persons who can think clearly and independently about professional problems—who know the reason for their procedures and can explain these reasons to others.

Through your years of college you have been exploring the foundation areas upon which teachers draw in making professional decisions. You know something of the traditional role of the school in the United States democracy. You have studied the changes taking place in our modern industrialised society and the implications of these changes. Your courses in educational psychology and human development have deepened your understanding of the boys and girls with whom you will be working—their needs, the way they grow, and the way they learn. Your first full-time classroom experience will provide a major opportunity to think through in detail how the large issues and general principles derived from such background studies actually affected day-by-day decisions. You will discover that learning to teach is more than acquiring a "bag of tricks" useful in keeping a class interested, busy, and cooperative. Unless you learn to think as a professional person, such a "bag of tricks," no matter how amply stocked, is not likely to give you the help you will need as you face one new problem after another, day after day on the job.

This chapter examines briefly what is involved in decision-making in education. It is intended to help you to identify some of the fundamental issues with which teachers are dealing today and to become aware of the direction of their proposed solutions. It aims to assist you in thinking about the skills that *you* must develop if your are to become a professional person—a person able to make competent decisions regarding professional problems.

What is Expected of Schools in the United States Democracy?

The United States has a long and proud tradition of faith in education. Early in our national history the principle was established that elementary schooling should be free for the children of all of the people. The public schools in this country, therefore, have been delegated a major responsibility for producing citizens who are competent and willing to make their contribution so that our democratic way of life may flourish. The public schools have also been delegated a major responsibility for equipping future citizens to live in our modern. Industrialised society. How the schools can best discharge these obligations poses many problems. What your believe about the meaning of democracy; about the attitudes, skills, and knowledge which individuals must have to lead effective an satisfying lives, and about the place the school should occupy in our national life will influence your professional decisions. These decisions you cannot avoid if you are to be an effective teacher.

Schools in the United States have an obligation to help young people grow in the ways of democracy. Democracy in a term that means different things to different people. For some, it refers rather strictly to the processes through which those nations classified as democracies are governed and to the rights and responsibilities of their citizens. For many, democracy is more than a form of government; it is a way of life. Those who accept the latter definition believe that the most effective an satisfying personal values can be achieved only when we extend democratic concepts and ways of working to every aspect of living—to family life, to classrooms, to church and club groups, to professional organisations, to our relationships with friends and neighbours and to fellow citizens whom we have never met.

Certainly, the schools in a democracy are responsible for acquainting youth with the processes of their government and with their rights and responsibilities as citizens. Our democratic tradition has established a legal pattern which respects the rights of the individual but which also protects the welfare of the group. We have a from of government under which we relinquish some of our personal freedoms for the sake of orderly ways of living together. It is a form of government which allows us to establish for ourselves the rules under which we live and provides ways of changing these rules when they no longer prove satisfactory. Under our Constitution we are guaranteed the right to vote; equality under the law regardless of political affiliation, race, social or economic status; freedom to participate in the religion of our choice; freedom of speech and the right to be heard whether we belong to the majority or to the minority.

Helping prospective citizens to understand the basic forms of their government is a far bigger job than merely teaching courses in civics or the United States' history. It will be your responsibility to identify the ways in which boys and girls can become familiar with democratic government in action. What lessons in democracy are there when six-year-olds learn to abide by school policies? What understandings might be developed when fifth-graders rebel against a school regulation that keeps them from crossing a busy street to the candy store at recess? What learnings should come to the safety guards who act as an arm of a law, enforcing body? What may we hope to teach through student council activities? These are only a fraction of the experiences through which youngsters meet democratic government in action. A well-informed, sensitive teacher makes the most of them.

Teachers who believe that democracy is more than a from of government—that it is a way of life—need to analyse carefully what this means in practice. Sometimes discussions in social groups indicate that the definitions on which we are operating are somewhat limited. Occasionally there is a hint that the speaker is thinking only about a majority vote. ("If we were to try to be democratic about it, the children would vote to take a holiday, and then where would we be?") Sometimes the speaker seems to be thinking of equality in the sense of making sure everyone is treated exactly alike. ("The talents of our children are being wasted if we try to be democratic and teach everyone exactly the same thing." "Colleges should be more democratic about parking privileges. Why should the faculty have reserved parking? Make it first come, first served.") Sometimes it sounds as though the speaker thinks it is undemocratic to take any leadership responsibility whatsoever. ("I know it's not democratic, but how else could you get an orchestra playing together?") Or that democracy means the right of the individual to do exactly what he chooses, regardless of the group ("You can't be too democratic with children, you know, or you'll have some of hem climbing out of the windows.") Or that it is a matter of letting pupils think they have made decisions, even when this is not actually the case. (We work it out democratically in my room, but, of course, I always know where they're going to come out.")

Obviously, what we mean when we talk of democracy as a way of life is more significant than the quotations in the preceding paragraph imply. Analysing what democratic ways of working actually do mean for daily living is one of the most challenging and significant tasks that you as a teacher will face. It is a lifetime job. In your classroom, situation after situation will arise where you will stop to wounder what is the democratic thing to do.

What are some of the values held by those who think of democracy as a way of life? For one thing, we have in our democratic tradition a belief in the unique worth of the individual. We hold that we should be able to establish ways of living and working together that will allow each person to develop to his own maximum potentiality while he makes it possible for others to do the same. What it means to recognise the unique worth of each individual poses a number of challenging problems. For example, what type of school curriculum will actually make it possible for each boy or girls to develop to his own maximum potentiality? What system of grouping and promotion will be most satisfactory?—should we segregate the very able or the very slow? retard youngsters not up to grade level? promote those who are advanced? How do we go about helping an individual to reach his own goals and still teach him that he has an obligation to assure the same opportunity to others? How do we help children and youth to develop respect for those who differ—in race, religion, economic status, talents, interests?

If such problems sound complicated when stated in theoretical terms, they become even more so when they arise in the classroom setting. Sixth-grade John refuses to work with the subcommittee which is to locate information about industries in modern England, but he volunteers to do an independent report on the effects of the Industrial Revolution. What democratic values should be taken into account in appraising his proposal? Fourth-grade Jeanne is a talented musician. Is it undemocratic to release her from her arithmetic lesson to take private music lessons? First-grade Belinda loves to paint and makes a dash for the only easel every free-choice period. What should she be helped to learn about the ways of democracy? In choosing characters for a play, fourth-graders ignore Andy, who lisps. Should this be talked through, and if so what issues should be raised? In planning to exchange Christmas gifts, several youngsters argue that everyone should be allowed to spend just as much money for a gift as he wishes. Is it undemocratic to veto this proposal? These problems all have at their base the fundamental issue of what it really means to respect the unique worth of each individual. They are typical of the practical situations you will face as you try to determine your own attitudes and decide what attitudes your pupils should develop.

In our democratic tradition, too, is the belief that each individual has both a right and an obligation to contribute to the solution of problems in which his well-being and that of his group are involved. In our government, we do this through universal franchise. Those who see democracy as a way of life extend their faith in the cooperative solution of problems to clubs, to committees, to classrooms, to family groups. What it means to involve those concerned in the solution of a problem is, in itself, a difficult question. Certainly the effective solution of many of the problems we face in today's complex world calls for more than a majority vote. There are many times when we must rely upon the advice of an expert. We must help young people to develop bases for deciding when to look to an authority for help and how to appraise the competence of the persons to whom they turn, Furthermore, there are often varying degrees of maturity and insight among the persons concerned with a common problem. We must develop techniques of cooperative problem-solving that will enable each individual expert or uninformed, mature or immature, to make his appropriate contribution. We must also perfect the skill needed if the members of a group are to work effectively together—leadership skills; techniques for communicating with others, for identifying issues and resolving conflicts, for arriving at consensus. In addition, there are problems of how to safeguard the rights of the minority—of deciding when the will of the majority should be accepted and when a minority has a right to dissent, of using minority voices to best advantage in working toward more effective solutions of common problems.

As you begin to think about helping boys and girls to operate as effective group members you will uncover a number of challenging points to ponder. What does this mean for pupil-teacher planning? Should the pupils (who certainly are vitally concerned) have a share in deciding classroom procedures? To what extent? What happens if the pupils proposal runs counter to your well-laid plans? Suppose it runs counter to a board of education rule?

What leadership role should you play? Mr. Smith is helping his class perfect a song for the school assembly. Miss Adamson is working to develop more proficiency in basic arithmetic processes. Miss McCabe's pupils are crying to decide how to decorate their classroom for Halloween. If each teacher is to be democratic, will his procedures be exactly like those of his colleagues? Miss Simonds' sixth-graders come bursting in with a proposal that they build and launch a rocket. It is undemocratic for her to ask them to stop to examine the difficulties involved? Mr. Sampson sets up an exhibit of all his Mexican souvenirs and then asks his pupils to think about the social studies unit they should start with first. After a brief discussion (in which he points out how much more interesting it will be to study Switzerland later in the winter), they vote to study Mexico. Has he been democratic?

In our democratic society we also believe in freedom of inquiry and a research approach to the solution of problems. We do not accept with out proof the pronouncements of the so-called "expert." Our books do not distort the evidence in order to support a political faith. We value our laboratories and our research workers, and we expect them to be able to pursue their investigations without coercion or fear of reprisal. We face a very important task in helping boys and girls to develop a healthy respect for methods of scientific investigation and of rational thinking. Still more crucial, we must teach them how to use these methods in the solution of new problems.

Teachers who wish to develop in their pupils respect for a scientific approach to the solution of problems face some challenging questions in deciding how to teach. When should classroom time be devoted to activities in which pupils use an experimental approach to solve a problem, when to reading for answers in a textbook? What authority role should the teacher play? What teaching techniques seem most likely to help pupils develop the problem-solving approaches of the various subject disciplines?—to acquaint a pupil with the research techniques of the scientist? the economist?

Pupils learn what they experience. This is an obvious but often forgotten principle of education. It means that we must *teach* what we want pupils to learn—that we must provide experiences so that they will learn. If we want to insure that boys and girls will grow in their understanding of democracy, we must make certain that they experience democracy in action. One of your most important professional decisions will be to determine for yourself what it means to practice democracy in your own classroom.

Schools in the United States must equip young people to live in this modern world. The pupils in the classrooms of 1960 will be in leadership positions in the year 2000. Deciding what attitudes, information, and skills will prepare them to cope successfully with their world would be relatively easy in a simple and static culture. However, we are living in an extremely complex society and in a world that is changing rapidly. How to equip the young people of today to live intelligently in the world of tomorrow is a matter of grave concern to those who teach in the United State's schools.

You do not need an extended analysis to remind you of some of the problems which the pupils whom you are now teaching will have to face. Radio, television, and jet propulsion have made us next-door neighbours to the entire world. Whether our democracy as we know it will exist when the youngsters we teach have grown up may depend on how successful we are in building international understanding, in learning to communicate with other nations, in developing techniques for the cooperative solution of international problems. How best to equip children and youth to make their contribution to international understanding poses some major problems for educators. What should we emphasise in studying other cultures? Should political ideologies other than our own be examined in our schools? What should be our attitude regarding the teaching of foreign languages? These are only a few of the questions which require professional decisions. How we, as teachers, answer them will help to determine the course of our national life in the years ahead.

Through the agencies of radio, television, and the press, children and youth today are exposed to widely divergent and conflicting value systems. They see a western marshal use his gun to stop a criminal. They hear newscasts reporting the number of cars owned by the current singing star and the failure of the local bound issue for new school buildings. They read of the fourth marriage of the actress who is their current heroine. In this complex and contradictory milieu families do not exert the same kind of stabilising influence they once did. You may be astounded to discover how many of your pupils come from broken homes, how many mothers are working, how many youngster have no regular church affiliation. Teachers belong to the one agency that touches the lives of all children. Is the teaching of values a task we must assume? Perhaps it would be more accurate to ask whether we can escape it even if we wish to do so. How is it best accomplished-by teaching religion in the public schools? by developing reading skills through stories with morals? is it an emphasis that should permeate all our teaching? How? Whether you are conscious of it or not these are professional questions that you answer time after time by the way in which you deal with day-by-day problems in your classroom.

The vast communication network that links farm to city and east cost to west poses another type of problem for our schools. Never be force has it been possible for a single television personality to touch the lives of so many, for advertisers to come into such a large number of homes, for news analysts to make their opinions so widely felt. Here are we going to equip young people to cope with the bids being made for their attention, their time, and their money? Should we teach observation and listening skills as well as reading skills? Should we be concerned about developing skills of critical evaluation in reading. Should there be training in propaganda analysis? consumer education projects to help in the interpretation of advertisements?

If present predictions are borne out, the pupils you teach will face job opportunities and working conditions very different from those of today. We read much about the need for top-flight scientists, but our society will also require many persons in professions calling for expertness in human relationships—teachers, physicians, nurses, psychologists, social workers, personnel executives. On the other hand, with increased automation it seems likely that machines will take over many of the routine tasks once assumed by the less well-educated. In all probability most people will have more leisure time than ever before. Does this mean that we should be paying increased attention to the creative arts? to the development of personal interests and hobbies? Questions such as these may seem to require the use of a crystal ball, but they must be answered. You will be associated with colleagues who face seriously their professional responsibility to find the answers.

Perhaps the most challenging phenomenon of all is that our pupils will live in a world of rapid change. Certainly, we want to equip them with the knowledge that will render them effective in their chosen professions and in their daily living, but what we teach as fact today may have to be reinterpreted tomorrow. Even basic physical and chemical principles may be rewritten as new discoveries are made in the physical sciences. In the biological and social sciences there are many problems still unsolved. If the speed of our transition from telegraph to radio to television, or from the model-T to the jet plane, is any indication of the changes to come, our pupils will be called on to weigh new evidence, appraise new principles, and solve new problems beyond our boldest predictions. What kind of classroom situation will provide a learner with existing knowledge and still prepare him to meet new challenges? How can we teach so that our pupils leave us equipped to locate new information and arrive at new generalisations for themselves. How can we teach so that our pupils leave us equipped to locate new information and arrive at new generalisations for themselves? How do we prepare our slower learners to secure competent advice when they face situations with which their training in school has not equipped them to deal?

As you listen to discussions of educational problems and read professional literature, you will discover that serious attention is being given to the question of what role the school should play in preparing boys and girls to live effectively in tomorrow's world. Some teachers argue that the schools have all they can do to equip children and youth with the traditional and established elements of our cultural heritage — reading; spelling; writing; calculating; and basic scientific, historical, political, economic, and social facts and principles. Others hold that this is not sufficient, that too many important applications of basic principles to present day problems will be left to chance. They maintain that it should be possible to focus more directly on the pupil's present world without sacrificing essential elements of the cultural heritage. Again, you will find teachers who believe that the major responsibility of the schools should be to develop the problem-solving skills and techniques for acquiring new information essential in a world of rapid change. Occasionally, you will read a plea that teachers make a blueprint of the future world they desire. These are not points of view to accept or reject on the grounds of prejudice or bias. They should be the basis for thoughtful reading and study as you meet the day-by-day situations that reflect these larger issues.

Schools in the United States are expected to meet the needs of all children and youth. In the United States it is taken for granted that the schools shall serve all children. It is our tradition that all boys and girls be given an opportunity to climb the same educational ladder. We do not sort out, at an early age, the college-bound student from the one destined for industrial and service occupations. We have extended compulsory attendance age limits to sixteen years of age—to eighteen years in some states. All this presents many problems in actual practice. How do you provide a worth-while education for all boys and girls—the bright and the slow, the well-adjusted and the emotionally disturbed the privileged and the underprivileged, the healthy and the physically handicapped?

Teachers in the elementary school are deeply concerned about the ways in which they can meet this challenge. You will find them experimenting with schemes for grouping learners in classes and in sub-groups within a class in an effort to provide the best possible educational environment for every boy and girl. This is not nearly as simple in practice as it sounds in theory. How many years can a child be retarded before he is such a social and physical misnt that both he and his classmates suffer? How much should we accelerate those youngsters whose skills and reasoning ability are ahead of their age group? Inasmuch as not all the capacities and potentialities of a given individual develop evenly, would it be better to group by ages and then to vary the educational offering for individuals? These are problems for which there are no categorical answers. There are democratic values to consider as well as psychological implications. Can it be argued that the unique worth of each individual is being honoured when all children in the same class read the same texts when lessons are geared to the understanding of the pupil of average ability? On the other hand, should able pupils not have the opportunity to learn to work with those who think more slowly? And does the less talented child not need to be in some situations where he learns to acknowledge the contribution of his more able colleagues? Whatever the basis for setting up class groups in your school, you will still find yourself working with a range of abilities in your room and trying to decide how to meet your obligation to help each pupil grow. Your psychology courses have taught you to expect this, but the first class you actually work with closely will show you how complicated the task really is. As one beginning teacher phrased it, "I'd heard about individual differences all the way through college, but I didn't realise what it would mean to meet forty sets of individual differences until I began to teach."

What is the Direction of Our Efforts to Solve Educational Problems?

Many important educational problems are solved on a day-by-day basis in the classroom, but back of these decisions are major theoretical considerations. Some relate to the curriculum design—the pattern that indicates the scope of the experiences to be provided for boys and girls, the areas of study under which these experiences are to be grouped, and the sequence in which they are to be studied from grade to grade. Others refer to methodology—to the ways in which teachers guide the learning experiences of boys and girls. Thoughtful teachers have always worked toward improved curriculum designs and methodology. Problems related to these two major areas of concern are under serious consideration in many school systems today.

What kinds of educational programmes are resulting from our efforts to define the functions of schools in the United States's society, to translate these general objectives into specific goals, and to decide what teaching procedures will best achieve these goals? Although there are many areas of agreement, there are no absolute answers. This will not surprise you if you stop to think of the major problems about which value judgments have to be made—what is means to teach the ways of democracy, how best to equip young people to live in tomorrow's world, what it means to meet the needs of all the pupils in our schools. Serious educators may, with good reason, disagree on issues such as these.

Many types of curriculum designs exist today. Class discussions and school visits prior to student teaching will have taught you that schools are operating today under a variety of curriculum designs. You may be placed as a student teacher or first-year teacher in a school system using a curriculum design very similar to that under which you, yourself, went to school. On the other hand, the pattern may be very different. Whatever the design, it represents a thoughtful decision regarding how best to meet the educational needs of boys and girls. It is important for you to become thoroughly familiar with the values held by the persons with whom you are teaching and with the decisions thy have made regarding the curriculum design they feel to be most effective for their situation. It is important, also, if you are to grow into a teacher with a broad professional outlooks, that you be able in identify the values that lie back of other proposals for curriculum designs—proposals that your colleagues have not accepted. It is all too easy to classify a position you do not understand as "traditional," "progressive," "subject-centered," thereby brushing aside a thoughtful educational proposal with an emotionally laden label.

The curriculum design with which the majority of beginning teachers will be most familiar from high school and college days and perhaps from elementary school also, is the one in which *separate subjects*—history, geography, composition, literature, physics, chemistry—are the centres about which classroom work is organised. When the separate subject design is used, aspects of the subject are usually assigned to grades. Problems near at hand and present-day are dealt with in the primary grades—community helpers, family life. Older pupils go farther back in time and farther afield. Typically, a topic is repeated in more complex form abut every three or four years—the United States' history, for example, in fifth, eighth, and eleventh grades. Typically too, subject lines are adhered to more firmly as pupils grow older, with separate teachers for each subject and opportunities to specialise common at the upper grades in the high school. Separate subjects are the traditional way of organising the essentials of our cultural heritage. They encompass, however, more than groupings of knowledge; they also represent ways of thinking and of solving problems. Problems of historical research demand procedures different from those of the science laboratory. A sociologist has ways of working different from those of a mathematician. Those who plan the school curriculum by designating aspects of various subjects for specific grades make this choice, in part, because they feel that the best equipment young people can take into the world is a thorough understanding of the traditional fields of knowledge that are their cultural heritage and the ability to use skillfully the ways of thinking and solving problems that are unique to these subject areas.

Persons who feel that there are more effective bases than separate subjects for organising the experiences of children and youth sometimes claim that teachers of subjects tend to follow textbooks too closely and give too little help in applying knowledge from basic subject areas to present-day problems. This could be a danger, especially if the textbook contains an extensive amount of material to be covered. However, it would not represent good teaching. If you are working under a curriculum design organised around separate subjects, you will find your colleagues particularly concerned about helping pupils to see the values the subject has for their lives today. You will find them planning with pupils and developing problem-solving activities that will encourage boys and girls to think for themselves. You will discover, also, that teachers of separate subjects are much concerned about helping pupils see interrelationships among subject fields. Good teaching has many common elements, regardless of the curriculum design.

Next most popular, country-wide, are the patterns in which related subjects are pulled together into *subject fields* or *groups of related subjects*—history, geography, and civics may be grouped as social studies; nature study, physics, and chemistry become general science; and so on. As with the sequence where subjects are taught separately, younger pupils tend to work with the near at hand. In fact, the experiences considered appropriate and worth while for primary children are so similar from one curriculum to another that it would be difficult to tell by walking into a kindergarten or a first grade just what the design for the school system is. Subject fields are more frequently the organising centres for learners' experiences at the elementary than at the secondary or college levels. However, if you have had a courses in Survey of Western Civilisation. Survey of Science, or Survey of Mathematics in college, you have had experience in working broadly within a subject field. What are seen to be the advantages, as against teaching within the boundaries of individual subjects? Persons who feel that subject fields are the most appropriate bases for organising curricular experiences value highly, among other things, the opportunities this plan provides for helping pupils to see interrelationships among separate subjects. In developing a problem related to an aspect of the United States' history, for example, a teacher can draw upon as much background as is needed from geography and political science.

Educators who object to the grouping of subjects into related fields do so on several bases. On the one hand, some fear that the thoroughness with which a separate subject would be studied may be lost. In a sense, this may be true. If you elected the Survey of Western Civilisation in college rather than European. History, you probably explored historical backgrounds more broadly but not as deeply at all points. You did not, however, necessarily learn any less thereby; you simply acquired a different set of understandings. On the other hand, some educators maintain that even the subject-field type of curriculum does not provide sufficient opportunities to explore extensively with their pupils. The courses of study in school systems where the curriculum design is built around groups of related subjects are developed so as to overcome, at least partially, this criticism. For example, helping pupils to understand newspaper articles reporting a plan to prevent the pollution of the local river may call not only for geographical and historical background, but also for concepts from such fields as bacteriology and chemistry. Actually, if you are working under such a curriculum, you will find your colleagues concerned about challenging your pupils to explore each problem they undertake as thoroughly as their maturity allows. It is not a proposal that allows for superficial learnings. You will also find your colleagues concerned about helping pupils to draw extensively upon areas of knowledge not encompassed by the subject field. Charts are often included in courses of study, for example, showing the points at which the suggested work in such fields as the natural and the social sciences can be correlated.

Very different from the curricular patterns in which subjects or subject fields are designated as centers for study are those in which an attempt has been made to study *broad areas that cut across subject fields*—areas which would allow for the organisation of knowledge from many fields around the types of problems pupils actually will face in life. In these patterns, subjects are drawn upon as extensively as needed but the problems designated or study are grouped under such areas of living as homemaking, earning a living, recreation, communication, conserving goods and resources, transportation, housing. Problems related to simpler aspects of each area are assigned to the elementary school grades, more complex problems to the upper grades. In some high schools a series of appropriate units are assigned to a "core" block of two or more periods, and subject electives are provided for the rest of the programme. If your college methods courses have been consolidated into one large time block within which you and your instructor have been free to take up topics in the order you felt most crucial, you have had some experience with such a core. It is quite possible, also, that you have had experience with a certain number of units of work that focused on problems of daily living even under a curriculum design developed around fields such as social studies and science. For example, there may have been a unit on transportation proposed for the fourth grade or a study of the national election insetted into the old-world focus of a sixth grade. Why advocate a curriculum that is so different from the pattern under which most teachers have received their training? Those who have given this type of proposal their thoughtful support see many advantages. Among the most important are the greatly increase opportunities to provide experiences through which boys and girls can learn to bring information from all needed subject areas to bear on the day-by-day problems they actually face.

If your schooling has been under a traditional curriculum pattern, you probably will be voicing many of the typical questions that are raised regarding a curriculum proposal that departs radically from this pattern. How will such a plan ever lead to a through knowledge of anything? How will the pupil who has studied conservation, communication, transportation, homemaking, ever get along in college? On the other hand, if specific topics are definitely assigned to the various grades, what have you really gained? Won't these topics be just as far removed from pupils lives as blocks of work selected from subject fields? Actually, you will need to examine courses of study carefully to realise how broad and deep the activities developed of study carefully to realise how broad and deep the activities developed under such a design, you will realise that your colleagues take great pains to explore each area under discussion in as much detail as is appropriate to their pupils maturity and to make sure that the total experiences for the year contribute to a balanced programme. You will also find that there is considerable effort expended to keep the potential contributions of subject areas in mind, to use time lines to provide historical perspective, to develop needed scientific principles. You will discover, too, that the total curriculum plan provides a number of opportunities for upper-grade pupils and for high school youth to explore specific subject areas under the guidance of specialists.

In contrast to educators who would assign specific subjects topics, or units to each grade are those who feel that the most useful understandings will be built only when a teacher is completely free to work with the *problems or concerns of a group.* Under such a curriculum design it would not be possible in advance to say for certain exactly that the year's activities of a group would be. Teachers would be responsible for studying the needs, the strengths, the weaknesses, the experience backgrounds, of their pupils and for deciding cooperatively with them the areas for study for the year. The teachers most likely to be working in situations where such freedom exists will be those in college laboratory schools or in public school systems noted for their experimental approach or curriculum design. In some schools there may be available rather elaborate studies of typical problem faced by pupils of various ages as guides in providing for a well-balanced programme. In others, teachers may be expected to draw upon their total professional background in deciding what areas for study will prove the most effective learning experiences for their classes.

Educators who want to give teachers maximum freedom of choice are deeply concerned about equipping future citizens with a broad foundation of knowledge. They feel, however, that intelligent teachers can make the most effective choice of exactly what areas of study are most likely to contribute to maximum growth. This certainly would not mean that minor and incidental problems in which pupils happen to express an interest would necessarily be developed into elaborate units regardless of their potential educational values. Teachers would evaluate carefully possible topics for study. Nor would opportunity be lacking to explore subject fields extensively. At both upper elementary and high school levels, there would be science laboratories, art studio-social science seminars, writers' clinics, to which pupils with special interests or concerns could be referred. Obviously, such a programme demands extremely competent and sensitive teachers with great depth of subject matter background and broad understanding of the present-day world.

This brief sketch will not have done much more than help you identify the curriculum design under which you are working and perhaps start you thinking about how and why it contrasts with the one under which you went to school. You will have to do much more studying before you will be able to decide where you stand, and why. Particularly, you are going to need broad reading and experience to understand the values to be achieved through those curriculum patterns that are unfamiliar to you. We would not be human if we did not tend to prefer ways of working similar to those which provided us with our most satisfying experiences and to have trouble recognising. The potential values of procedures with which we have had little experience. If you wish to grow as a professional person, however, do not accept any one answer too quickly. Keep studying and keep asking *why*.

There are many common emphases in methodology. A first look at contrasting proposals for organising the experiences for pupils often suggests that teaching methods differ widely. Sometimes the terms were use to describe differing curriculum designs add to the confusion. Occasionally we talk about "subject-centered" designs as opposed to "child-centered" ones, as though those who teach within subject frame-works have little concern for the pupils they teach and those who are working in terms of the needs of pupils don't care at all what information is learned. Sometimes "subject" and "experience" curriculums are contrasted in such a way as to give the impression that those who teach subjects draw on no concrete experiences and that those who work from the experiences of children never have them read for information. Actually, although there are differences in emphasis, depending on which values are considered to be most important, there is much agreement on what represents a sound educational programme for boys and girls regardless of the curriculum design.

In the first place, all teachers today try to provide *purposeful learning experiences*— to help pupils to see the purpose of what they are learning in school. This is just as important to the teacher of a college preparatory course in high school physics as it is to the teacher whose pupils want to learn enough about electricity to do a good job of wiring a model log cabin. This is a point at which psychological research in the area of motivation has made a major contribution. Early studies were largely concerned with extrinsic motives—gold stars, honor rolls, grades. Recently there has been much more emphasis on understanding how the learner views the situation. In your own case, for example, you defined the way you would work in a college class in terms of the way you sized up the value of the class to you, the grade you hoped for and the instructor's requirements that would have to be met to earn it, the relative importance of other classes and other grades, and probably the importance of social engagements and campus leadership responsibilities. Your pupils will likewise define the way they work with you in terms of the goals they understand. You will hear much discussion of the role of interest in learning. Interest is important, but this alone can hardly guarantee all the learnings for which schools are responsible. The basic question is how to make the work more meaningful or purposeful, how to tie what you are teaching to problems in the pupil's world. No matter what your grade level or your teaching field, you will need to develop skill in helping your pupils to establish vital purposes for what they learn.

Every teacher who cares about his subject field works seriously and conscientiously to secure *maximum carry-over to life outside of school.* There is not much point to spending hours studying the battles of the War Between the States if one cannot bring generalisations from this study to present-day tensions. Neither is there much value to acquiring ways of manipulating numbers in arithmetical processes if one cannot apply basic understanding of the structure of the number system intelligently to a new mathematical process. Perhaps one of the most important contributions of psychological research to teaching lies in the evidence that *how* we teach is crucial in determining what is learned. This is the problem of transfer of learning. We cannot be certain that a series of lessons in grammar and punctuation will result in polished writing unless we aim for this. A course in the United States history will not guarantee a more intelligent voter unless we deliberately and carefully teach toward this goal. No matter what you are teaching, you will find your cooperating teacher or supervisor anxious to help you learn how to work so that your pupils will arrive at concepts and generalisations that can be applied to new situations.

Occasionally articles stressing the importance of pupils' applying what they learn are interpreted to mean that the authors are concerned only with the knowledge needed to handle day-by-day problems. Actually, all teachers are concerned with *sound scholarship.* The group rigging the lighting system in the log cabin would be held to as accurate thinking about electricity as would the pupils in the physics laboratory. There are differences of opinion, of course, as to what learnings are most important. In some school systems Latin requirements may be giving way to modern languages, or extensive studies of the Western world may be curtailed to make room for acquaintance with the Far East, but whatever the area chosen for study, teachers are concerned that each pupil be challenged to extend himself to the limits of his ability. No matter what the focus of your work, you will need to learn how to hold for your pupils standards as high as their maturity will allow.

Whether your curriculum design is organised around topics that allow all subject areas to be drawn upon as needed or planned so that each teacher works within a separate subject field, you will find concern that pupils be helped to develop *awareness of interrelationships among subject fields,* It is impossible for any teacher today to do a good job if he concentrates only on health, or history, or arithmetic. A health problem related to good nutrition has science implications. Realistic arithmetic problems touch on consumer education and economics. The history of the early explorers does not make much sense without the application of geographical principles.

You will also find that teachers under all curriculum designs stress the development of *competence with fundamental skills.* It may surprise you to realise how broadly the word "skill" is interpreted. Your cooperating teacher or your supervisor will urge you to work toward higher levels of ability in reading, language, and numbers, but he will also be thinking about listening skills, observing techniques, and group-process skills. He will be helping you to analyse your lessons to see whether you are teaching effective problem-solving techniques—to think about how to handle a situation when a pupil says: "The mountains would be about a mile high. I guess," or states blithely, "there are, too, men on Mars; I saw it on television."

Furthermore, he will want you to recognise the variety of skills a pupil may need for competence in a single subject area. In arithmetic, for example, there are specialised skills not only in mathematical processes, but also in reading skills peculiar to the reading of problems and to the interpretation of charts, graphs, and tables. Similarly in science or history, there are specialised vocabularies with variant meanings and specialised techniques for finding additional information and evaluating data. You will not be a teacher very long before you find that the teaching of skills is an important aspect of your work in every field or area.

Because each human being has his own unique pattern of strengths, weaknesses, and experience background, you will find your colleagues giving much thought to achieving the *maximum development of each individual,* whether they are following the topics in a single, adopted text or are free to choose with their pupils the points of focus for their studies. You, too, will be expected to bring all your previous training to bear in identifying the needs of your pupils, and to develop a programme flexible enough to allow you to give help both to the pupil who grasps ideas slowly and to the able learner. In most classrooms, this will mean learning to utilise small groups and individual projects for part of your work as well as to individuals your attention when you are working with the class as a whole.

Whatever the pattern of your course of study, you will soon realise that the teachers with whom you are working are thinking about *democratic values.* They will not count it a waste of time to stop in discuss better ways of settling an argument, to talk out the reason in a school rule, or to listen to a student-counsel report. They will be involving pupils in planning and using teaching techniques that allow-pupils to develop effective skills as leaders and group members. You will find that those responsible for your supervision are as concerned about the democratic atmosphere in your room and the interpersonal relationships you develop as they are about any other aspect of your teaching.

There are, then, many points of agreement regarding the direction in which we should be moving in order to provide effective learning experiences for boys and girls. There is no room for complacency, however. A wide gap exists today between the best and the poorest of the United States' schools. Furthermore, each turn of events on the national or international scene is a challenge to re-evaluate present practices. Each educational advance suggests a host of new problems. If you want to become a professional person, you will equip yourself to do your share to assure the continued improvement of educational programmes and practices.

What Skills Are Needed for the Effective Solution of Educational Problems?

Whether or not you will make a sound contribution to the development of better education experiences for boys and girls—either your own classroom or as a member of a curriculum committee—will depend upon the effectiveness of your problem-solving skills. Just as research chemist must be able to use the scientific method or an historian must be skilled in the techniques of historical research, teachers need to acquire those skills basic to the effective solution educational problems.

Sometimes you will hear, even from professional people, comments which suggest that we do not always use effective problem-solving procedures in the field of education. You may hear someone talk about "the pendulum swinging" as if we tended to go from one extreme position to another.

A teacher may describe his procedures as "middle of the road"—a position which seems to imply that he does not deep his colleagues to be as sound as he in their points of view. You may even hear some well-meant comments about the "gap between theory and practice" which, in effect, means that you have not been taught very much that is practical. On the other hand, your colleagues may ask. "What does the college believe?" as though, to be up to date, one must accept the philosophy of the prevailing authority.

If we are realistic we must admit that some of our educational practices are determined by factors other than thoughtful, impartial study. In some school systems, what teachers consider to be a desirable programme has to be balanced against what they feel must be taught for the purposes of standardised tests. There are situations where the quality of the educational programme is conditioned by the classroom space available, the textbooks adopted, or the salaries which teachers can be offered. In some places the concerns of special community groups will determine what is taught. Although such factors need to be reckoned with, lasting gains in terms of better programmes for boys and girls will be made only as more teachers become skilled in analysing and solving educational problems. You will have experiences that help you to develop such skills every time you plan a lesson, consider your next move when a problem of behaviour has arisen, or analyse your role as a playground leader or club sponsor.

Teachers must be able to analyse the educational potentialities of complex situations. One of the most important skills for you to acquire is the ability to analyse complex situations for yourself. Beginning teachers are often baffled and frustrated when they seek help on their classroom problems. Typically, instead of saying "Do this" or "That's right" or "That's wrong," principals and supervisors say "Let's study the situation." This is a much slower process, but it is at the heart of a professional solution to an educational problem. There are few black or white answers in the field of education; there are many shades of gray.

To creative teachers, the fact that educational problems are rarely simple is one of the most challenging aspects of the profession. Consider for example, Mr. Bantam, who is planning a sixth-grade science unit on how sound is produced and transmitted. Certainly, he wants his pupils to end up with accurate information about sound—but is this all? Whether he realises it or not, he is also teaching attitudes. He may be turning able youngsters toward or away from science as a career. By the way he teaches, he may be encouraging independent exploration and building appreciation of the scientific method, or he may be developing the attitude hat the word of experts (in this case, Mr. Bantam and the authors of the textbook) is to be accepted without question. He must think about the reading skills he is teaching and the discussion techniques and skills in cooperative problem-solving he plans develop. Even in conveying accurate information about sound, he must decide whether he will be satisfied if his pupils can give back the express words of the textbook or will take steps to assure that they can use the information accurately. All these decisions and many more will influence his lesson plans—how he will present the problem to his class whether he will let pupils experiment, how he will use his textbook whether he will lecture, what time he will allow for present-day applications, on what bases he will evaluate pupil growth.

Even a problem seemingly as simple as working with a third-grade reading group has many facets. As Miss Antonio makes he plan, she needs to consider what special reading skills she wishes to stress—word analysis techniques; ability to locate accurate information, skill in summarising what has been read, oral reading skills. She, too, is building attitudes—reading interests, feelings of competence, case before an audience, habits of reading critically. If certain youngsters are having special problems, she may find herself helping others in the group to develop attitudes of sympathy and tolerance. All these considerations combine to determine how Miss Antonio plans her reading lesson and works with her group.

Problems of developing effective inter-personal relationships in the classroom call for just as careful an analysis. Three of Mr. Jackson fourth-grade boys habitually interrupt in group discussions. There must be causes for his behaviour and as Mr. Jackson and his supervisor sit down to consider next steps they analyse the situation to see what these might be. Perhaps the boys simply lack discussion techniques and need specific instruction regarding how one behaves in a group. It could be that they lack basic respect for other individuals and need to be helped to develop this attitude. Possibly being the center of attention is satisfying basic needs—needs for affection, for group status, for the satisfaction of intellectual curiosity. It could even be that Mr. Jackson, as discussion leader, is allowing more freedom than he realises and the boys are simply following his cues. Once Mr. Jackson has decided what the undesirable behaviour means and what his goals should be, he will have a sense of direction in deciding hat to do next. All three youngsters could respond to the same approach, but it is possible that the behaviour stems from a different cause in each case. If so, the procedure used to effect changes in behaviour must differ.

These examples are no more complex than many of the everyday problems teachers face. Deciding what to do in any situation involves thinking of the attitudes and values the pupils will be acquiring, the ways of working they will develop, the attitudes that will be built toward other persons in cooperative or authority roles, precisely what information or skills they will learn. Whether or not the day's activities are as effective as they should be will depend on how positively they contribute to all the potential learnings in the situation. How good a science teacher is Mr. Bantam, for example, if his pupils pass with flying colors tests over the facts in the book and never apply scientific ways of working to their own solutions of problems? How well has Miss Antonio done if her pupils analyse words with great skill and never take home library books to read? How good is Mr. Jackson's discipline if his boys behave only when his eye is on them? One of the most important contributions that your student-teaching experiences can make to your eventual success as a teacher is to help you to develop more sensitive insights into the classroom problems you face.

Teachers must be able to translate goals into behaviour. Beginning teachers often fail to achieve desired goals because they do not define exactly what they are after. You will have to learn to translate your general objectives into specific behaviour. Watch three student teachers helping their fourth-graders learn a ten-word spelling list. Ruth Glad-stone goes at it by giving a pre-test, helping the children to identify the words difficult for them, and then analysing the sight and sound elements in each word with them. Dave Martino tells his class to write each word ten times for homework; he has no discussion of how to study and gives no help in analysing words. Sam James decides that the children will do better if they are interested and plans a spelling bee where those who miss a word go to their eats. Each of these plans hints at the teacher's conception of the characteristics of a good speller.

You will need to translate goals into behaviour if you wish to teach information effectively. What would you accept as evidence that your teaching in a fifth-grade unit on safety has been a success? Do you want your pupils to be able to list the exact points in the textbook? If they can write their own stories about safety, or make posters, is this the evidence you seek? Do you expect changes in behaviour on the playground? In what ways?

Behavioural goals are equally important in developing group relationships. At the beginning of his student teaching Bob Anderson was very enthusiastic about the responses he was securing in his class discussions. When his supervisor visited he found a very lively discussion indeed where everyone was trying to outshout everyone else. Comments such as "You're crazy" or "Oh, shut up" were frequent; unfounded opinion were defended heatedly even in areas where ample evidence was available. Do these suggest behaviours that relate to good discussion requires? How clearly has Bob defined the democratic value of respecting the unique worth of each individual? If you would have your lessor effective you must learn to make your goals precise.

Teachers must be able to use effectively research regarding human growth and development. The solution to almost every educational problem calls for answers to three questions: (1) What are our goal (in terms of our best insights into the needs of individuals, the needs our democratic society, and the potential learnings in a given situation? (2) What do these goals mean specifically in terms of behaviour? (3) What are the most efficient and economical means of reaching these special goals? Research in human growth, development, and learning makes major contribution to this third step.

Once in a while you will hear comments which indicate that the contribution of educational psychology to good teaching is not very clearly understood. A parent sometimes is heard to say, "I used at the psychology I knew and then I spanked him." A beginning teacher may be advised, "At first, forget your psychology and show them you are in control." A leader persuades a group to do something about which they are not too happy and reports. "All it took was a little psychology." Or a mother hears a psychologist talk at a Parent-Teacher Association meeting and wonders whether the speaker would "take look at Sammy." Actually, of course, our insights into human behaviour make a much more basic contribution to effective teaching than a ball of tricks for persuading people to do as we wish or a crystal ball to understanding deviate behaviour.

As you work with your pupils, try to identify the situations in which you can apply what you know about maturation and readiness: about basic needs and developmental tasks; about motivation and the nature of learning: about individual differences; about transfer of learning about the effects on behaviour of broken homes, social class structure family patterns of permissiveness and authoritarianism; about growth dynamics and democratic social climates. These are among the research areas on which you will draw over and over again as you face the realities of teaching.

Many a beginning teacher (and many an experienced teacher, too) described to a supervisor the way he handled a class situation or problem with an individual child and then has asked. "Was I right. As you learn to analyse the situations you face, to spell out your goals precisely, and to apply appropriately what you know about the ways in which children grow and learn, you will become better and better able to answer this question for yourself.

Teachers must be able to use research techniques in solving new problems. As you study more closely the research underlying modern classroom procedures, you will discover that many of our ways of working are deduced from basic psychological studies. For example, our general knowledge from laboratory studies of the effect of the learner's purpose on the way he works suggests that it is important to provide for pupil-teacher planning so that pupil purposes will be clear; what we know about transfer of learning suggests that the way we teach will make a crucial difference in what our pupils actually learn; what we have learned from research in child-study laboratories has helped to define our concept of readiness for learning. If our progress toward better educational programmes is to be continuous, teachers must become more and more skillful in testing basic educational principles in the classroom setting.

In recent years serious thought has been given to the possibilities of involving teachers in classroom research. Typically, in the past the research pattern was designed by college professors, research bureaus, or doctoral candidates, and if teachers had any share, it was largely to carry out instructions. Today there are many school systems in which individual teachers, the members of an entire school faculty, or the faculties of several schools are engaging in research projects. You may well find the teachers in your building testing out a proposal for an individualised reading programme; comparing the results of a spelling programme built around words pupils actually need with those of a programme which follows the adopted text; investigating ways of gearing learning activities more effectively to pupils experience backgrounds; studying how to help children develop-more effective problem-solving techniques. One of the most exciting advances in the field of education is our realisation that teachers themselves can make an important research contribution to better programmes for boys and girls.

Research involves complicated techniques for identifying and clarifying a problem, advancing hypotheses, collecting and analysing data, drawing conclusions, and testing them further as necessary. An effective research project calls for a high level of skill at all these points. In your first years of teaching you probably will not find yourself involved in much extensive research. You can, however, learn to approach your classroom problems with a scientific point of view. You can learn make hypotheses as to why a procedure worked well or failed and to text your hypotheses. You can use objective techniques for studying pupils to collect concrete evidence of the success of your teaching. You can also learn to withhold judgment and study a situation rather than saying to quickly and glibly, "I believe in this" or "Of course, I don't how with that at all." Teaching offers endless possibilities for growth for those who choose to take a scientific approach to educational problem. Every day suggests a new hypothesis to test and new types of data to be collected.

Developing Your Own Educational Points of View

Philosophies of education like philosophies of life, keep on growing. No one has the insights at twenty that he will have at forty. No one at sixty, if he has maintained his interest in professional problems will think exactly as he did at forty. To all the richness of experience which comes through dealing creatively with professional problems must be added the challenges of a changing world. Who knows but the new evidence in psychology, psychiatry, and medicine in the next quarter of a century may change our ways of looking at human nature Certainly, few teachers in 19930 dreamed that developments in the physical and social sciences would soon cause them to reappraise their attitudes about the world in which they live in the light of the atomic age. As a beginning teacher, you are taking early steps in the lifelong process of building a sound professional point of view. How can you guarantee that your student-teaching experience and your first years on the job contribute to this goal as richly as possible?

Do not expect "snap" answers." Your expectations of what it mean to learn to teach will help to determine how much you grow. If you are looking for pat answers and simple solutions, you will not more very far in the direction of solving professional problems effective for yourself, and you may find student teaching and your first years under supervision in a classroom of your own very frustrating, indeed. Learn to think about the situations you face. Even responsibilities the seem routine and simple merit a careful analysis. You will grow in your ability to solve professional problems for yourself to the degree to you make yourself work at it.

If you are expecting to do a perfect job every day and to receive nothing but praise from your cooperating teacher or supervisor, you are also in for disappointment and frustration. The more complex the teaching responsibilities you undertake, the more likely it is that something unforeseen will go awary in spite of your most careful planning. This is part of the challenge of teaching. If you want to grow, take on the difficult tasks and welcome opportunities to analyse your mistakes. Even your most experienced colleagues, you will discover, face each new day as a challenge and an opportunity for professional growth.

Keep asking why? Preparing yourself day after day to

give leadership to thirty or more boys and girls offers unparalleled opportunities to develop skill in educational planning. Make yourself think by asking *why* as you develop your lesson plans. It will be a temptation at times to adopt blindly the procedures of a colleague or even, in despair, to recall how Miss Hannabell did it when you were in the fourth grade. However, you will find that the time you spend thinking through goals and outlining your plans in detail will pay off in feelings of security as you teach. There is nothing more difficult than trying to give a class a sense of direction if you yourself are not sure where you are going.

Ask your cooperating teacher or your supervisor *why* also. If your first full-time experience in the classroom is as challenging as it should be, you will discover that you cannot always identify in practice principles that seemed quite clear in college classes. Because each new group of boys and girls poses a different teaching problem, your co-operating teacher and your colleagues will almost certainly be using some teaching techniques you did not talk about in your methods courses. Perhaps you will find yourself in a classroom where both curriculum and teaching methods are quite different from those you remember from your own school days. You may be tempted to reject those practices that do not look familiar. "After all," you may be saying. "I had an excellent education, and my teachers did not go in for all of this. It is strange that the very person who extols the virtues of progress in medicine and points with pride to how much better protected is the health of his children today sometimes argues vehemently for a return to the "good old days" in education. Actually, in most cases, there will be good reasons for the procedures you are now observing and for the suggestions of your supervisors. You should fed a professional obligation to ask for help in interpreting what you have seen. The persons supervising your work can spell out the reasons back of their objectives and procedures if you will let them know where you are puzzled.

It is equally important, however, that you do not feel compelled to accept completely everything you see. There are genuine differences of opinion as to what learnings are of most value for boys and girls. You will not grow if you reject too quickly ideas that are unfamiliar but neither will you grow if you bend all your efforts into making yourself a carbon copy of your cooperating teacher or of the colleague next door. Keep on ferreting out explanations, but at the same time match your best thinking against that of the experienced teachers working with you.

Keep yourself up to date! Teachers do not grow unless they actively seek new ideas. It is a common complaint of beginning teachers that they have far too little time to sleep, let alone to read and think. To some extent this is true, but your first years of teaching should also be years of thoughtful study. You must continue to grow in your insights into human nature and the society in which we live—two of the foundation areas upon which all teachers draw. If you have never stopped to think what you mean by "democracy," this is the time to do so. You will be vague and uncertain about many of the steps you take in developing effective human relationships in your classroom if your goals in teaching democratic relationships are not beginning to clarify. Your preoccupation with college classes may have left you woefully ignorant of what is going on in the world today—even of the television which your pupils watch so avidly. If you are going to help your boys and girls understand what is happening in the world around them, you may have to set yourself a definite reading programme. You will also find that you will need to continue to examine basic psychological principles. No matter how rich your college background in this area has been, your first hand experiences with youngsters will deepen and sharpen many of your concepts. This is your year to dip back into book on human relationships in the classroom, on the influence of social class backgrounds, on meeting the emotional needs of pupils, on working with the exceptional child.

It is also important for you to grow in your sensitivity to the major educational problems which concern the members of your profession. In many schools, student teachers are invited to participate in faculty meetings, workshops and other in-service projects, Parent-Teacher Association meetings. As a beginning teacher you will be expected to make such activities part of your professional life. You may wish you could decline these invitations under the pressure of your college classes, campus obligations, or the weight of all your new responsibilities in your first year in a classroom of your own. If you are anxious to become a top-flight teacher, however, you will arrange your schedule to include such professional meetings. They offer priceless opportunities to learn firsthand the types of problems that are receiving the attention of educators today. This is your chosen profession and these, your colleagues-to-be, are anxious to help you feel that you are an accepted, full-time member of it.

REFERENCES

Cole, Lawrence E., and Bruce, William F. *Educational Psychology*. Revised Edition. Yonkers-on-Hudson, N.Y.: World Book Co., 1958, pp. 720.

Counts George S., *Education and American Civilisation*, New York; Bureau of Publications. Teachers College, Columbia University, 1952, pp. xiv + 491.

Cronbach, Lee J., *Educational Psychology*, New York.: Harcourt, Brace and Co., 1954, pp. xxvii + 628.

Jersild, Arthur T., and associates. *Child Development and the Curriculum.* New York: Bureau of Publications, Teachers College, Columbia University, 1946, pp. xi + 274.

Research for Curriculum Improvement. 1957 Yearbook of the Association for Supervision and Curriculum Development, N.E.A. Washington, D.C.: The Association, 1957, pp. x + 350.

Rugg. Harold, and Withers, William, *Social Foundations of Education.* Englewood Cliffs, N.J.: Prentice-Hall, 1955, pp. x + 771.

Saylor, J. Galen, and Alexander, William M., *Curriculum Planning for Better Teaching and Learning.* New York: Rinehart and Co., 1954. Pp. xiii + 624.

Stratemeyer, Florence B.; Forkner, Hamden, L.: McKim, Margaret G.; and Passow.

A. Harry, *Developing a Curriculum for Modern Living.* Revised Edition. New York: Bureau of Publications, Teachers College, Columbia University, 1957. Pp. 740.

Teachers for Our Times. Washington, D.C.: American Council on Education, 1944. Pp. xix + 189.

13

The Right Teaching Position

After four years in college preparing to be a teacher, your most important concern, except, of course, that of obtaining your degree, will be find the teaching position in which your can be happy and success. Securing the right teaching position is not ordinarily a matter of bad or good luck. Once you begin to consider this important step obviously you will find the task more complicated than you had thought to be. One does not go blithely to a superintendent of schools and for a job. There are professional channels to be followed and find rules to be observed.

In some colleges, there is a definite programme designed to inform prospective teachers concerning professional opportunities. If this has been uses in your institution, careful guidance and pertinent informations have been given to you from the time you first entered the teacher-education programme. As a freshman you may have been told, for simple, about trends in job opportunities—that positions were more likely to be available in some teaching areas than in others. At that teacher or perhaps later, you may have been advised that your background experience and your personal characteristics might better suit your success in one teaching field than in another. Undoubtedly, your operating teacher, your college supervisor, and perhaps the principal of the school in which you do your student teaching will also counsel to you regarding the type of position for which you seem best fitted. For this is evidence that those who have worked closely with you in a preparation for teaching are interested in your future success in teaching profession.

During the time that you are engaged in student teaching you will begin to work actively toward securing the type of position which your own self-appraisal and the advise of other have led you to believe you will be successful. In many colleges, those who are responsible for teacher placement will be ready to help you at that point. This is not to say that you cannot secure a teaching position entirely by your own efforts. It has been done. You will, however, by working with the placement director and your faculty advisor, stand a better chance of securing the kind of position in which you can be successful and happy.

This chapter contains specific suggestions regarding how to go about securing the position you want—how to make effective use of your college placement services; how to make application to superintendents of schools and how to decide whether the positions they have available are right of your; and what professional amenities to observe in making applications and signing contracts.

MAKING EFFECTIVE USE OF YOUR COLLEGE PLACEMENT FACILITIES

In most colleges, the persons who work most actively in helping students to secure teaching positions are those charged with the responsibility for teacher placement. The exact name of the office will vary from college to college. The more common titles are *Bureau of Placement, Bureau of Recommendations, or Office of Teacher Placement.* The title of the office is really not important to your. What a important is the kind of services, information and advice available through the persons in the office. Ordinarily the director of the placement office maintains close relationships with school officials within the college area and knows something about teaching opportunities at a greater distance. Usually he will have a definite procedure for bringing together personal information, college records, and writers statements regarding your performance as a college student, as a student teacher, and a person. He will also be able to advise your about certification, not only in your own state but in other states as well. During your senior year, and especially in your final quarter or semester, he or his assistants will be at your service to answer your questions and to advise your regarding what steps to take in securing a teaching position. You should not be hesitant about asking question or seeking advice. It is not only to your best interests, about to the best interests of the college that you be placed in the position most likely to guarantee that you will become a successful teacher.

Find out about teaching opportunities. Your first step will probably be to consult with someone in your college placement office about the teaching positions available. Regardless of all the publicity about the shortage of teachers, there are some localities in which there is actually an oversupply at some grade levels or in some subject areas or special fields. Fortunately, as a person preparing to be a teacher in the elementary school, this is less likely to be the case for your than for some of your friends whose teaching interests are at other levels. It appears that there will be a need for you in almost any part of the country for the nest several years.

Because of the shortage of teachers at the elementary level, your placement director will probably know of many available positions. He will have direct acquaintance with the needs of local school officials. Numerous inquiries will also have come to his office from school distinct in neighbouring parts of the state and from superintendents at a greater distance. In the course of a placement season he will receive notices of vacancies from the far corners of the United States and sometimes from overseas. He will also know when representatives of school systems plan to visit your campus for the purpose of interviewing prospective teachers. The methods by which this information is made available will vary. Sometimes notices of vacancies are posted on a bulletin board for general inspection. Sometimes you will be informed personally if the vacancy seems particularly suited to your preparation and personal characteristics. This, of course, is one reason why you should register with the placement office and talk to the placement director rather early in your last semester.

Although the teacher placement office is likely to be the best source of information about teaching vacancies. There are other possibilities about which you should know. Among these are your own acquaintance with school official in your home community and leads given a friends or relatives. Such sources of information are, of course, legitmate, but you should be careful in exploiting them. Usually it is not to consult your placement director before you proceed very far in supplying for a teaching position located through such sources. Often cases he will have information about these situations which you do not possess. He may, for example, know of conditions within the school system which would make it inadvisable for you to make application. He may also know enough about the specific position to be dubious regarding its suitability for you. In any event. He will have some worth while suggestions regarding steps to take in making application which will be helpful if you are genuinely interested in the vacancy.

Prepare credentials carefully. When you talk to a

school official, he will ask about your *credentials.* This may be a new term to your. It relates to a copy of the registration forms you complete for your placement office together with copies of the statements secured from the persons you have listed as references. Placement officers routinely ask graduating students to prepare sets of registration papers—usually in quadruplicate. These forms will ask for such information as your present as well as your permanent address and telephone number. You will also be asked for certain personal data—age, height, weight, marital states, educational background, and work experience. In addition, there will be professional data requested. You will be asked to indicate the kind of certificate you now have or will have after graduation. Other kinds of professional information may include the kind of teaching positions you would like to obtain and the grade level or special subjects or areas in which you feel best qualified. You may also be required to indicate special abilities or activities in which you have participated. Do not neglect these. Sometimes they mean the difference between obtaining a position before graduation and waiting until later in the summer. Some registration forms also provide space for the lisitng of courses, credits and grades. If you are not asked for this information, you will certainly be required to submit copies of your college transcript.

By this time, and certainly by the time you have completed the registration forms, you will be asking "Why all this bother?" The answer to this question is simple. All the bother enables the placement director to have at hand several copies of your credentials for his own use and for the use of prospective employers. In these days of rapid communication, the telephone is used more and more frequently is teacher placement. Often a superintendent will describe the teaching position over the phone and ask for a certain kind of teacher if this placement director does not know you well he will study your credentials and perhaps read them to the superintendent. If the school superintendent comes to the campus he will usually have studied your credentials before he interviews you. On the other hand, if you are being interviewed at the office of the superintendent, your credentials will often have preceded you. Whatever the specific practice, your credentials will certainly be studied by your prospective employer before your are offered a contract.

You can now understand why credential on, as they are sometimes called, "confidential folders" are so important Incidentally, the true "confidential folder" is perhaps even more appropriate them credentials." Your credentials are confidential and are never submitted to or aspected by anyone other than persons interested in you as a prospective teacher. Since the registration forms that you have filled in as part of your credentials often provide your employer's first impression of you, you must be very careful in completing these forms. Be sure that the information is accurate and complete. If a statement regarding your reasons for wanting to teach is requested, write it thoughtfully. Do not take a poor impression by careless writing or sloppy typing.

Use care in listing persons who know about you and your work. Legislation forms typically contain a section in which you must list games of persons who can write a statement about you. These statements are an important part of your credentials. You should do some careful thinking about the individuals you list. It is usually best to give the names of persons who have knowledge of your in different kinds of situations. You will certainly give as references your faculty advisor your cooperating teacher, and perhaps the principal of the school in which you were placed for student teaching. You will also want to list one or more professors who know your competence in academic fields. Sometimes, too, you may want to give names of persons for whom you have worked and perhaps the names of your physician and your minister priest, or rabbi.

Persons named by you and from whom your placement office secures requirements are known as *references*. It is courteous to request permission of these persons before you list their names on the registration form. Requesting permission serves a double purpose; it establishes your reputation as a considerate, courteous individual and at the same time identifies you in the mind of the reference. It may surprise you, of some people cannot associate names with individuals. They may have forgotten who you are or they may remember—you vaguely as he quiet little girl in the front seat."

Ordinarily the placement office will send the reference from direct to a person you have named as a reference, but sometimes you may be asked to deliver the form yourself. In any case, do not expect to see what has been written about you. The statement is a highly confidential and professional document; it tells such points about you as scholarship, estability, judgment, leadership, personal appearance, health and other social qualities, loyalty, attitude toward work, and probable getting success. Your references would not write frankly were they are sure that their statements would be treated as confidential.

Although you will never see the statements written about you, it had there been vague and mildly flattering statements telling nothing. Not all evaluations, of course, are written as carefully as those you just read. However, a series of statements written by persons who know you well and in different situations does serve to give the placement director and the employing officer a rather good picture of what you can do and the type of position in which you should be placed.

Submit a good photograph. Nowadays you are not likely to obtain a teaching position without a personal interview with the employing school official. Even so, there will probably need to be a photograph submitted with each set of credentials. Your placement officer will tell you how many prints you should file. The photograph requested by your placement bureau will probably be approximately 2 x 3 inches in size, to avoid delay in registering with the placement bureau, you ought to secure these some months in advance of the time when you will be actively seeking a teaching position. When you submit your photograph, write your name and the date it was taken on the back of each print. A nameless photograph usually — and sometimes quickly—funds its way into the waste-basket.

Your photograph should be appropriate and in good taste. Further more, you should look like yourself. Snapshots are ordinarily not acceptable. If you have a photograph that is not of the proper size, your placement bureau can probably supply you with the name of a photographer who specialises in making reproductions. The cost of these is nominal—usually not more than tow or three dollars per dozen. Here again, however, it is better to have a new photograph taken than it is to use one which is inappropriate. A few dollars well spent may pay large dividends. Oftentimes obscure and intangible impressions make the difference between getting the position you want and having to accept one not quite as desirable.

Ascertain when a commercial teachers' agency can help you. In these days when positions for elementary school teachers are relatively plentiful, your own college placement bureau will, under ordinary circumstances, provide all the help you will need in securing the teaching position you want. There are, however, certain instances were you may require additional assistance. One of these might be when you are looking for a teaching position you want. There are, however, certain instances where you may require additional assistance. One of these might be when you are looking for a teaching position which is outside of the usual placement territory of your own college bureau. In such cases it might be helpful to avail yourself of the services of a commercial teachers agency. This is a private business which serves somewhat the same purpose as your own college placement bureau, but which charges a fee for as services. The free is usually a percentage of your first year's salary in the teaching position obtained.

Commercial teachers' agencies have different names and different titles, but their purpose is always the same— to secure teaching position for you for which a fee is charged. If you decide to use the services done of these firms, you would do well to inquire about its status. Ensure, also, that you are aware of the conditions of the contract you will have to sign. Read it carefully and be sure you understand it. You will be wise to talk to your placement director before you register with a commercial teachers' agency. He will know the names and addresses of responsible firms and will be able to give you sound advice regarding the circumstances under which you should use them.

Apply for the proper teaching certificate. One of your most important responsibilities if you plan to teach in the public schools is a make application for your teaching certificate. In some teacher-education institutions you may be furnished with the proper certificate without application, but more often you will have to secure the appropriate forms, complete them as directed, and return them to the college certifying officer. Some time before graduation, information will probably be sent to you regarding exactly what procedure to follow. Do not neglect this advice or fail to inquire if you do not receive official notice. Some beginning teachers have been delinquent in this, only to discover later that their first month's pay check is being held up pending confidence that they possess a valid certificate.

As you pursue the teacher-education programme in your college the success are that you will be meeting the requirements for the appropriate teaching certificate concurrently with preparing for your degree. A college degree, however, does not *necessarily* mean that your will have met certification requirements. You, yourself, should make attain that you will not be caught short when you are ready to apply for teaching position. Study the college bulletin carefully. Both degree and certification requirements may be outlined there. If not, there may supplementary information, mimeographed or printed, which will you what you want to know. If you still cannot find the right answers, ask your advisor or the certifying officer designated by the college authorities.

In most states, certification for teaching is a prerogative of the state department of education. Your college probably follows the requirement set forth in the directives of this department. There may, however be some variation. In some states, too, a college which has been approved as a teacher-education institution has been delegated the authority to recommend its graduates for certification. If so, you, as a graduate, cannot secure a certificate without the recommendation of the college authorities. This is often the reason why you must apply for a certificate through the certifying officer of the college.

You have, no doubt, already learned that each state has slightly different requirements for certification. If you plan to teach in a state other than the one in which your college is situated, you will be wise to inquire long before you last semester of work about its certification requirements. There may be, for example, such state requirements as knowledge of the state constitution, a course in state history, a special course in education, or a background of specific academic courses. Meeting these requirements is, of course, your responsibility. Your college officials can, however, advise and help you.

IDENTIFYING AND APPLYING FOR THE TEACHING POSITION IN WHICH YOU CAN BE SUCCESSFUL

Registering with your placement office is only a first step in securing a teaching position. You still have ahead of you the exciting (and sometimes tedious) process of identifying positions which are right for fulfiling applications for them, and being interviewed. In this process your college authorities can be of major help. They know you: they also know superintendents and school systems. Professional placement officers do not see their responsibility as securing just any position for an applicant. They want you to be located in a situation where you can make a truly professional contribution to the education of boys and girls.

Decide for yourself what type of position will be right for you. As you approach the time when you are actively to enter the teaching profession, you will be the recipient of much gratuitous and unsolicited advice concerning the kind of position you should accept. There will be some, for example, who will tell you that there is more status as teaching in a large city. Others will say that there is less status if you work with slow-learning or underprivileged boys and girls. Listen as such kinds of advice politely, but then make up your own mind. You are the person (with the professional advice of your college supervisor and your placement director) best equipped to decide what position will be best for you.

By the time you have completed your teacher-education programme. You should have had wide experience with children of varying ages. Intellectual levels, and socioeconomic backgrounds. You also should have had occasion to observe the ways in which schools are organised and how teachers and administrators work together for the benefit of boys and girls. You may have had some opportunity to work in a city school, a suburban school, and a school in a rural area. All such experiences will help you to reach some general decisions regarding the type of community and school in which you are interested.

To proceed intelligently in locating a teaching position in which you will be successful, you should be working from more than a general impression of the type of situation your prefer. You should have done same careful evaluation of your own strengths and weaknesses. Persons who will make an outstanding contribution in one situation will not ways be equally successful in another. If you have some skill in working with underprivileged children, you should consider carefully a position where you will have an opportunity to help them. If, on the other hand, you are somewhat short of patience with children who do we handle verbal materials easily, you should look for a position where you can work with pupils more able academically. Likewise, you may have found that you are happier in a small community than in a large area. If this is so, perhaps you ought to seek a position in a suburban school or one in a rural or semirural area. There will be many other each factors to consider. It is not a sign of incompetence on your part indicate, frankly to your placement officer or to an employing official types of situations in which you feel least comfortable. Nor is it a an act of egotism to be equally frank regarding the circumstances under which you feel that you can do your best work. Employing officials are just as anxious as you are to see that you secure a position in which will be successful.

Write business-like letters of enquiry or of application if these are enquiry. When you have clarified you own thinking regarding the position you want and its location, you are ready to consult your placement director regarding specific opening in your location and how to go about applying for them. If the position to have the placement director make it tendent is interested in your qualifications, arrangements for an interview may be set up then and there.

Most placement officers have access to a national directory of school systems and superintendents. If the director of your placement bureau has no information about the school system in which you are interested, he will know the person to contact to secure the information you want. He may write a letter for you, but he is quite likely to suggest that you, yourself, write a *letter of inquiry* to the superintendent. This letter should state that you are interested in a position at your selected grade level, but it should also indicate that your are qualified to teach at certain grade levels. It is usually best to enclose a self-addressed stamped envelope. An example of a letter of inquiry is given here, but you would, of course, make necessary modifications to fit your own background of experience and training.

When you complete an application form, you should be a careful as you are when you write a letter of inquiry or of application or fill in your registration blanks for your placement office. Write nearly or use a typewriter, check spelling, and above all read the application carefully and answer the questions honestly. If the form requires the submission of a photograph, be sure to attach it securely. Cellophane tape or a staple will serve the purpose. Do not use glue or a paper clip. A photograph separated from the application form is useless.

Some school system may require supplementary information and documents with your application. One of the documents which you are likely to be asked to supply is an official college tanscript. Employing officers want to know what grades you have attained and the pattern of courses which you have taken. Of course, if you are applying for a position before you last semester or quarter has ended, your transcript will be incomplete, but this is not a serious matter. The official will be able to judge your work from the record available.

Another document which may be required is a birth certificate. Retirement may seem in the far distant future, but you will join a retirement scheme when you accept employment, and proof of your age is likely to be needed. Different states have different offices for the registry of births and you will have to ascertain where to apply. Even if you are not required to submit a birth certificate in order to obtain employment, there is certain to be a time in your life when you will need one. You should know how to go about securing it.

The third document which you will need is the appropriate teaching certificate. You are not, however, eligible for this until you have completed your programme of teacher education. It is probable, therefore, that you will have to attach a statement to you application to the effect that you do not yet possess the appropriate certificate but that upon graduation you will be eligible for it. The exact name of the certificate is important. Find out from your placement director or collage advisor what the correct title of your certificate will be.

If you have been in the military service, the employing official will want to examine your certificate of service in many school systems you will be given credit on the salary schedule for military service and your papers will be used to substantiate what your length of service has been. Although your military papers will usually be returned to you, it is wise to supply photostatic copies rather than the original documents.

Completing the necessary application blanks and supplying the required papers may seem to you to be a lot of trouble, but remember that a decision regarding whether or not to call you for an interview is likely to be made on the basis of your application. Remember, too, that offers of positions as well as appointments for interviews are sometimes delayed if the necessary papers have not been received. You can not be too careful if you really want a teaching position in the school system where you are applying.

Respond thoughtfully in your interview with an employing official. It is unusual for a school superintendent or employing official to offer in individual a teaching position without a personal interview. From our own point of view, it is unwise to accept a position before you have visited a school and community and have had an opportunity to ask questions. For your prospective employer, the interview serves as a means of judging your personal appearance, voice, interest, and adaptability and of securing your reaction to possible teaching assignments, local conditions, and school regulations. An interview, however, is not a one-sided affair conducted only for the benefit of the employing official. It enables you to gain information about the demands of the position for which you are applying, the community, living conditions, salary, opportunities for advancement, and local teaching regulations. You will not, of course, appear at a board of education office and expect to be interviewed without an appointment. Make your appointment head of time and then be sure to be *on time,* or preferably a few minutes early.

Naturally you will want to appear at your best at the interview. The initial impression you make on your prospective employer is conditioned by many factors. Among the most important are your attitude, your apparent interest, your use of the English language, your posture and carriage, and the appropriateness of your dress and grooming. One of these are factors well within your control but others are not, false front, assumed merely to impress, can be identified rather easily. The employing officer will be attempting to discover what kind person you rally are and how well you will fit into his school system. It is far better that he do so in the interview rather than discover it after you have been on the job for three months.

Some specific hints as to how you may make a good impression will not be amiss. Probably of most importance is good grooming and appropriate dress. One would not, of course, dress as if attending of formal college function, nor, on the other hand, should the informal dress sometimes seen on college campuses be worn. Young men in sport shirts and unpressed trousers and young women in slacks have been known to appear for interviews with consequent disastrous results to their job aspirations and repercussions in the college placement office. It does one no harm to prepare for the interview by having one's half nearly combed, or in the case of a young woman to use lipstick and make-up in appropriate moderation.

Your poise, the ease with which you converse with a stranger, and your general manner contribute to a good impression. It is not unusual to be nervous and ill at case prior to the opening of an interview. Remember, however, that most employing officials will try to conduct the interview in a friendly, informal manner. You, too, can be friendly and informal as long as you are serious when the discussion demands it. You will create the best impression if you are as natural and as frank as possible. In general, the employing officer will be the one to direct the course of the interview. Allow him to speak as freely as he desires without interrupting unnecessarily. At the same time, be prepared to pick up the conversation rather than have an embarrassing pause occur. You will probably have questions to ask about the school or community and points you would like to make about your own qualifications of interests. Do not hesitate to insert these as the occasion permits. Be a good listener, too. Watch for indications that the interviewer wants to bring the interview to a close. If you are sensitive to the general atmosphere of the interview situation, you will not attempt to carry the interview beyond that point.

What should you be prepared to talk about? There is no way of telling, for sure. Employing officers have many ways of getting to know people. Frequently they are as much interested in your frankness your sincerity, and your poise as they are in the exact answers to their questions. In general you should be prepared to discuss such professional topics as your educational philosophy and perhaps some recent books on education, especially those in your own teaching field. You could be asked about some of the topics of the day, such a television programmes, current movies, popular novels, sports, and national and international affairs. It is quite likely that you will be asked about your professional aspirations. You cannot possibly prepare yourself, a few days before an interview, to talk intelligently on current affairs about which you have not been reading consistently, but you *can* be prepared to talk definitely about your professional plans and the ways in which of expect to improve yourself professionally. Certainly you should not hesitate to ask questions—after all, the interview is for your benefit is well as for the benefit of the employing official.

Listen now as Sarah Yancey, personnel director in a large city school system, carries on an interview with Ellen Wilson who has applied for a position in the intermediate grades.

Sarah Yancey

Miss Wilson, we know quite a lot about you from your letter of application, the application form, your credentials from your college placement office, and your college transcript. What we want to do today is to get better acquainted with each other and give you an opportunity to find out something about what we have to offer you. Let's begin by asking what grade you would really like to teach and why?

Ellen Wilson

Well, I think I like the fifth grade best of all. Although I have had some experience with second grade and sixth grade, I did may student teaching with fifth-graders and I think I really did my best work there. I like ten-year-olds very much. I found it much harder to work with primary children.

Sarah Yancey

Your faculty advisor says you worked with some rather able fifth-graders. How do you think you might get along with slow-learning children?

Ellen Wilson

Oh, I think I could work with them, too. I was with slower groups last year. Your have to be a little more patient and, of course, you don't expect nearly as much. But I don't rally think you teach differently.

Sarah Yancey

You know, of course, Miss Wilson, that this is a large city and we have elementary schools in communities representing many different socio-economic levels. In what kind of school do you think you would like to work?

Ellen Wilson

Well, I don't think it would matter much as long as they were not primary children. Of course. If I had my choice I would like to looks pupils like the ones I had in student teaching. That was a higher economic level. I wouldn't hesitate to try a class in an underprivileged district, through.

Sarah Yancey

Of course, we have many assignments to make. I couldn't tell you just now where you will be placed. You have been very helpful, though, in indicating your feelings about it. We would want to assign you where you would be happy and make your best contribution to boys and girls. Let's change the direction of questioning a little. Have you done much work with children outside of your work in college?

Ellen Wilson

Yes, I've been a camp counselor and a playground leader. Then I have worked with the church school and for one of my college classes I worked with underprivileged children in a settlement house.

Sarah Yancey

That's fine. Have you belonged to any organisations in college?

Ellen Wilson

Yes, I was a member of the Elementary Education Club and served on the student council. I've always been active in the YWCA, and I have served on several campus committees.

Sarah Yancey

What kind of reading do you do in your spare time?

Ellen Wilson

Well, since this is my last semester I've been pretty busy and haven't had much time for anything but school work. I really haven't read any novels this year. I do try to look at news magazines, but I must confess I don't have time for much more than the front page of the newspaper I try to listen to the news on the radio, though, and I find time for some of the music programmes on television.

Sarah Yancey

Where would you say the greatest public concern about education is today.

Ellen Wilson

From what I've heard and a little reading, perhaps programmes for gifted children and perhaps science in the schools, or may be both of these together. It seems to me, though, that people need to visit schools more. I thought the teachers worked very hard at it where I did my student teaching.

Ellen Wilson

I might just as well confess that I haven't I did hear one television panel.

Sarah Yancey

Miss Wilson, so far I have been asking all the questions. Perhaps you have some you would like to ask.

Ellen Wilson

Yes, I do. If I come to your school system, what would my salary be?

Sarah Yancey

Here's our salary schedule. You can see what your beginning salary would be. Of course, you must figure on some deductions such as income tax and teachers' retirement.

Ellen Wilson

I was wondering, too, how large a class am I likely to have?

Sarah Yancey

Well, we try to hold our class load to thirty pupils, but we can't always do that. It will depend somewhat on the way the principal organises his schedule.

Ellen Wilson

As you know, Miss Yancey, I do not live in your city. What kind of living conditions can I expect to find here?

Sarah Yancey

We try to help you find a suitable place to live. Mrs. Nelson in our office has a list of places available. Sometimes two or more of our teachers rent an apartment together. Is there anything else. I could tell you?

Ellen Wilson

No, those were the questions which bothered me.

Sarah Yancey

I think, then, that this covers most of the items we have in mind. I believe you would be happy in our school system and we are pleased with you. However, we always take a little time to think about you after we have seen you, and I know that you will want to think about us. You will hear from us definitely in a few days. When you do receive your contract, be sure to return it promptly.

Sarah Yancey

I shall. Thank you very much, Miss Yancey I've enjoyed meeting you.

From the report of the interview you can surmise the easy, informal way in which it was conducted. Miss Yancey took the leadership, but, at the same time, Ellen had an opportunity to express herself and to ask questions. Do not expect, however, that all interviews are conducted exactly in this way. The structure of the interview and the questions asked will vary from situation to situation. Some interviews will be cozy and informal, others stiff and formal, and there will be those in between. After a few experiences, you will be able to "spot" the techniques and adjust your approach accordingly.

MAINTAINING PROFESSIONAL ETHICS IN SECURING A POSITION

Determining the professional procedures in applying for and accepting a teaching position is not always easy for the beginner. Until voa-actually begin to apply for positions, the process may seem to be simple and straightforward—you complete the needed forms, you are interviewed, if you are offered the position, you say "yes" or "no". Actually however, you are very likely to find yourself facing situations that are complicated and confusing. As a matter of fact, even the veteran teachers is sometimes at a loss regarding the ethical step to take. Many of the problems involving professional ethics about which you may find yourself uncertain will enter around whether to apply for more than one position at a time; how much information to give employing officials; how long to delay in signing a contract if one is offered to you; and how and under what circumstances to ask to be released from a contract already signed.

Apply for as many positions as you wish. You may hear comments in professional circles that imply that it is unethical to apply for more than one position at a time. Just what reasoning is back of this in uncertain. Perhaps it stems from a belief that when there is a shortage of teachers it is unfair to arouse false hopes in the minds of four or five employing officials at once. Certainly, in times when teachers were abundant and positions scarce, persons just out to college often applied for many positions before they found employment. The fact that conditions of supply and demand have changed does not make it any less proper for teachers today to apply for several positions at once. It is better to turn down an offer or two than not to secured the tape of position you desire because you wait for Superintendent Smith to make up his mind before you file your application with Superintendent Brown.

The ethics of applying for teaching positions are simple. Apply for a many positions as you wish. Do not panic, however, and "broadcast" applications to school systems which seem unlikely to offer you the kind of position in which you feel you would be successful. Be selective. investigate carefully, using the most competent advice available to you, and then apply only to those school systems in which it seems likely that you will become a successful teacher. At least until the shortage elementary teachers has abated considerably, you stand and good chance eventually locating the type of position you prefer unless factors beyond your control restrict severely the geographic area in which you must be located.

You should make every effort to be courteous and tactful in your relationships with prospective employers, whether or not you are offered position. Certainly, you should show enthusiastic interest in every position for which you are interviewed, even though the tenor of the interview makes you increasingly dubious as to whether you would accept employment if it were offered to you. It is a thoughtful (and prudent) move to write a letter thanking an employing officer for giving you an interview, even though you are not offered a position. This is a courtesy that will cause you to be remembered favourably and perhaps contacted the next time there is an opening.

You also have a professional obligation to keep everyone who is interested in you—including the director of your placement office—informed of your progress. After you have accepted a position, be prompt a notifying other employers who are still considering your application that you are no longer interested. By so doing you may save busy school officials unnecessary expenditure of time and efforts and yourself embarrassment. Little things sometimes make big and lasting impressions. Is not brand yourself in the eyes of placement officials and of empowers to whom you might at a later date be applying for another position as someone insensitive to the administrative problems faced by employing officials.

Be honest, open, and aboveboard with school officials. Because you inexperienced in applying for teaching positions, you may have tendency to withhold information which, in reality, might be helpful to you in securing an appointment. School officials want the facts from you. They respect straightforward and above board statements. kindness and honesty will react in your favour. If there is any type of teaching situation in which you doubt your competence, say so. In a school system to any size, your prospective employer may be able to consider another assignment for you. In a small system, it may at least be possible to plan to give you special help at your point of weakness. Certainly, if there are elements in the situation which make your probable success very dubious, it is best to discover them before you accept employment.

Be equally frank if you are asked about other position for which you have applied. An employing officer often faces a difficult task in filling his vacancies. He has a right to know what his chances of securing you are likely to be. Particularly is it important that you be honest with him regarding your intentions if you definitely prefer another position and would consider what he has to offer only if the other job does not materialise. Furthermore, employing officials within a reasonable geographic radius are likely to match notes on candidates for positions. An attempt to keep several persons "on the string" by concealing your moves often leads only to building in every body's eyes a reputation for being unprofessional.

Above all, do not be afraid to ask questions. In your desire to secure a position and your inexperience with employing officials, you may be hesitant in asking for information which you must have in order to make an intelligent decision regarding whether or not to accept the position. Questions which deal with school organisation, salaries, supervision, promotion policies, pensions and retirement, professional improvement, and housing are among the types that you might ask. The only restriction is that you be courteous, tactful, and cheerful and that your questions be in good taste.

Decide promptly whether or not to accept the position offered to you. Once you have been offered a teaching position, you have a professional obligation to decide promptly whether or not you wish to accept it. This does not mean that you must accept at once if offered a contracts at the conclusion of the interview or that you must return it with your signature by the next mail. You should, however, make up your mind within a reasonable time. Sometimes the employing official will specify a time limit, for example, three days or five days. If this is the case, you must be prompt, for the official may want to offer the position to someone else. The fact that the contract was sent to your indication that you were the first choice. Often there will be a second choice person waiting to hear. You have no right to be dilatory beyond the time limit.

Occasionally circumstances beyond your control will cause you want to delay your decision beyond the deadline given you. You may be waiting to hear from another position slightly more to your liking or there may be personal factors which cause you to be doubtful regarding how long you will be in the community. You need not necessarily refuse a situation because you cannot make up your mind within the time limit. First, talk it over with the employing official. If he feels that the deadline must stands, then you have no choice but to make to your mind. He may, however, be able to extend the deadline or to employ you on the understanding that you will be released without prejudice if the factors which you feared might force you to break our contract do materialise. It is quite within the bounds of professional ethics, too, to contract a second employer from whom you have been hoping to hear and ask when you can expect to have his decision. you may raise ethically with an employing officer any problem you face of deciding whether to sign a contract. The only unprofessional move is to conceal information which you know has an important bearing upon you to make up your mind.

After four years in college, living with some very natural doubts regarding whether you will be given an opportunity to practice your profession, there is always a tendency to accept the first position that you were offered. This is a tendency which it will be well to resist unless the position is exactly what you want. There are cycles in teacher placement about which you should know. Many superintendents prefer to the teachers before May 15, and you may be one of those who is employed prior to that date. There is another cycle immediately after education. By that time, the school year is ending and superintendents have had a better opportunity to inventory their vacancies for next year. Your may be the one to secure a position at this time—between June 15 and July 1. After July 1, superintendents usually take vacations, concerning in late July and early August to find additional vacancies. Placement directors know that some of the best positions are available 4 August. If you have the fortitude to take a chance, you can usually get just what you want even this late in the summer. This advice is given not to encourage you to wait until August, but to reassure that you can usually locate exactly the position you want if you have each offer carefully, make your decisions within the limits special and refuse to be panicked if you do not find just what you desire immediately.

Consider carefully before you ask to be released from a contract. A contract is a document which binds both parties concerned to certain obligations. It cannot be broken without the consent of both parties. It is assumed that when you sign a contract you intend to fulfil your obligations and you have the right to expect the board of education which offers you the contract to do likewise. You should never break a contract without the consent of the board of education and then only for the most compelling and urgent reasons. You do not, for example, ask to be released from one contract simply because you have received an offer of a better teaching position. You might, however, ask to be released because the urgent personal reasons—marriage, removal to a distant community, or personal or family illness.

If you do find it necessary to ask for a release from your contract discuss the facts frankly and honestly with he appropriate school official. School officials are reasonable people and will release you without prejudice if they are convinced of your sincerity and good intent. They will usually release you, too, if you don't have good reasons, but such action is often to your disadvantage. Sometimes a derogatory memorandum is place din your file and your placement office notified that the school system considers you an unreliable prospect.

If you are to become a respected member of the teaching profession you must take care to maintain your professional reputation. This you can do if you are honest, frank, and judicious. Everyone—employers college officials, supervisors—is as anxious as yourself to see you placed where you will be successful. Fulfill you obligations with matriculation care.

REFERENCES

Eye, Glen C., and Lane, Willard R., *The New Teacher Comes to School.* New York Harper and Bothers, 1956, Pp. xii + 376.

Huggett. Albert J., and Stinnett, T.M. *Professional Problems of Teachers,* New Yark: The Macmillan Co., 1956. Pp. ix + 468.

Richey, Robert W. *Planning for Teaching,* Second Edition. New York: McGraw Hill Book Co., 1958. Pp. xv + 550.

Yauch, Wilbur A.; Bartels, Martin H.; and Morris, Emmet. *The Beginning Teachers,* New York: Henry Holt and Co., Pp. xii + 339.

14

Helping Beginners to Grow

"We plan together right from the first. I try to help the student to feel that he is only responsible for the classroom. As the year goes on, he takes on more and more responsibilities for carrying out the plans."

"I try to draw the student into all discussions with the children so that they will become used to the idea that two of us are there to help them."

"Every Friday afternoon we have an hour's conference when we do most of our actual planning."

"Our student teachers worked right along with the regular faculty on special programs."

"Our principal takes time to acquaint the students with over-all school policies. We also try to find time for them to work in the office and to visit other classroom."

"My student and I checked the college rating sheets independently and then referred about them."

"Three-way conferences with the college supervisor have been very valuable; so are the duplicate copies of notes made by the college supervisor."

The student's reports on the discussions in the student-teaching seminar were most helpful. I value the new ideas."

Increased participation in teacher education by public school personnel through student-teaching programs is a significant indication that education has "come of age" as a profession. This important development is not merely a matter of necessity where the numbers of prospective teachers have overtaxed the available classrooms in the laboratory and demonstration schools. It is, above all, recognition that all members of a profession have a mutual responsibility for inducting europhytes into that profession. From the standpoint of the teacher-education institution, the establishment of comprehensive student-teaching programs indicates an increased awareness of the value of providing extended contacts with many types of school situations. Working closely with an experienced professional colleague is one of the most significant aspects of the education of the teacher-to-be.

Actually the practical experience known as *student teaching* is part of a continuum which begins with planned contacts with children and schools in the first days of the prospective teacher's college work and extends into the early years of his professional employment. In this continuum those professional teachers who share their classrooms during what is ordinarily the potential teacher's longest and most responsible contact with a group of children have a particularly important part to play. It is in recognition of this role that many prefer the title "cooperating teacher" to that of "supervising teacher" or class teacher." The education of teachers today is truly a cooperative enterprise—school officials, classroom teachers, college faculty members and students, all working hand in hand. No matter how carefully related to the classroom previous college courses have been, there is a high hurdle to be taken when the student teacher attempts to transform professional theory into classroom practice appropriate to the needs of a particular group of pupils. This is the point in the student's growth where the experience of working cooperatively with a skilled classroom teacher becomes invaluable.

Students may be assigned to cooperating teachers in a variety of ways. In laboratory and demonstration schools, working with students is a responsibility which is an accepted part of the job. In some public schools, cooperating teachers are invited to participate in the student-teaching program by the college personnel. In others, the superintendent, the principal, or the supervisor makes the assignment. Ideally teachers should be consulted before the responsibility for a student is added to the not inconsequential professional obligations which are already their lot—for responsibility it is, regardless of the satisfactions and rewards it brings. Whatever the procedure by which they are selected, conscientious teachers frequently have misgivings regarding their ability to be of help. What kinds of experiences will have to be provided? How much responsibility should the student be asked to take and how rapidly? What type of help will a cooperating teacher be expected to give? What will be the expectations of college personnel?

The purpose of this chapter is to assist cooperating teachers in providing suitable experiences for students, but students themselves and college supervisors may also find it useful. To be effective, the student-teaching program has to be the result of cooperative planning. Experiences of cooperating teachers can be shared. Students usually have worth-while suggestions. College supervisors have the advantage of years of experience in working with successive groups. Each of the key persons involved needs to understand the goals, problems, and methods of the others. An open-minded attitude on the part of each person concerned is the foundation of a functional program of practical experience for the potential teacher.

WHAT KINDS OF EXPERIENCE WILL THE STUDENT TEACHER NEED?

What should be the objectives of the student-teaching program? The kinds of experiences that will be needed by any specific student will be determined by several factors. Among these are the time allotted to the student-teaching program by the college, the nature of the student's previous contacts with children, the ways in which theory has been related to practice in his college classes, the amount of transfer from college courses to the actual classroom situation, and the student's personal traits and attitudes. Just how each of these factors would be weighed depends on the particular student.

There is, among teacher-education institutions, no commonly accepted allotment of time for organized field experience. The plan followed by the individual college will be influenced by such factors as the existing philosophy of education, the availability of teaching centers, the number and kinds of professional programs, and in some cases, the type of daily schedule which can be worked out for the individual student. Some student-teaching programs provide classroom experience lasting for a year, others for a semester or half-semester. Some students are required to live in the community—often at a considerable distance from the college—and to spend full time in the school. Others may do their student teaching for a half-day and attend college classes during the other half. Students may even be assigned for less than a half day—period or two—or for two or three half-days a week, or perhaps for one or two full days a week. It is not unusual to find variations in time allotments even within the same college. Such variations make generalizations regarding how best to utilize the student's time in the classroom almost impossible.

The trend today is toward providing extended contacts

with children or to student teaching. Notwithstanding this students will come with varied background experiences with boys and girls. These may include playground or club work, orientation visits to schools, guided observation in a variety of classrooms, and quite often participation experiences with a single class or group of children for an extended period. On the other hand, there will be some students who have had little or no experience in the classroom. Such diversity will result in very different needs, especially in the early part of the student-teaching experience. Some students will be ready to take over the class after a short period of familiarization; others will require a more gradual initiation to full-fledged responsibility.

One does not learn to teach from the textbook alone. Watching children learn and relating theory to practice are obvious accompaniments of a well-rounded program of teacher education. Nevertheless, college courses will vary widely in the degree to which the work is correlated and integrated with classroom experience. In some colleges, separate methods courses may be taught by three or four different instructors with little parallel classroom experience or even relationship among the courses. In others the work may consist of an integrated "core" program with extensive coordinate classroom activities. In some institutions, this core may be simultaneous with student teaching. Under this plan, the student will be making his first theoretical analyses of teaching procedures at the same time that he is becoming acquainted with his own classroom. Students from such varied backgrounds will come with widely divergent needs for guidance in their first contacts with their student-teaching assignment.

Even in the case of two students with identical college backgrounds there will be differences in ability to apply what has been learned to the new situation. One of the most challenging problems in teacher education is that of assuring maximum transfer from the college classroom to the student-teaching classroom. In common with other learners beginning teachers develop concepts gradually; there will be differences in the degree to which they see as applicable what was talked over in the college class last year. Although the trend toward providing classroom contacts which parallel closely the college psychology and methods courses has been of major help in illuminating what might otherwise be purely academic discussions, both student and cooperating teacher must expect that many principles and procedures will have to be worked through again in relation to the student-teaching situation.

To the possibilities of differences in professional competence must be added personal differences in academic accomplishment, in talents, in sights, in ability to adjust to new situations. Perhaps more important, students will bring differing feelings of adequacy in human relations and differing levels of aspiration. For some, any day that seems less than perfection may represent a major threat to self-esteem. Others, from the start, will take in stride the challenges, satisfactions, frustrations, and surprises of learning to work with thirty or more youngsters.

Just as the needs, capacities, and previous experiences of the individuals in a classroom determine the specific goals for the year, so the professional and personal qualifications of each student influence the objectives of his student-teaching program. Ideally, the student-teaching program should be flexible, continuing for as short or as long a period as is needed for the student to achieve a desirable level of competence. Practically, in most cases, the length of the experience will be defined, and the problem will be to start where the student is and to help him proceed as far toward attaining competence in dealing with the professional problems of teaching as his capacities and previous experience will allow.

What are the major professional problems with which beginning teachers (and, for that matter, all teachers) must be able to cope? Student teachers, as well as cooperating teachers, would do well to think about the goals suggested in the remainder of this section. Awareness of the types of competence they will be expected to acquire can help students to make the most of the classroom responsibilities they are asked to assume.

It is important that students have experience in developing effective human relationships in the classroom. Among the problems that cause beginning teachers to consider leaving the profession, discipline ranks high. The student teacher must have ample opportunity to learn how to establish himself as the democratic leader of his group. He needs security in his ability to help pupils develop increasing self-control. He must acquire as automatic a goodly number of those common-sense procedures by which experienced teachers achieve a classroom atmosphere conductive to happy living and smooth working relationships.

Establishing good work habits and a democratic classroom atmosphere only part of the problem of developing effective human relationships. Every teacher is likely to have in his class one or more individuals those inner tensions make it difficult for them to adjust to the patterns of behavior expected of the group. It is essential that the student teacher have experience in helping to guide these pupils, in being responsible for studying them and deciding what to do in group situations in such youngsters find it difficult to operate. He needs to see how parent conferences may be used to help such children and to become familiar with the services of the professional workers who can assist him. In short, in so far as he is able, the student teacher needs to take responsibility for every aspect of the problem of developing effective human relationships in his group.

Experience in guiding the learning activities in the classroom is needed. Responsibility for the growth of a group of boys and girls means guiding their learning—in the development of skills, in the acquisition of information and the formation of concepts and generalizations, in creative expression. If he is to feel secure in his decisions in his first full-time position, the beginner should have had experience in planning independently for each step of the teaching process—evaluating the needs and present level of competence of his group deciding what new goals are appropriate, deciding how he will achieve these goals, locating his resource materials, and executing and evaluating his plan. He needs to feel secure in planning activities as simple as an effective spelling lesson and as complicated as an extensive and highly organized unit of work.

Sometimes a beginner who can formulate effectively the plans for a single lesson meets his Waterloo when it comes to scheduling the activities for the day or managing the experiences of groups and individuals working at many levels of competence. Although the student teacher will undoubtedly assume responsibility gradually, before his assignment has ended he needs to have learned what it is like to take full charge of scheduling and guiding the activities of his class—for deciding how his time as the teacher is to be spent, for worrying about the half-dozen children who finish early and stand at his elbow asking what to do next, for deciding whether to wait for the youngster who invariably finishes last, for making sure that all the groups working on special projects have their plans clearly in mind. In other words, he must become aware of just how much planning has to go into an effective day.

Not all learning activities are confined to the regular classroom schedule. The beginning teacher will have to decide how best to help his pupils profit from attending an all school concert, from cooperating in a school service project, from abiding by school regulations in the lunchroom. Then there are Halloween, Thanksgiving, Christmas, Valentine's Day, birthday celebrations, special assemblies. Some pupils may be on the student council, the safety patrol, an office helpers' list. All these extra activities must be worked into the school day. The prospective teacher needs to know how to do this. He must be able to plan for a regular program, but his life in the first classroom of his own is likely to be miserable indeed if he does not know how to adjust his carefully laid plans to the exigencies of unforeseen events.

Experience in evaluation and reporting to parents is essential. Taking full responsibility for deciding what shall go into a day involves evaluation—identifying pupils' strengths and weaknesses and deciding upon appropriate next steps. This calls for sensitivity in studying children while they are at work as well as ability to evaluate written work and skill in using a variety of teacher-made and standardized instruments for measurement. Perhaps most important, it calls for ability to set standards—to judge what can appropriately be expected of individuals, to decide what new levels of achievement to hold.

Every teacher must also be able to translate what he knows about individuals into symbols or words that will convey accurate meaning to the child, his parents, and the next teacher who works with him. How to conduct a conference with a parent, what precautions to take in writing a letter home, what to say in a home visit and how to invite oneself to a home, how to interpret the school program to parents during a school open house or a class program—these are all problems a first-year teacher must face. Such problems are handled with security only after there has been firsthand experience.

Proficiency in handling housekeeping and clerical responsibilities must be acquired. Many a first-year teacher is overwhelmed by the multitude of minor details that must be taken care of in the course of a normal day. Moneys have to be collected, attendance reports kept, supplies ordered, visual aids secured, special requests from the office met. It is all too easy for cooperating teachers to continue to share these responsibilities on the basis that two pairs of hands can get chores done faster than one. This is not, however, a favor to the student. Beginners need to become thoroughly familiar with the types of records that may be expected of them. They must also be helped to realize their obligation to carry out their own clerical responsibilities promptly and accurately. Perhaps most important, they must learn, through ample firsthand experience, how to manage the classroom program so that work proceeds smoothly while administrative responsibilities are being met.

The student teacher needs to participate as a member of the faculty. Some of the beginning teacher's anxieties relate to school. The student-teaching experience should provide activities that prepare for operating as an effective faculty member. The new teacher must understand the principal's role and the responsibilities of teachers to him. He needs to be aware of the interrelated functions of the school nurse, the custodian, the lunchroom personnel, and other persons who also have some responsibility for the welfare of boys and girls. Lunch room supervision, hall duties, special assignments—these are obligations which are part of the teacher's work. Some knowledge of them is essential. Perhaps equally important, the beginner needs the "feel of the interpersonal relationships characteristic of a closely knit school faculty—the ways committees operate, the problems that are discussed around the luncheon table, the social events, the joking and easy in formality that make for group morale. These are important experiences if the student is to be a contributing faculty member next year.

Skill in self-evaluation must be developed. The ultimate objective of the student-teaching program, then, is to provide the student with the varied and wide experiences which will permit him to operate as nearly like a full-time faculty member as his assignment and his capacities will allow. The student-teaching experience will not have made its fully contribution, however, unless the student has learned to evaluate his own competence and to plan for his own further growth. He needs opportunities to look objectively at his strengths and to identify those areas in which he feels least sure of himself. Where the student teaching program makes its maximum contribution, the student share actively in planning for his own growth experiences. Only the student, with the help of his cooperating teacher and college supervisor, can determine the combination and proportion of activities which will insure optimum growth.

HELPING STUDENT TEACHERS FEEL AT HOME

How to help the student teacher to feel that he is accepted in the classroom is a first and very practical concern of many cooperating teachers. Much depends upon the feelings of security developed when the first contracts are made. In some situations the student teacher will be responsible for meeting the cooperating teacher before he reports to the school. This makes a preliminary conferences possible, perhaps at the schools where the student can see the classroom and become acquainted with some of the teaching aids. Sometimes the student-teaching assignment will begin with the first day of school. This frequently alleviates some of the tensions of beginning, since all are concerned with becoming acquainted—pupils, cooperating teacher, and student. There will be other situations in which the student comes after schools has begun, and there is a very little opportunity for any preliminary contacts. In such cases care must be wisely exercised to insure that the student becomes a part of the group as rapidly and as easily as possible. Whatever the plan governing the beginning of the student-teaching assignment, cooperating teachers will face problems of how to help the beginning teacher to feel secure and easy in his relations with themselves; how to assist him in becoming established as a teacher in the eyes of the pupils; and what steps will help him feel at home in the schools faculty and the community.

The beginner needs to feel secure in his relations with his cooperating teacher. It is safe to say that most beginners approach the student-teaching experience with two major concerns, both within the area of human relations: how they will get along with their cooperating teachers and how they will be accepted by their pupils. It is important both for cooperating teacher and for student to realize that the cooperative relations they desire will not usually emerge full-blown the first day they meet. Adjustments by both persons are likely to be needed before easy working relationships are achieved.

In the first few days many little things can contribute

to a student's feelings of security in his relationships with his cooperating teacher. Students report with satisfaction comments such as, "I am always so glad to have someone to share the responsibility for these children"; "I enjoy very much working with you people from the college"; "There are so many things we can do for these youngsters when there are two of us"; "We've been looking forward to you; the children were quite disappointed when we had no one last semester." On the other hand, too frank a sharing of concerns during the first few days can arouse anxieties. "I wondered if a I should have a student when this group is so slow, but Mr. Jackson talked me into it," "I'm afraid you'll find the dreadfully old-fashioned; I've been away from college for a long time"; "I must confess I was a little concerned when I heard you were coming; Miss Simonds worried so much about here student last year." Phrasing expectations in overly glowing terms in an effort to help a student to feel secure can also cause tensions. "I'm counting on you to show me all the latest methods, you know"; "I'm glad to see that you play the piano; we'll expect some wonderful experiences in music this year."

Students comment with appreciation on many specific steps taken to help them feel at home. Knowing whether to hang one's coat with the children's or in the teacher's closet, where to sit, whether to put one's books on the teacher's desk, whether to borrow the teacher's copies of textbooks or to take some from the shelves for children, whether classroom books may be taken home—these may represent more crucial problems when one is anxious to be accepted than they would appear on the surface. Knowing whether to move about the room while the children are working or to sit still and whether to answer the questions of children who come to one for help, raise other dilemmas where specific indications of what to do can be very reassuring. There can also be uncertain moments during recess or lunch breaks. Should one "tag along" or seem to have one's own plans made? Is the teacher's room for the use of students, too? Although students typically will have been advised in college pre-planning sessions not to hesitate to ask when they are uncertain, it can sometimes be quite a struggle to decide whether to raise a question that might make one appear hopelessly naive and uninformed. The first steps of becoming acquainted can be made much easier if cooperating teachers will be particularly aware of the values of being outgoing and definite in their advice.

It is a major contribution to a beginner's feelings of acceptance to realize from the start that he is going to have a share in planning for the well-being of the class. On the other hand, there needs to be reassurance that he is not going to be left without support. "She asked me what kind of news I thought they should have on their first bulletin board," reported Arnold Stevenson. "How could I know?" Most cooperating teachers develop ways of thinking their plans aloud during the first few weeks so that students become involved in the process without having to make the full decision themselves. "We probably should try to have a fairly good ideas of how well they read by the end of the week." "Have you seen teachers make a tally of language errors from a set of papers like these? I think we would find it revealing." "Perhaps we should take time tomorrow to reorganize their seating. Did you notice how badly that group in the corner fell apart?

The typical beginner often comes apprehensive about how rapidly he may be asked to take on responsibilities and sometimes fearful lest he not be capable of carrying out his first assignments. Cooperating teachers can ease the tension considerably by indicating some of the procedures they have found most helpful in working with students. It is reassuring to hear from the lips of the persons with whom one is to work closely that there will be time for cooperative planning, that one may start with an activity in which one feels secure, or that one is to be inducted into responsibility gradually.

Perhaps no procedure demonstrates more clearly that one has a place in a new classroom than being given a job to do, even though it may take only a few minutes. On the first day of school this may involve helping children to fill in registration forms, preparing name tags to paste on desks, going with two children to deliver materials to the office, helping individuals with spelling as the youngsters write a short autobiography or a description of their summer activities for their new teacher. If school has already begun, pupils may be invited to go to the student for help in a specific area, a committee may be asked to seek his advice in setting up a bulletin board, the student may be involved by telling something about his college or sharing experience—from his special background.

In giving the student teacher his first taste of responsibility, it is advisable to be specific. Even though the activity seems likely to be one in which he has been engaged before, this is a new situation and there can be understandable anxiety about doing things just right. Advice on how to proceed can often be directed toward the children as well so that there is no seeming coaching from the side line. "Let's all look at the sample here to see just how these cards are to be filled in; then I shall check this half of the room and Mr. Dick will do the other." "Miss Grayson will serve as our resource person in spelling today. Let's see, Miss Grayson, won't it be easier if you come to them when their hands are up rather than having everyone come back to you? And would someone like to tell Miss Grayson how we're trying to use spelling to help us learn to use the dictionary?" "We're lucky Mr. Anson came today. This is just when we needed somebody new to look at our mural. Mr. Anson, the mural committee has the list of things we said a good mural should accomplish. Would you like to help them discuss one point at a time?"

The beginner needs to feel accepted by the class. How shall the student teacher be introduced to the pupils? It is safe to say that regardless to the exact phrasing used older pupils, particularly, will recognize at he is from the college and that he is there to learn more about teaching. Sometimes their devotion to him and concern for his success are touching. "What did you think of your student?" asked one alert to grader of the college supervisor. "Don't you think he deserves A?" Don't worry, Mr. Jackson," said one group that normal lighted in seeing how precarious they could make the situation, "when your supervisor's here we won't let you down." "We like Miss Sharp," said a second-grader. "Can't you fix it so she can stay with us all year?"

Even though the pupils are often aware of the student teacher's status, it is helpful to introduce him as a teacher rather than as a student. ("Mr. King is going to work with us this semester. Next year he'll have a class of his own. We should accomplish a lot with two teachers to help.") A number of steps can be taken to demonstrate from the start that the student is, indeed, another teacher. Drawing him into the discussions helps. His advice can be asked in areas where he is known to have competence. Involving him in activities where he can be of service to children, such as those indicated in the preceding section, does much to establish him with the group. When this is done, it is important to see that pupils actually do turn to him for help in whatever areas he has assumed responsibility.

("Mr. Smith is helping you with that; suppose you ask him.") It is also helpful to plan early activities which place the student teacher in front of the class as a whole in situations that are not too likely to tempt the venturesome to try to discover how much latitude he will allow. Depending on the particular situation, experiences with the total group such as the following may be considered: taking attendance, reading a story, sharing a special experience, dictating a list of spelling words, escorting the class down the hall to the library, walking out with the lines at noon.

A student teacher can establish himself more rapidly with a group if he knows names. He will probably have been advised to make his own seating charts. Procedures that will aid him in matching names and faces can be helpful. Children can be encouraged to introduce themselves as the student works with a small committee. In the early fall games to help children learn one another's names can involve both cooperating teacher and student. Seeing that each child writes his name clearly on his written work enables the newcomer to spot the names as he moves around the room giving help. Even the rather routine secretarial activities of preparing attendance books, taking roll, and checking registration cards may be of value.

Individuals begin to stand out more clearly when one knows a little of their backgrounds. Students will probably come prepared to study pupils intensively when the occasion offers. In the first few weeks projects for the children such as writing a short autobiography or developing a bulletin board of pictures and descriptions of home and families can be particularly, he is beginning to know pupils as individuals. It can also be of value to have access to cumulative records, although these are often best looked at first in conference situations where the cooperating teacher's insights can temper the student's judgment. In addition, many cooperating teachers use a good share of the early conference periods to discuss with students the needs of individuals.

It is important to be sure that the student is acquainted early with specific classroom regulations—agreements regarding when pencils are to be sharpened, how people are to be excused to leave the room, when one may get a drink. When the student knows of these specific agreements, he is better prepared to forestall ingenious attempts to play one adult against another. Beginners need to be advised specifically with regard to their responsibility for the behavior of individuals when a cooperating teacher is at work with the class. Everyone is to have books away, but Johnny has a comic book on his knee; Billy has been taking delicious tugs at Janie's braids with one eye on the newcomer in the back of the room; people are supposed to be paying attention to the planning session, but Caroline is addressing explanatory comments under her breath to the intriguing new source of adult attention; the cooperating teacher is called into the hall and everyone begins to get silly—what is the newcomer supposed to do? Unless there are unusual circumstances, most cooperating teachers expect the student to make the appropriate move as a teacher in such situations, but without specific reassurance he may be uncertain whether this will be acceptable. Isn't is a little presumptuous for a student to motion to a child to put a book away after the cooperating teacher has already asked for this? Won't this give the impression that one thinks the cooperating teacher does not know what is going on?

Ultimately, of course, the student teacher must establish himself with the class on the strength of his own leadership. Often it is helpful to leave him with the class for short periods of time—to walk in a little are, leaving him to get people in their seats and ready to work; to run an errand while he is teaching; to send him ahead to the library with the children. Well-meant efforts to control the situation from the side lines often contribute to the student's feelings of insecurity and inadequacy and sometimes convince the class that here is someone with little or no authority in his own right, establishes part of the student in many aspects of human understanding, good teaching, and common-sense organizational ability.

The beginner needs to feel at home in the school. A student teacher needs to feel a part of the school as a whole as well as a member of the classroom to which he is assigned. Principals have developed a number of devices that help in this. In many schools the student's name is entered on the regular faculty roster. If teachers sign in the time of their arrival, so does he. If there is a handbook for new faculty the student is supplied with one. In some schools, principals find time for an early conference with the student teachers in which background information about the school and community is given and school policies are outlined. Sometimes folios of the various forms used in the school system—absence records, order blanks for visual aids, attendance forms—are provided. Students have also been invited to attend faculty meetings. In some situations, it has proved helpful to take the student out of his assigned classroom long enough to enable him to get the "feel" of the school by visiting in other rooms, observing in the offices of the nurse and other special personnel, and perhaps spending a half-day working in the principal's office.

Cooperating teachers can also make definite efforts to help students become acquainted with other teachers. Inviting the student to stay at the school for lunch, if his is a half-day assignment, is a gracious gesture. Normally, the typical intervisitation that goes on before school begins and during breaks offers other opportunities for the student to meet individual faculty members. In some situations students have been included in faculty social affairs. Students have also reported appreciatively opportunities to work with their cooperating teachers on special faculty projects—sharing responsibility for part of a Christmas program, helping with the faculty planning for a Halloween entertainment.

Problems sometimes arise as to how far to involve a student when faculty members face problems of semiconfidential nature that need to be talked through. If the student feels welcome in the lunchroom and in the teachers lounge, he is almost certain, before the year is out to be present when vigorous disagreement with a request from the office is being expressed, concern is being voiced regarding the difficulties of the new teacher down the hall, or information is being shared about problems in the home of some child. There will also be times when another teacher drops by the classroom to discuss a problem that cannot be aired in the hall or the lounge. Such situations can prove awkward for all concerned, and there is no easy formula for handling them. One general guide might be that the give-and-take of normal faculty disagreements can provide important preparation for participating as a regular faculty member next year, provided there is an opportunity for the student teacher to discuss these professionally afterwards. A second guide probably should be that it is important to explain to the student frankly whey certain types of information cannot be shared with him and to give him advice regarding what his behavior should be when situations arise that seem to have confidential aspects. Should he go on working with his bulletin board or stop to be sociable when the principal walks in? If he doesn't come over to that will he be thought shy or distant? It is helpful to be told specifically that it is quite in order to greet the visitor and then go on with one's work. It is reassuring, also to be invited specifically to join a conversation when this is appropriate. Before entering upon student teaching, students probably will have engaged in discussions regarding professional behavior in a school. Here again, however, the aid of the cooperating teacher is needed in making the transition to the specific situation.

The student teacher needs to be accepted by parents and community. Over the semester, it is important for the student teacher to come to feel that he is acquainted with the community and accepted by the parents. In some situations, cooperating teachers will face the problem of explaining the importance of the student-teaching program to parents and of gaining the acceptance of the student as a person who is to have at least partial responsibility for their children.

There are many ways of helping the student to feel that he is coming to know parents. Attending Parent-Teacher Association meetings and doing present at an open house when parents are visiting the classroom are among the most obvious. Many cooperating teachers also arrange to take the student with them on a certain number of home mates.

What can be done to interpret the student-teaching program to parents? Probably nothing is more useful than concrete evidence that pupils are benefiting from the presence of another teacher (unless, perhaps, it is the successful job done by a first-year teacher who has graduated from the same program). The way in which the student teacher is introduced to the pupils (and is talked about at home) can contribute to his acceptance. So can his first classroom responsibilities if they are successful and interesting to the pupils. It is usually possible, also, as parents visit to point to a project that has been the student's special responsibility. In most elementary schools it is customary to plan at least one class project to which parents are invited. This provides another opportunity to point out the share the student has had in the development of the project. Often, the student's presence makes it possible either for student or cooperating teacher to give time to a group in need of special help. Parents whose youngsters have been the recipients of this attention tend to value the student-teaching program. In addition, it can be very reassuring to parents to be told the ways in which the student and the cooperating teacher are working together the planning sessions, the conferences, the cooperative teaching, that insure a rich program for pupils. Faculty supervisors can frequently help in giving such explanations. College resources may also be tapped to enrich other aspects of the school program and parents apprised of this. The school which opens its doors to student teachers is assuming a major professional obligation. The success of this cooperative undertaking must be judged by the degree to which the lives of youngsters are enriched here and now as well as by the later success of the student.

HELPING BEGINNERS MOVE INTO FULL RESPONSIBILITY

It would be most unusual if cooperating teachers did not have some misgivings when they face the responsibility of guiding the student teacher through the full range of the professional experiences necessary for a successful first year on the job. An invitation to become a cooperating teacher typically signifies a reputation for devotion to children and exceptional skill in meeting their needs. Naturally there is some trepidation when it comes to trusting the well-being and progress of the pupils to the inexpert hands of a beginner. Nevertheless, the welfare of many future groups of pupils depends on the thoroughness and effectiveness of the student-teaching experience.

Pupils need not suffer, however, if the student teacher's induction into full-time responsibility is skillfully executed He needs to be helped to take on increased responsibility at the pace at which he can handle it successfully. If student teaching is a gradual induction process. The beginner typically brings to each new responsibility a zeal, a desire to provide challenging activities, and a genuine fondness for children that more than counterbalance any lack of adeptness in teaching techniques. What procedures on the part of the cooperating teachers will contribute to successful progress toward full-time teaching?

Early experiences should build security. For what types of activities should a student teacher first take responsibility? There are probably many answers to this question as there are student-teaching situations. A combination of factors may influence the decision in any one room of the student's own feelings of confidence, his competence, the needs of the pupils and the projects in which they are engaged, the way in which the cooperating teacher feels most secure in delegating responsibility.

Ideally, the student himself should express a preference regarding the activities with which he would like to begin. However, some may be reluctant to make suggestions lest they interfere with the cooperating teacher's plans. Others may view every possibility with trepidation, and some will not recognize the hazards involved in their proposals. In the beginning, the cooperating teacher often must be the one to assign specific responsibilities. These early experiences should be selected with two objectives in mind:

to give the student the security that comes from success and to develop the children's ready acceptance of him as a leader because of the quality of his contribution.

Whether or not a student's first major responsibility should be with small group or with the class as a whole depends on the particular student and on the situations that present themselves in his class. Although it is helpful to the student in establishing himself with the group to have some early responsibilities that put him before the class as a whole—talking attendance, escorting the group to the gym, reading a story—an all-class contact more extensive than those just mentioned can be threatening to some students unless it is preceded considerable experience with small groups.

Often a student's special talent makes a good starting point. Janet McCardy reads aloud very well and takes over a primary story and rest period as her first major responsibility. Janice Watson is a talented musician and starts by teaching her first grade some songs. John Abernathy is a veteran whose overseas experiences make it appropriate for him to supervise the sixth-grade group in preparing a map of Europe. Anna Mae Simpson is at home in art and creative dramatics and takes over the group preparing a puppet show. Sally Zelinka has spent several years as a playground leader and feels competent to take her third-grade class out for games.

Frequently, the responsibilities assigned to the student teacher to help him become acquainted with pupils lead directly into his first definite teaching assignment. Kathleen Anderson has been helping with individual spelling problem; now she takes the responsibility for directing the study of a set of words. Jonathan Maxwell has been helping a small group to arrange a current events bulletin board now he works with them to develop their reports to the class. Belinda O'Neill starts by helping a group to appraise their mural and then goes on to guide the work of these youngsters as they plan to add more details. It is not usually a matter of being an observer one day and a teacher the next. The process is gradual, and the difference between the independent responsibility taken on today and that assumed tomorrow can often scarcely be noticed.

Cooperative teaching can provide a smooth transition to increased responsibility. From a student teacher's first venture, the steps which lead to full responsibility for the class may be large or small, rapid or slow, depending on the student, the class, and the cooperating teacher's feeling of security. Cooperative teaching is often helpful in assuring a successful transition to full-time teaching. Both persons work actively with increasing responsibility for leadership being assumed by the student.

In classrooms where pupils are involved democratically in planning and evaluating their activities, it is easy to include the student in planning sessions even while the cooperating teacher is assuming major leadership functions:

Cooperating Teacher

Mr. Cardy and I thought about your projects last nigh; it seemed to us that one good work session would finish them. What do you think?

Alec Cardy

John, you were absent yesterday. We're farther ahead than you think.

Cooperating Teacher

Then you think John's group can wind their work up today, Mr. Cardy?

Alec Cardy

I think so. What do you say, Belinda?

Soon the student will be sufficiently involved in aspects of the program so that it is a simple matter to turn over to him more responsibility for leadership of the planning session:

Cooperating Teacher

Mr. Cardy, the big thing today is to get the play under way, isn't it?

Alec Cardy

That's right. Boys and girls, let's check yesterday's plans here and see what's most important.

Janie

We still don't know whether we want costumes and what scenery we want.

Alec Cardy

Shall we put that down to settle today, then?

Often student teachers take on, as their first independent teaching responsibility, the direction of the work of an arithmetic, a reading, or a spelling group. This is a situation that lends itself readily to cooperative teaching. While the student works with a group in one corner of the room, the cooperating teacher works with a second group in another. Under such circumstances, it can be a valuable experience to the student to be responsible for seeing to it that both groups report of their teachers with the equipment they need and for keeping an eye and those at their seats. Because transitions are awkward for beginners, can be a valuable experience, too, for the student to call the groups back at the end of the period and to supervise them as they put books back and get ready for the activity to follow. If the student merely works with his small group and leaves the cooperating teacher to supervise gathering in papers and getting out materials for the next person, he is failing to develop skills that can make a major contribution in the smooth running of his class next year:

Sand Mix

> Let's look up here, then, so that we'll know what we're doing. Billy's group were going to finish their pictures about the story—is that right?
>
> (Several voices from Billy's group say "Yes, Ma'am.")
>
> Will you get out your pictures right now, please? Now, Miss Sampson wants her people in the back of the room. Do they need anything. Miss Sampson?

Miss Sampson

> Yes; bring a pencil. We're going to try ourselves out on our new words today.

Sandy Mix

> All right. And I want my people to come up here. John, will you get the books for us? Now, before my group begins, is there anyone is Billy's group having any difficulty getting started with your picture? Suppose you finish ahead of us, what might you do next?

Cooperating teaching can also provide a smooth induction into full responsibility for developing an elaborate unit of work in the content fields. In the first unit, the cooperating teacher may take major responsibility for planning with the pupils with the student assisting in clarifying problems and deciding on ways of working. Once plans are laid, both student and cooperating teacher give help. Sometimes each may take specific responsibility for guiding the work of two or three subcommittees; sometimes both circulate, giving help wherever it is needed. Responsibility for all-class activities may be shared. The student may set up a series of demonstrations or work with visual aids in areas where his competence is strongest; the cooperating teacher may take over for others. At the end of the unit, a short culminating activity might be developed under the leadership of the student. Later, the student takes over the complete responsibility for planning, setting up work procedures, and deciding on visual aids and the cooperating teacher serves merely as a resource person as specific committees go to work.

Establishing an atmosphere of cooperative teaching from the beginning has advantages over and above the support it offers to the student as he makes the transition to full-time classroom responsibility. It makes it possible for the cooperating teacher to continue to give special help to individuals without seeming to encroach on the student's area of leadership. There is always a talented child who could be stimulated to venture into new fields if time for individual conferences only permitted, a bright youngster whose zeal for science should be encouraged by a special reading program, a pupil whose difficulties in reading or spelling could be cleared up if only there were time for individual help. Although the student teacher should cope with this range in ability without help before his assignment ends, it would be a tragic misuse of the talents of the two teachers in the room if such youngsters did not receive extra help while it is available.

Cooperative teaching also makes it possible for the cooperating teacher to resume the leadership of an activity for a week or so without seeming to the children to be showing any lack of faith in the student teacher. Thus can be highly desirable when the student has reached a point where he recognizes his own inadequacies and feels the need to observe an experienced teacher's techniques. It is sometimes also desirable for the cooperating teacher to take over an activity in which a student has shown proficiency in order to allow him more time for planning and locating the materials related to a new project. By the end of the student-teaching assignment, of course, the student needs to know from firsthand experience what adjustments in one's personal life it will take to assume full responsibility for planning every aspect of the program. His progress toward successful full-time responsibility may be more rapid, however, if he is afforded temporary relief at points where he must solve a new teaching problem of major proportions.

Increased responsibility should be accompanied by careful planning. As the student begins to take on increased responsibility, the experience ought to offer more than merely an opportunity to experiment with his own ideas about how to teach. There should be joint planning sessions which will enable him to grow through thinking through classroom problems under the guidance of an experienced teacher. These sessions should help to forestall at least some types of difficulties so that the plan the student actually puts into effect results in a richer experience for youngsters (and a more satisfying one for himself) than would have come from his initial inexperienced suggestions. It is true that we learn from experience, but the intellectual consideration of a problem can be a type of learning experience.

In spite of considerable emphasis in college classes, students do not always realize the detail that must go into an effective lesson plan. A common error is to make a plan which gives an outline of facts to be presented but which does not show how the pupils are to be involved to what problems they will be asked to solve, what practice materials they might need, and what help they might be given as the lesson proceed. As any experienced teacher knows, such vague notes in the name of lesson-planning as "take up spelling," "read next story," or "group work" can lead to disaster. Cooperating teachers should not hesitate to request, and students should expect to supply in writing, plans sufficiently detailed for the security of both parties. These should include both unit plans and plans for the day. In contrast to earlier times in teacher education, the student may not have been required in college to use any set pattern for writing his plans, the assumption being that they are an instrument for his personal use and that the form that might be helpful to one person could be relatively ineffective for an other. The cooperating teacher should expect, therefore, to give the student some assistance in developing the type of plan appropriate to the needs of the particular situation. It is often helpful, also, for the student to examine the cooperating teacher's written plans. It is always reassuring to know that experienced teachers actually put into practice what they recommend for others.

Learning to select activities appropriate for a particular class can be a major hurdle for some beginners. It is often helpful if the first planning sessions are cooperative, with teacher and student jointly evaluating the strengths and weaknesses of the children and projecting next steps. What will unscramble the confusion of this social studies committee?—what factors seem to be causing the trouble? are there individual conflicts to take into account? do they lack important skills? with what aspects of their work should they be given special help the next time they meet? What types of reading experiences do these able children need?—what skills seem well mastered? in what areas have they had limited opportunities? Should we be discouraged that yesterday's lesson on capitals seems not to be reflected at all in today's stories? —what follow-up is needed? how many times must a point be repeated before everyone gets it? How should the performance of this class in writing letters be evaluated? —from a college point of view it seems inadequate, but is it appropriate for third grade? Planning sessions such as these, in which the student is encouraged to share his insights and to propose next steps, can make a major contribution to the security with which he begins to plan on his own.

As the student begins to assume more responsibility for independent planning it can be particularly helpful to him to have ample time to formulate his plans. This is not possible for all aspects of the program but there are many points at which generous time for preparation can be allowed. It may be that the units of work in science social studies, and health are outlined in the course of study. If so, the student can be allowed to select well in advance those for which he will assume major responsibility. This will enable him to explore resources fully, to make his block or unit plan in careful detail and to review the subject matter involved. The plan can then be evaluated by the cooperating teacher and discussed with the student while there is still opportunity to make changes.

What does the cooperating teacher do if a student teacher's plans do not develop as his own would? If the plan seems likely to work out successfully, the student should certainly be congratulated on thinking for himself and encouraged to try his wings. If there seems to be an obvious weakness, the problems can be discussed with the student and alternative procedures worked out. Two cautions are in order here. First, the student needs to understand why the alternative procedure is suggested and precisely what problem it is likely to forestall. Second, because it is difficult to use another's idea effectively if it is only half understood, he needs time to think through the new proposal in detail and to incorporate it into his plans. The temptation to suggest that a student change completely his plans for the day, if it is now 8:45 and the youngsters are walking in the door; should be resisted unless he is known to be exceptionally secure and versatile. However fraught with pitfalls, a plan which is the student's own and clearly understood by him has a better chance of success than one suggested by the cooperating teacher whose purposes and reasoning have not been comprehended.

Even though student teachers typically regard student teaching as a learning experience and expect to be given help, there will be some who experience difficulty in accepting suggestions. There will be the occasional student who is so unsure of his own ability that the slightest attempt to raise questions regarding his plans is taken as evidence that he has already failed. Faced with this situations, the cooperating teacher is probably well advised to give praise and encouragement until the student has developed a greater sense of security. There are other students (probably also insecure if one could get below the surface) who find it very difficult to accept the possibility that their proposed course of action might not work. In the face of such resistance, a cooperating teacher may have to grit his teeth and endure failures until the student reaches the point where he can be more objective about advice. Let it be said in defense of this procedure that it is extremely difficult to have so bad a single day that the pieces cannot be picked up tomorrow. Cooperating teachers, too, on their own worst days, have cause to be grateful for the resiliency of youngsters.

Help from the side lines can be made constructive. How does the cooperating teacher occupy himself while the student teacher is in charge of the group? Dare he interrupt if an error is made? Should he try to pass a note to the student or signal with raised eyebrows that something is amiss? Suppose the lesson is dragging far too slowly—can anything be done to speed it up? How far does he allow a disciplinary situation to build up before he steps in?

The answers to questions such as these depend on the complex constellation of factors in the immediate situation. The student's sense of security is a major consideration. With some student teachers, a word or a gesture from the cooperating teacher indicating that something is awry may result in panic. If this seems likely, the only defensible procedure is to take up the problem in conference later, counting on some effective reteaching by the student to rectify the error. Other students think readily on their feet and welcome the help, preferring to be "tipped off" to a point they are missing rather than to have a lesson loess effective than it would otherwise be. Where there are sound relationships between student and cooperating teacher, it is to be hoped that students will feel free to say how they feel regarding interruptions. If the questions is talked through, an understanding can be reached so that both the student and cooperating teacher know how to proceed when the emergency does arise.

The general classroom atmosphere can also make a difference in the ease with which a cooperating teacher can enter into the lesson. If the situation has been one where children, student teacher, and cooperating teacher have been used to cooperative planning each feeling free to contribute his best thinking, it will not seem unusual to the children to hear the cooperating teacher offer a suggestion. At another point, it may be the student who is contributing from the side lines. The following interchanges may illustrate. Linda Nash's cooperating teacher refers to class plans in order to give help:

Linda Nash

Look at the picture on the next page. How do you think the Pilgrims did their washing?

Bobbie

They're right on the ocean. They must have used sea water.

Sally

But if they did, why couldn't they wash their clothes on board ship?

Linda Nash

Let's read what it says about the picture and see if it helps.

Andy

It doesn't say what water they used. But you can't get soap suds from salt water.

Cooperating Teacher

Miss Nash, that's a good question for these people to add to their list, isn't it? I think you'll find some of the other books will tell you.

Linda Nash

All right, let's put it down so we wont' forget it. Thank you for helping us, Mrs. Crosby.

College personnel, too, are sometimes brought into an informal discussion, as was Janie Williams' supervisor.

Bobbie

But we've got to turn him loose or he'll starve. [Bobbie is speaking of a snake brought to the third-grade classroom in the late fall.]

Susan No, he won't. He'll just sleep and if he sleeps outside he'll freeze to death, won't he, Miss Williams?

Janie Williams

I don't know for sure, Susan. Miss McDermit, can you help us?

Cooperating Teacher

I know Mr. Johnson has kept some snakes in the science laboratory, but we'd better talk to him to make sure what they need. What do you think, Dr. Rose?

College Supervisor

I think you folks had better talk to Mr. Johnson. Will you tell me what you found out when I come back next time?

Janie Williams

We'll remember, won't we, boys and girls?

The student's relationships with the children also need to be considered in deciding whether the student had been weak and the lessons dull, one would not add from the side lines another piece of evidence confirming the pupils' feelings. Sometimes, help from the cooperating teacher at the point where the student's relationships with the group are precarious can pull the class entirely away. Many a cooperating teacher has added a comment from the back of the room in a well-meant effort to help, only to find the entire group facing him while the student stood in the front, alone and foresaken. On the other hand, a secure student is often able to establish an "everybody makes mistakes" atmosphere where the pupils themselves help to correct him. "*I think* you've spelled that wrong," says John. "Will you look it up to be sure, John?" replies Sarah Gayner; and, as John makes the correction. "Thank you, John; I'm so glad you caught that before we all wrote it down."

A certain amount of role playing has its advantages in making corrections or additions smoothly at crucial points. The cooperating teacher signals for the floor as would any other pupil, and asks a question or adds a point. "Miss Smith, we're still confused back here. Are we to draw the design for our covers on notebook paper first so that you can see it before we use the colored paper?" "Miss Johnson, several people near me don't seem sure what they're to do until their reading group meets." "Mr. Adamson, I saw that geyser last summer. I wonder if you'd like the boys and girls to hear a little more about it."

Probably the most difficult type of situation in which to work from the side lines in such a way as to give genuine support to the student is in the area of interpersonal relationships—discipline in its broadest connotations. This is an aspect of teaching where it is virtually impossible to enter actively into the situation in order to strengthen the student's hand without, in the long run, weakening it. In the end, he must be the one to demonstrate to the group where his boundaries lie and how firm they are. Although the cooperating teacher can undoubtedly maintain any degree of control he wishes from the back of the room, this typically does not establish the student as a group leader.

In a situation involving classroom control it is possible, by a role playing approach, to alert the student to potential confusion which he has been too engrossed to notice. "We could hear better back here, Mr. Ronson, if the bulletin board committee would use softer voices." "Miss Black, I believe these people used up all their story time because they forgot our plan about putting books away." "Excuse me, Mr. Keller, but three people have been back to ask me what to do next. Would you mind taking a minute to straighten them out?" It is possible, also, to give very firm support aloud to whatever the student teacher has requested. "Not now. Miss Black is waiting for you to put your books away" "Miss Clarkson said only two people at the easel, John. You'll have to wait until she has room for you." "If Mr. Edwards thinks you were too noisy to work in the hall, that's all there is to it. We warned you, remember?" Even though the student's decision reveals his inexperience, it is usually more helpful to group morale to support him and talk it out later than it is to contradict him. Divided discipline is as ineffective at school as at home. Where the student has not realized a school rule exists, it is often still possible to correct the situation without seeming to override him. "I'm sorry, Mr. Garson; I completely forgot to tell you that the traffic is so heavy here we must let these people cross the streets before the safety guards go home. But if you feel they were wasting time, I think we should cut short our story time tomorrow to finish this work."

There are times in the life of any teacher when he must ask other authorities to help with a child presenting unusual behavior problems. For the student teacher, the cooperating teacher may be the one to lend the weight of established authority to the student's newer voice in the case of the youngster who is having difficulty in working cooperatively with others. Typically, it is wise to map out procedures ahead of time. What type of appeal, for example, should be made in the presence of the child? What support should the student expect and the cooperating teacher be ready to give? What follow-up of the cooperating teacher's action should the student plan?

Sandra Polly

I'm sorry, Miss Cresky, but Billy can't seem to leave other people alone. Could he sit here by you and read?

Miss Cresky

Certainly he can. You've had a bad day, haven't you, Billy? Do you want him back, Miss Polly, if he feels he can work with you?

Sandra Polly

Yes. Billy is a very nice painter, and I'm sure the committee will be glad to have him when he's ready to help.

Beyond question, the typical student will need time to make his own mistakes and to establish his own leadership. It would be unwise (and, for that matter, impossible) to guide and supervise his work so carefully that nothing ever goes wrong. Over and above on-the-spot assistance through skillful cooperative planning and teaching, it is important to provide conference time to analyze situations with the student in detail, pointing out as clearly as possible the elements that contributed both positively and negatively to the goals he desired. This important means of helping students to grow is discussed in the next section.

The foregoing presupposes, of course, that college advisory systems prior to student teaching have guided those not suited for the profession into areas more appropriate to their capacities. Where there is no solution that seems to contribute to both the growth of the student teacher and the well-being of the pupils, the youngsters, of course, must come first—and the college supervisor be consulted.

Observation can be a valuable aid to learning. What is the place of observation in the student-teaching experience? Certainly, the full resources of the classroom have not been utilized unless opportunities are afforded to observe an experienced teacher at work. However, the points in the student-teaching sequence at which observation is provided and the specific purposes of the student make a difference in the effectiveness of the experience.

At times, cooperating teachers have placed the entire observation period early—students watch for two or three weeks, perhaps, before the take any active leadership responsibility with the children. This plan has not always been satisfactory, even when a student teacher brings to the experience considerable know-how from classroom contacts the preceding year. The day tends to grow very long, and there seems to come a point of diminishing returns when the subtler aspects of what is going on are lost partly because the student has not had enough close contacts with the youngsters to sense when their needs are being skillfully met and partly because he is not always able to appreciate how effectively another person is avoiding pitfalls until he has tried to handle a situation himself. Students undoubtedly need some opportunities to observe in the early weeks of getting acquainted with a new class and a new cooperating teacher. These observation periods can be profitably interspersed, however, with the types of short-term responsibilities discussed previously as desirable ways to help the student to establish himself with the children.

The focus of the student's first observations should be on problems of getting acquainted. There are names to learn; procedures to acquire for passing papers, collecting books, getting wraps; and countless other activities where some sensible and fairly automatic rules and regulations are needed if thirty or more individuals are to live together peacefully and effectively. Beginners also need the reassurance of having seen the general techniques used by their cooperating teachers in planning with children, handling a reading group, or helping a social studies committee. Students will frequently come armed with general lists drawn up in college classes suggesting what to observe, but it is most helpful in these beginning weeks for cooperating teachers to point out specific aspects of the program or specific ways of working with individuals where it is deemed advisable for the student to follow similar procedures.

Observation can be extended with profit well beyond the beginning days. In situations where there is cooperative teaching some opportunities to observe are achieved in the natural course of events. Often it can be helpful if the cooperating teacher resumes a specific responsibility after the student has had an opportunity to experiment with it. It is reassuring to the student to know that such requests are expected and will not be taken as evidence of his inadequacy. Gladys Robinson feels that her planning sessions have been dragging and asks her cooperating teacher to take over for a few days so that she can try to analyze what makes the differences. Suzanne Jones asks for time to observe her cooperating teacher at work with a reading group in order to see how she handles problems of word analysis. John Arthur panics at the thought of helping his pupils to write Thanks-giving poems and his cooperating teacher volunteers to demonstrate for him.

Some students and cooperating teachers have reported that it is worth while to plan for an increased amount of observation as the student-teaching period comes to a close. In addition to giving the student a last objective look at expert teaching, this procedure may help to return the class smoothly to the leadership of the cooperating teacher. If the student-teaching program closes before the school year is out, this transition should be thought through cooperatively for the sake of the children.

Observation can also be used to help both student and cooperating teacher to gain better understanding of individuals. While the cooperating teacher leads the discussion, the student makes a tally of the flow of comments. While the cooperating teacher gives help to social studies groups, the student collects anecdotes on the activities of Jerome as he interrupts group after group. Sometimes the situation is reversed, the student teacher taking over the leadership responsibility while the cooperating teacher carries out the study of individuals. Such experiences can add much, both to the student's insights into the needs of individuals and to his data-collecting skills.

In some situations, observation has also been used effectively to enrich the student's total experience in the school. He may follow his group to the gym or to the music class to see how they are handled by another teacher, or if he is responsible for the physical education or music programs himself, he may follow the class in which he has the greatest concern back to their regular teacher. If he is on a half-day assignment, he may profit from returning to observe the program for the full day. It may be that the class next door presents behavior problems totally different from those of his group. Mrs. Sanderson down the hall may be experimenting with a tape recorder, or Mr. Bandy in the sixth grade be trying out an individualized reading program. Such visitation can add much to a student's insights, particularly if it is planned late enough in his experience to insure that he brings considerable depth of understanding.

Obviously, any observation is more valuable when its purpose is clear and there is guidance regarding the particular points to note. The problems which suggest the need for observation should be identified ahead of time in conference and some foci for observation thought through. Then the observation should be discussed dispassionately after the student has an opportunity to do some thinking about what he has seen.

MAKING THE MOST OF CONFERENCES

Opportunities to talk things through are essential if the student teacher is to derive maximum benefit from his classroom experiences. Undoubtedly there will be much informal consultation during the regular school day—a few minutes before school opens, a quick reaction at noon, a suggestion offered or question answered during a recess. Such short conferences are essential where people are cooperatively responsible for the well-being of thirty or more youngsters. However, these brief contacts do not provide the time required to help a student think through all the complex problems that confront him. He needs to be helped to grow in his ability to analyze classroom problems, in his insights into broad educational objectives, and in his ability to evaluate his own strengths and weaknesses and to understand himself.

The ways in which student teachers and cooperating teachers have managed to find time for conferences are many. Ideally, administrators should realize that accepting responsibility for a student teacher calls for an additional expenditure of time and should release the cooperating teacher from other duties shared by the school faculty to allow for conferences. This, however, is not always done. On the contrary, in some schools the presence of a student teacher is taken to mean that the cooperating teacher will be free for extra assignments. Nevertheless, conference time is important. Sometimes the weekly schedule provides an open period when the class is working with another teacher. Occasionally the student and cooperating teacher agree to use a lunch hour for this purpose, or set aside an afternoon once a week. Whatever the plan, it can be helpful to both people in working out other aspects of their busy schedules if the arrangement is definite and the length of the conference agreed upon. It can be discouraging to a conscientious student to plan time after time for a conference only to find that his cooperating teacher has been called to another meeting. In view of the cooperating teacher's heavy professional obligations, it should, in most cases, be the student teacher who takes the major responsibility for adjusting his schedule to provide for the most convenient conference time. There may, however, be certain college obligations which cannot be set aside. The student should be urged to make these known so that he is not placed in the position of being criticized for failing in his responsibilities in one situation because of his efforts to be cooperative in another.

Conferences can have many points of focus. Conferences can serve many purposes. Undoubtedly, most will focus on teaching problems. Some will be devoted to cooperative planning; others to thinking through alternatives to the proposals in the student's plans as he begins to take on more independent responsibility for the day's activities. It is also important to use conference time to help the student analyze his performance—to note places that went well and activities that were ragged; to figure out why it was that a plan that looked excellent did not work out as foreseen.

Conferences can profitably be used for purposes other than the demands of the particular classroom. Some sessions may well be devoted to helping the student understand general school policies. Some of the details of the school organization and specific regulations ought to be explained relatively early. Later, it may be helpful to discuss such problems as the method of reporting to parents, steps to take in helping the severely disturbed child, means of securing visual aids and other equipment, the teacher's responsibilities on professional committees the local system of reporting attendance and keeping other types of records. Granted that such topics also receive attention in college classes, there are many details that must be acquired in the actualities of the school situation.

It can be helpful to the student to have opportunities to talk with school personnel with whom he may be expected to work a year hence—the principal, the attendance officer, the school psychologist or visiting teacher. Where there are several students in the school, group conferences for such purposes can often be set up, perhaps by releasing the students to sit in on conferences regarding an individual child so that he can have firsthand experience with some of the problems of working cooperatively faced by parents, cooperating teacher, and perhaps the principal, psychologist, or social worker.

Conferences can also serve to help the student look a year ahead, especially in areas where his school or his class tend to be atypical. The number of pupils in his room may have been unusually large, or unusually small. How would one work if next year's situation were different? The children may have been exceptionally cooperative or the student may have joined the group after patterns of classroom behavior were established. How would one go about securing good work habits in the early fall? And what would one do if three or four children proved to be facing difficult problems of adjustment? The youngsters may be very bright and have a wealth of experiential background. What adjustments would one have to make if one's first assignment were to a community where youngsters had more limited resources? Using the day-by-day experiences in the present classroom as a starting point, cooperating teachers can often give students valuable, realistic help in facing contrasting situations.

Conferences regarding teaching procedures should help to build feelings of security. How to plan cooperatively with a student teacher, how to acquaint him with over-all school policies, and how to help him become aware of problems he may face next year are aspects of conferring with students that cause cooperating teachers very little concern. Such problems are objective. It is a challenge to share one's professional insights. But how does one go about helping a student to face up to his own strengths and weaknesses in classroom performance? Will he be unduly discouraged if the inadequacies of a lesson are pointed out? How does one conduct such conferences so that they are of maximum value?

Students will have been urged in college classes to seek help—to consider their student-teaching experience as a time to make mistakes and an opportunity to grow through constructive criticism. Nevertheless, each comes with his own particular necessity to be successful, his own concept of the ideal teacher he would like to be, and his own personal feelings of security. No two students will react to supervisory conferences in exactly the same way. While certain general principles can be suggested as a guide to such conferences, exact procedures will depend on the personal relationships between each student and his cooperating teacher. Whatever the specific procedures, the student should come away from the conference feeling that he has received help and a little more confident about assuming his leadership responsibilities in the classroom.

Perhaps the most important guide line for conducting a conference in which the student's teaching is to be analyzed is that he, like all of us, needs to know where he is succeeding as well as where he needs to improve. Occasionally, in his zeal to help an individual acquire a new technique, a cooperating teacher forgets to point to other aspects of the day that went extremely well, assuming that the beginner will recognize these for himself. Even the most adept and seemingly most secure student, however, does not always realize when he has done a good job. In fact, like the talented experienced teacher whose insights always lead him to see more possibilities than he can execute, the skillful beginner is quite likely to underrate his performance. Conferences should be conducted, then, so that the student has specific reassurance about aspects of his work that were successful.

Conferences should do more than dwell on a student's strengths, although with an insecure student who seems unduly discouraged by suggestions as to how he might improve the emphasis in early conferences might, for the most part, stress successes rather than failures. The typical student, however, knows that he has much to learn; he can grow uneasy if his cooperating teacher seems never to mention his inadequacies. Perhaps the cooperating teacher feels that he can't take criticism? or is it that he's so poor he is not worth assisting? or perhaps his cooperating teacher is just too busy to help? Cooperating teachers should not hesitate to analyze quite frankly with students the rough spots in the day's work.

The cooperative planning sessions of the first few weeks when the cooperating teacher's successes and failures are often the focus of discussion can help to establish ways of identifying solve difficulties that can be utilized later when the student's efforts are evaluated. The student should be encouraged to offer his reactions to the way various activities unfolded. He can be involved in watching an individual child or a special group to pick up clues as to why they are having trouble. He can, with the cooperating teacher, examine a plan that did not work and learn firsthand that experienced teachers themselves do not always have successful days. It is also possible to take a first step toward self-criticism by asking the student to report on his efforts to help individuals.

Mr. Johnson

That little group I had in the corner was really having trouble. I'm not sure our plans were clear. How did your group come along?

Sandra Kane

All right, I think. At least they seemed to go right ahead, so I think the plans made sense to them. But then Barbie asked me if she could go off on a project on her own. I said I thought she should stay with the group and she just bothered them from then on. Was I right?

Mr. Johnson

You might like to keep an eye on Barbie for the next day or so. I'm not sure anything we've done for her could be called exactly "right." Did you try to help her see how she could fit in?

Sandra

Well, no, I guess I just told her. I was afraid to give her much chance to argue....

It is helpful, as the student begins to assume more teaching responsibility, to encourage him to take the lead in explaining his plans and raising questions. This procedure tends to forestall any tendency to say "Well, how did it go?" or "I was terrible, wasn't I? and then to wait meekly for criticism. Some students may need to be urged to take responsibility for initiating requests for help, especially if they are not yet quite at ease in the situation. One does not, after all, ask a question that might reveal naivete unless the listener is trusted. Once two or three questions, however trivial they may seem, are analysed thoughtfully and with due respect to the student's desire to know, the ice tends to be broken. Cooperating teachers, of course, will certainly sense, and need to raise, problems of which the student is blissfully unaware. Starting a conference with the concerns uppermost in the student's mind does not preclude the discussion of other topics.

The cooperating teacher's attitude toward an activity that goes poorly can do much to help the student accept and profit from his difficulties. It is reassuring to realise that mistakes are expected. Sometimes, in spite of all his preceding college discussions, the student thinks of his teaching as testing experience, a situation in which he must demonstrate complete competence no matter what he attempts. As a matter of fact, a lesson that misses fire can sometimes contribute considerably more to increased teaching skill than one that goes perfectly, provided it is properly analysed. Elizabeth Parker plunges into an art lesson without thinking through how she is going to distribute the needed materials. In order to make one last point, John Anderson carries a discussion fifteen minutes beyond the time when his sixth-graders are obviously becoming restless. Janie Sampson assumes, without looking, that the map in the social studies text will serve her purposes and suddenly has forty bewildered fourth-graders asking for help at once. Sarah Welsh says rashly to her first grade, "If I hear one more crayon drop we'll just put our Thanksgiving cards for our mothers away and not finish them"—and a whole box of crayons topples off shy little Sandy's desk with a clatter. These are situations that should lead a cooperating teacher to say quite sincerely, "I'm so glad that happened this year while you had someone to help you analyse it," and a student to say equally sincerely, "I certainly learned something today."

Students frequently need to be helped to identify the outside influences that can cause the best of lessons to go awry. A conscientious student (and sometimes an earnest cooperating teacher, too) often desires from children a level of self-control and cooperation that would tax the most mature adult. A rainy day does make a difference. So does Christmas, or Halloween, or the noontime discussion about Janice's birthday party. It's natural to relax a little while papers are being passed, or to reach the point where one must wiggle even if the lesson is still going on. Then, there are in most classrooms one or more youngsters who are facing unusually difficult problems of personal adjustment—who desperately need recognition, even though it is a scolding, or whose span of attention is unusually short. It can be reassuring to students to be helped to distinguish between situations such as these and situations where the basic difficulty lies in their own lack of skill. Not that an experienced teacher merely blames the situation under such circumstances—actually, he makes all the adjustments in his programme and methods that he thinks will help. He also sets his expectations realistically, however, and does not call himself a failure if his best efforts do not succeed completely. "I thought I'd lose my mind trying to figure out what I was suddenly doing wrong," reported Jane Adams just before Christmas, "until I went down to lunch and listened to everybody else. I guess you just have to decide to enjoy Christmas even if you don't get anything else done."

Students also need to be hoped to realise that increasing the complexity of their responsibility also increases the possibilities of difficulty. This is a fact that cooperating teachers may also need to recognise, especially if they are concerned about the reactions of the college supervisor. Dictating a spelling list is not fraught with nearly the possibilities for error that are inherent in guiding the plans for a unit of work. Far from working toward a day that his cooperating teacher would call perfect, the student teacher who is gaining skill works toward more challenging situations in which to try his wings. His activities, therefore, offer increased opportunities to analyse with him the fine points of skilled teaching—to point out possible refinements in his techniques. This is a point of view that is not always easily achieved. Some students state quite frankly that years of working toward an *A* or a perfect paper make it very difficult to accept the fact that in their chosen profession further growth is always possible. "I'm beginning to see what you mean," said Nancy Smith. "A really creative teacher never stops wanting help in doing a better job. Why, even Mrs. Jones says she always learns many new things from us, and she's taught for years."

Unnecessary feelings of frustration and insecurity can develop because students do not realise how long it sometimes takes to make new ways of working automatic. For their own sense of security, cooperating teachers also need to know that achieving the smooth coordination of all the skills that make up the complex act of teaching is a lengthy process. Often the student's concentration on achieving one goal will cause him to lose sight of another. It may seem as though the same problem has to be discussed many times over before it is solved successfully. Beginners may also need aid and reassurance in facing the fact that some types of errors cannot be eliminated overnight. This is especially true in the general area of human relationships.

Fifteen minutes of clear explanation can probably correct an error of fact in geography, but a discussion pattern in which it has been quite permissible for the pupils to chorus answers, shout for attention, and conduct side arguments will not be changed so easily. A beginner can become very discouraged when the new technique does not "pay off." Often perhaps without expressing his disappointment, he abandons a procedures long before it has had time to become effective. ("I *did* try waiting for them to be quiet, but it didn't seem to help much." "We did some planning together so that they would know what to do next, but they just made silly suggestions, so I stopped it.") Once a problem has been identified with a student, the cooperating teacher needs to be alert to evidences of improvement, however slight, and to draw attention to these. Succeeding conferences can be used to point to this improvement, to analyse new difficulties, and to suggest next steps as the student seems able to execute them.

Conferences should help students to understand basic educational principles. The student who can analyse in general terms what went wrong in a situation is not always able to make a concrete suggestion regarding what to do next. The suggestions made in conference should be specific enough to give the student a sense of direction. Merely suggesting a new procedure, however, is not always of sufficient help. The student needs to know why the alternative is recommended. There is a vast difference between a situation in which a technique is used by an expert who understands what he is doing and one in which the same technique is mimicked blindly by the beginner who does not understand its purpose. One of the most challenging aspects of working with student teachers often proves to be the stimulation offered to cooperating teachers to think through why they teach as they do.

The young adult who is learning to teach, like any other learner, builds his generalizations gradually. It is not always immediately apparent to him that the principles discussed in his college classes apply in the situation in which he now finds himself or that the procedure which worked well yesterday can also be used in a slightly different situation today. He must be helped to employ many of the same processes of inductive reasoning in arriving at new generalisations for himself that would be characteristic of younger learners. It should be possible, however, for the cooperating teacher to short-cut the reasoning process somewhat in the light of the student's maturity and background:

John Arthur

They always seem to restless, even when I ask them to cooperate.

Mr. Maxwell

I wonder if you realise how infrequently you do ask for the atmosphere you have in the corner talk among one another for a full ten minutes before you tried to pull them back.

John

You mean I should be harder on them. I know I should, but it seems so mean.

Mr. Maxwell

Take that a little further. What do you mean by being hard on them?

John

Well, scolding them or threatening to keep them in to make up the wasted time, or something else to show them I'm the boss. But I hate to throw my weight around.

Mr. Maxwell

Have you ever stopped to think why you want them to listen? Is it only to show you're boss?

John

Well, on they make it hard for everyone around them to hear, to say nothing of how little they learn. It's impolite, too, to the speaker, I suppose.

Mr. Maxwell

What would you do if it were a fraternity committee?

John

Use the gavel.

Mr. Maxwell

Would you feel mean? Would you be throwing your weight around?

John

No, that's the chairman's job. Say, is this what you've been driving at?

Mr. Maxwell

That's the general idea. It takes time; you're getting their attention when you're teaching much more smoothly now. These informal situations are the rough ones. What about it? Do you think you'd feel differently about asking for order if you saw yourself as a chairman rather than a boss?

John

I guess I might.

Mr. Maxwell

Let's make it concrete. What might you.

John

Well, you always say, "Are you ready?" And I've seen you stop the speaker and say, "Let's wait until everyone is listening." And I guess I haven't used our "good audience" rules very consistently, We could look at them. I suppose if I began to hear voices, I'd have to ask for quiet again.

Mr. Maxwell

Yes. You've given that group in the corner quite a bit of experience in being impolite. It's going to take some time to teach them a new habit. Shall I try particularly to analyse what they do tomorrow?

John

That'd help, I think. Time me again, too, will you? I think I get so wound up in the reports that I don't always see what's going on.

This discussion assisted John in identifying some basic principles of effective democratic leadership. Mr. Maxwell contributed illustrations which helped to sharpen the issues, but he led John to arrive at his own generalisations. It is important to note, also, that he did not stop when the generalisation was identified; he encouraged John to make the practical application that provided him with some specific classroom procedures. And he guarded against discouragement by pointing out that the children's behavior might not be changed instantly.

Conferences should help students to grow toward self-understanding. The excerpt of a conference just cited indicates another important kind of growth that all teachers need to be helped to achieve—growth in self-understanding. John didn't want to "throw his weight around"; he "felt mean." Seeing himself in the neutral role as a class chairman was a new idea to him. If teachers are to grow in their ability to understand others, they must gain increased understanding of themselves. Oftentimes the student's association with his cooperating teacher is one of the closest of all his college contracts. The discussions of specific classroom events offer many opportunities to help him to grow in understanding himself.

It can be enlightening to students to analyse the leadership roles they are assuming in the classroom. They can profitably be helped to examine their day-by-day classroom reactions for the light that these throw upon the roles that are being played. Which behavior from pupils proves the most irritating? At which points is there the highest tolerance for pupils' inadequacies? Why? Are there types of children of whom the student feels drawn? some by whom he feels repelled? What seems to be the reason for this? What is the nature of the student's leadership in situations involving problems of behavior? How does he feel after he has had to speak firmly? What is his reaction in situations where pupils do not follow his directions instantly? What is the pronoun when the student is playing a leadership role, *I* or *we*? If it's *we,* is it truly a *we* situation? ("I think it would be fun," said Alice Jay, "if we each wrote five sentences about our spelling words for homework.") Helping a student to identify clearly the role he is now playing is an important first step in assisting him to assume more effective roles.

A student's attitudes toward success and failure can have a marked influence upon his progress toward professional competence. Parents and previous teachers may have put such a high premium on success that supervisory suggestions are much more of a threat than they would appear to be on the surface. On the other hand, previous experiences with failure may have resulted in timidity, unwillingness to try out new ideas, clinging to the cooperating teacher's patterns. Students can be helped to look at their reactions to days that go poorly and to opportunities to try their wings. What is the response to a rugged day?—tears? a sleepless night? an optimistic change of plans? How much of the conference period seems to be devoted to letting the student justify why he proceeded as he did? to hearing complaints? What is the reaction to Ricky if he muffs an obvious question while the principal or college supervisor is in the room? to the group of boys who choose this time to show off? Are there delays or snags in situations where the student is to take over a new responsibility?— not quite enough time to start today? one more day needed to collect books? a problem in an area where the student is more secure that really should be attacked first? Ultimately a teacher must find challenges both in trying out new ideas and in analysing failures or his chosen profession will offer him few satisfactions. A student can be helped to take a major step toward becoming a professional person if he can learn to evaluate his work objectively.

Student teachers are often working closely with two supervisors. It can be important to help them look objectively at their attitudes toward supervisory suggestions. These will be compounded of a multitude of factors, many of which the student teacher may not be consciously aware. For some, previous contacts with others in supervisory positions—parents, teachers, college personnel—will have developed attitudes and expectancies leading to easy cooperation. For others, these early experiences may have built habits of unquestioning obedience. In a few, the last vestiges of adolescent rebellion may crop up in a "don't tell me, I'll work it out for myself" attitude. In some cases, the cooperating teacher or supervisor may resemble beloved Miss Jacobson who has represented for years the ideal teacher the student hopes to become. It is also possible, however, that something in the cooperating teacher's manner will hint of one of the student's previous teachers who aroused feelings of anxiety or failure. To all the attitudes stemming from previous experiences with older persons in authority roles must be added a host of impressions—many positive, some negative—contributed by other student teachers whose comments their peers are not always equipped to interpret. Every student has a very natural desire to succeed, to be thought well of by the cooperating teacher. It is important for cooperating teachers (who, themselves, take a very natural pride in their skill in building effective human relationships) to realise that such varied attitudes toward supervision can exist. It is even more important for students to begin to understand why they react as they do toward supervisory assistance.

Cooperating teachers are not trained counselors. Students can expect, however, the same help in understanding themselves that an experienced teacher would give to a pupil. The comments which the cooperating teacher might make in conferences would be designed to help the student to take a look at aspects of his behavior that are near the surface, not to pry. "Have you ever wondered why Bobby seems to worry you so much more than Jim?" You seem to expect every day to be perfect. Are you by any chance a student who never settled for anything but top grades?" "Teachers can feel under the weather, too. You need to know how to guard against your own fatigue so that children don't suffer."

In his need to grow in self-understanding, the beginning teacher does not differ much from the rest of us. We carry into our professional relationships with colleagues, pupils, parents, administrators, and supervisors equally complex expectations of which we are equally unaware. Certainly, cooperating teachers bring to the student-teaching relationship their own expectations, attitudes, and feelings of competence. These will influence their attitudes toward students' successes and failures, strengths and weaknesses, and toward their relationships with college personnel just as students' expectations and fears affect their relationships with children.

USING RECORDS EFFECTIVELY

Objective evidence is a valuable aid to supervision. Experienced supervisors and cooperating teachers know very well how many things happen in a classroom in a single busy day. In the confusion of all that there is to remember it can be helpful to have details in black and white so that they can be reviewed and thought over at leisure.

Several types of records will be needed in supervising students. Among the most useful are the records of the student's classroom performance. Sometimes conferences may be a week or more apart, or they may be postponed over the week end with its numerous interfering activities. If this happens, many of the details that would help to explain why a lesson went well or poorly tend to become fuzzy and indistinct. Yet in the details—the precise sequence of comments by the student or the exact steps that led to the breakdown of discipline—often lies the key to effective improvement.

It is not enough to keep records of what goes on in the classroom while the student is teaching. Some sort of record ought to be maintained by both student and cooperating teacher of the conference itself. By the end of a typical conference where problems have been raised, difficulties thrashed out, and plans reviewed and agreed upon, it is not always easy to be sure whether all is well or what the next steps are to be unless some memorandum is kept by the persons concerned.

Keeping records, of course, is not a one-sided proposition. The student must be prepared, even if not always required, to share his written materials with the cooperating teacher. Plans can be more constructively appraised if they are written out in detail. Not only this, but the fact that they are written out makes oral explanation easier and more precise. The student should also be expected to keep notes of his special concerns. If conferences are to be successful his problems and questions should be written out, not left to the chance of recall on the spur of the moment.

The kinds of reports required by the teacher-education institution will vary from one institution to another. Depending on the nature of the supervisory plan and the comprehensiveness of the record system they may range from a simple statement to a complex and elaborate series of check lists, evaluations, and written reports. In general, it may be anticipated that the less frequent the visits of the college supervisor the more necessary it may be for him to keep himself informed by means of fairly extensive records and reports. In all probability, both cooperating teacher and student will be involved in this process.

No two people keep records in exactly the same way. It is safe to say, however, that the longer the time lapse between conferences, the more important it is to note specific details. It is safe to suggest, also, that only those types of records should be made which prove useful either to the specific cooperating teacher and student teacher team or to the teacher-education institution. Neither cooperating teacher nor student has the time to devote to elaborate recording devices that do not serve the ultimate purpose—helping the student to grow.

Notes on the day's work can be useful. Cooperating teachers have devised a number of ways of keeping records of the day's work. On problems where a previous conference has helped to establish general principles and the student is relatively secure in what he is doing, brief memos—jotted down on whatever small bits of paper are handy—can often be useful. These are particularly helpful if time to chat during the day is limited. Sometimes the memo refers to an error in fact or to a confusion at a point where the cooperating teacher feels that interrupting the lesson would be unwise. Sometimes it points to something that worked particularly well. Sometimes it calls attention to a problem in personal relationships of which the student needs to be aware. Typical of such memos are the following:

> I wonder if they are all clear on what *zone* means? Would it be good to check again tomorrow to be sure?
>
> There are several books in our library that will help Andy's group. Ask me for them.
>
> Did you notice how much Ricky has grown in his ability to analyse words? Let's talk about giving him a more advanced book.
>
> Sandy has interrupted every committee. Let's talk about how to help him.
>
> Much smoother transition today. Keep it up!

Some cooperating teachers have used more complete and more consecutive notes in a log of the day which combines a record of what went on, reactions to it; and questions for further discussion. This is often kept in a notebook so that the full record is available at any time. The student is free to read the record at the close of the day; points of major concern may become the foci of conferences. This time of a record can be useful in orienting the college supervisor to the responsibilities being assumed by the student and the help he was being given.

Tuesday, November 12.

9:00 You remembered to wait until you had your audience today. Did you notice how well they are beginning to settle down now that you are working at it consistently?

9:10 Planning—nice job of using youngsters' ideas on crucial points today. Barnie was quibbling!

9:20 Spelling practice—much more pointed teaching today. Should you have plunged into possessives when you saw how vague they were? Let's talk about this—perhaps plan some language activities?

9:40 Library trip—should we do something special to encourage those who don't take books? Perhaps some individualised reading experiences? Any ideas?—This could be a nice unit for you. Could you be thinking ahead on this?

10:30 * * * * * *

At points where it is important for a student to be given help in concrete detail, a running record of what went on, as nearly complete as the cooperating teacher's writing speed will allow, can provide valuable data for a conference. Whereas logs such as the sample just cited often contain advice, questions, and problems to discuss the running record of activities will be more useful if it is an objective picture of what happened. When such notes are intended for a permanent file, a stenographer's notebook provides a convenient means of making a carbon for the student. Complete verbatim transcripts cannot be made unless shorthand is used, but it is at least possible to record the key comments that influenced the trend of the discussion, or if the problem is one of how to work with a particular youngster, to secure enough detail to make it possible to analyse his behavior. Because such notes contain few supervisory suggestions they usually require further analysis in conference to be of value to the student.

In order to incorporate supervisory suggestions within their running records of classroom activities, some supervisors and cooperating teachers have divided the page using the left hand side for notes of what went on and the right hand margin for an occasional comment. The following are a supervisor's running notes on a student teacher's planning session at a point in the student's growth where his concept of how to involve pupils in setting up the schedule for the day was merely to have them go through the motions of naming typical activities and voting upon a desired sequence. The student teacher's comments are recorded in full, but to save time in writing, the supervisor has adopted the device of putting the children's comments in parentheses without indicating names. The supervisor's evaluative comments appear at the right.

<table>
<tr><td>While Mamie collects the tax stamps, let's put our agenda on the board.
(Spelling.)</td><td></td></tr>
<tr><td>(Sharing.)</td><td>Need you take time to have them list routine aspects of the schedule?</td></tr>
<tr><td>(Can we have social studies?) Yes, we have our reports to finish.</td><td>Are you helping them do any real thinking about what needs to be done today?</td></tr>
<tr><td>(More dictionary exercises?)</td><td>Guesses like this suggest they don't have the needed backg round to make intelligent suggestions.</td></tr>
</table>

No, we didn't think you needed any more practice for a while.

(Can we have health?)

Well, we have our papers to collect, do we not?

(Could we see that movie?)

No, that has to go back; it wasn't for our group. Now what shall we do first?

(Spelling?)

You want your spelling first, then? [Vote]

Subdued cheer after each vote. Order depends entirely on group choice? No other reasons?

(Social studies?) [Vote]

The running notes that follow helped a student to see why her planning session at the beginning of a unit on Explorers went off on a tangent. The group had seen a movie about Columbus, and the supervisor's notes up to the point where this record begins show an extensive and challenging list of questions posed by the youngsters. The student's preoccupation with the end product which the children in their immaturity could not envision became obvious to her when the notes were reviewed in conference. The abbreviations in the original notes are given.

We're going to stop here—this list just a jumping-off point—you'll have a lot of reading to do to get all this information—now let's think of some way of organizing it.

Wonder if they have the background to decide?

(We could answer these questions.)

Yes, but this'll only be a small part—how could we *organise* all we learn?

Organiser

(Well, in science last year we worked in groups.)

Good, but we are trying to decide how to *organise* this information.	Leading them into something?
(Everyone could take 2 questions.)	
(Could we do a booklet on certain things?)	
Carry your idea a little further.	
(Each could do one ... or we could do skits.)	
(Yes, skits ... skits last year ... could use a box for a boat.)	
Just a minute. You did skits last year—so you don't want to do something new?	
(Well, yes ... but a skit could ... more reactions in a chorus.)	
Can I throw out an idea? Wouldn't it be better to read and *organise* our material first?	Organise! Can they decide intelligently until *after* they've read?
(You mean we can't do skits?)	

Cooperating teachers occasionally hesitate to do as much writing as these records suggest while the student is teaching. Much depends on the contents of the record. Probably most disturbing is the policy of taking notes only when something is going wrong. When the student, however, has had some satisfying experiences of being helped by brief memos or running notes and realises that positive as well as negative comments are being made, the flying pencil is soon forgotten. Most cooperating teachers talk over with the student the type of notes they would like to take and ask for a frank reaction if the note-taking process ever proves disturbing.

There are also possibilities of making tape recordings of the student at work. This would probably take a few days of preliminary experience so that pupils as well as the student could become used to the microphone. However, it could prove valuable in analysing the trend of a discussion and perhaps also in helping the student to appraise his voice and to identify any undesirable mannerisms.

When the college supervisor is making extensive notes similar to those just discussed, it is often helpful if the student shares the carbon copy with the cooperating teacher. In this case the carbon provides a second person's analysis of the situation. It may suggest problems upon which student and cooperating teacher may work for further improvement or points at which the student needs help in applying the supervisor's general suggestion to specifics of the classroom—specifics of which the supervisor may not be aware because of his infrequent visits. Often, too, a problem already identified by the cooperating teacher will be recorded in slightly different words which may help to sharpen the nature of the difficulty for the student. Even more important, however, such sharing of records helps the two persons supervising the student to coordinate their efforts in his behalf.

Students' records can be analysed. Students' plans and logs of their teaching experience may be helpful supervisory aids. These are perhaps most frequently used in conferences preceding the actual teaching experience, but they can also be helpful in evaluation. Bill Anderson's game ends in a riot because his rules were not clear. What do his plans show?—did he think through the rules in detail? had he listed alternatives if the youngsters failed to have the basic skills he assumed? Janice Simpson's first-graders mill about in complete confusion while she tries to work with a reading group. How carefully did she think through her plans for them?—did she list the materials they would need? had she thought about how detailed their directions should be? had she allowed any time for individual help? Problems such as these can be used by the cooperating teacher to document the value of detailed planning and to show the type of detail that is most useful.

The days of the prepared lesson kept on tap for emergencies and the messenger with the scissors or some other time-honored system of warning are a thing of the past. College supervisors are anxious to be of service. Whether their visits are long or short, frequent or infrequent, there are at least four attitudes that can be assumed. First, the college supervisor will view his responsibility in terms of facilitating the work of the cooperating teacher and student in whatever ways they deem his services to be most useful. Second, his aim will be to help the student operate as effectively as possible in the situation as he finds it, not to mold either student or classroom into a preconceived pattern of his own. Third, he will wish to be as sensitive as is the cooperating teacher to the needs of the student, his uncertainties, his aspirations, and his reactions to failure. Fourth, far from having all the answers with regard to how to work with children, the typical college supervisor will be most grateful for the contacts with actual classroom situations that his supervisory responsibilities provide.

It helps to see the classroom as it normally exists. How does a cooperating teacher make the most effective use of college supervisory help? Our basic suggestion is that the college supervisor needs to see the classroom situation as it is normally. This is true both of the total classroom experiences and of the student's specific responsibilities. Sometimes cooperating teachers are tempted to make changes in the programme when the supervisor arrives, either in a well-meant effort to show the supervisor a more interesting aspect of the day or to help the student appear to advantage. There may be occasions, of course, when the typical programme should be reversed because the college supervisor's time is limited and there are specific aspects of the student's work about which the cooperating teacher and student desire advice. A sudden change in plans, however, can be disturbing both to student teacher and to children.

Actually, every aspect of the day can be helpful to the college supervisor. If he is to be of assistance to the student, he faces the difficult problem of becoming well acquainted with the particular group of boys and girls and with the cooperating teacher's methods. A quiet work period can afford time to observe individuals. A lesson taught by the cooperating teacher can help him to sense the ways of working with youngsters with which the student is becoming acquainted. Watching a programme evolve, or the ground work for a committee's activities being laid, often reveals professional problems important to consider in college classes.

By the same token, every aspect of the student teacher's work can yield worth-while information. Observing the student at work in a situation that is difficult for him can often provide more clues to points where help is needed than watching him in a situation where he is proficient. Seeing how the student handles a rehearsal for a play will sometimes reveal much more clearly his skill in working with children than watching the finished production. The student's adjustment to an upset day or to the youngster who is having trouble frequently provides more information regarding his strengths as a teacher than does the smooth and eventless day.

Cooperating teachers are occasionally anxious lest the ragged parts of the day will not be understood by the college supervisor and will reflect unfavourably either on their work or the student's. It is important for both cooperating teacher and student to realise that the college supervisor brings considerable sophistication in classroom problems. He knows that a series of three or four rainy days can be reflected in pupil behavior, that the one youngster who loves the limelight may choose the occasion of his visit to monopolise a discussion, that a democratic planning session can lead to some unforeseen proposals, that a beginner's normal anxiety to do well can cause him to seem tense in situations he typically handles very well. One of the procedures most helpful to the student as well as to the college supervisor (and for that matter, to the cooperating teacher, also) is to make the college visitor a part of the classroom as rapidly as possible. One way to do this is to explain to the class who the supervisor is, why he is there, and then to bring him into the regular class activities. The supervisor, too, has a responsibility here. His task is to blend inconspicuously into the situation as he finds it.

Problems need to be raised frankly. The college supervisor comes to help both cooperating teacher and student. This he will not be able to do effectively if he does not know their immediate concerns. Although he can see for himself what problems the student is facing at the time of his visit, there may be other difficulties that the course of a single day does not reveal. Cooperating teachers sometimes hesitate to indicate these, lest the information reflect undesirably upon the student's general competence. It ought to be taken for granted that the college supervisor is as anxious as the cooperating teacher to see the student do well, and just as unwilling to have the difficulty of the moment become part of the student's permanent record. He, like the cooperating teacher, wishes to use time to advantage in the student's best interests.

Often it can be very helpful to ask a third person, in

this case the college supervisor, to study particularly a problem that has concerned a student and his cooperating teacher. There are times when it is not easy for either cooperating teacher or student who are close to the situation to spot exactly what is causing the trouble, although they can identify the area in which they are dissatisfied. Someone new to the room often catches a detail that the persons familiar with the setting have missed. From his varied experiences with beginners the college supervisor can often suggest helpful "hunches" regarding what typically causes similar problems. He knows, too, perhaps with somewhat more assurance than the cooperating teacher whether most beginners are likely to trip over the same problem or whether this student's difficulty is unique. Then, too, the way in which a new person phrases a suggestion may vary just enough from what the cooperating teacher has been saying to clarify the issue. It is often highly desirable, then, for the college supervisor to see those aspects of the programme in which student and cooperating teacher feel least secure.

Out of deference to the college, cooperating teachers may also hesitate to raise questions which seem to imply criticism of the college programme or counseling system. It may be that the course load or schedule are making it very difficult for the student to meet his full obligations in the school classroom. A student may also come lacking certain basic skills which the cooperating teacher believes could have been readily taught in college classes. College personnel should be made aware of such problems. It may be that the difficulty is unique with the particular student, or that it is one which only practical classroom experience can remedy. On the other hand, an effective change in college procedure may be brought about.

Frankness is also essential if the rating sheets and

requests for recommendations for placement papers are to be truly useful. Neither the college nor the employing officer receives much guidance in working with a student if the typical rating is high no matter what the student's performance has been. Some colleges have relieved the cooperating teacher of the responsibility of recommending a final grade for the student-teaching experience partly because it is difficult to do this fairly and objectively when working with only one person and partly because it can be destructive of the cooperating teacher's relationships with the student. Where grades must be given, or the cooperating teacher's rating sheet is to serve as one of the bases for the grade, it is essential for cooperating teacher and college supervisor to have talked together so that the rating system is clear and the bases for the cooperating teacher's ratings understood.

Three-way conferences should be utilised. One of the problems faced by both cooperating teacher and college supervisor is how to coordinate their efforts to help the student. Typically, the suggestions and the problems of the person who is working with the student day after day should have priority and the efforts of the college supervisor should be directed toward supporting the cooperating teacher. The college supervisor has, of course, a responsibility for sharing problems he senses or for suggesting other ways of working he deems will be helpful. Often, with the best of intentions, one person can misunderstand and misquote another, and the student who goes from a conference with his cooperating teacher to one with his supervisor can be trapped in the misunderstanding. Whenever time permits, therefore, three-way conferences can be helpful. Here issues can be pursued until all persons are agreed upon desirable next steps. Such conferences can sometimes be used for a cooperative analysis of the students activities that have just been observed. If the student has been having particular difficulty, it can be helpful to have the advice of a third person on how best to proceed. The reactions of the college supervisor to plans for the student's future experiences can also be secured. Where three-way conferences are not possible, both cooperating teacher and college supervisor need to keep the student informed regarding their discussions about him. Conversely, as he confers with either individual alone, the student has a responsibility to share the suggestions made by the other. In other words, every possible means should be utilised for coordinating and integrating the supervisory efforts of those most concerned with the student's growth.

College resources should be utilised. Cooperating teachers should expect help from the teacher-education institution over and above that given by the college supervisor. Often there will be a student-teaching handbook describing the programme and offering concrete suggestions. Sometimes such handbooks are written mainly for students, but even these can prove useful in alerting cooperating teachers to the orientation the student brings to his assignment. Frequently, the student teacher will be attending a seminar focused on his student teaching. Sometimes, too, he will have been in one or more professional classes centered in teaching problems. The bibliographies and mimeographed teaching aids from such classes can acquaint the cooperating teacher with the general nature of the student's background. Where such materials are not supplied systematically, the student can be requested to ask for duplicates. Often this process has worked in reverse and cooperating teachers have supplied special book lists or teaching aids that have been very helpful to college personnel.

Depending on the institution, there may also be special meetings for cooperating teachers—workshops, seminars, or college courses. In some places participation in such training sessions is considered to be essential before a teacher is invited to become a cooperating teacher. Sometimes such groups have prepared student-teaching handbooks in which they share their insights regarding an effective student-teaching experience. Certainly the common problems faced by cooperating teachers are many and meetings where ways of proceeding are shared can be of much help. The cooperating teacher, then, ought to feel that the college is offering its resources to him, and the college has a heavy responsibility in making him a part of its teacher-education programme.

The cooperative relationships developed between elementary and secondary schools and teacher-education institutions offer unparalleled opportunities to send into tomorrow's classrooms teachers with depth of insight into the needs of children and good judgment regarding how to meet them. This affiliation should do more. It should bring the resources of the teacher-education institution to bear on the professional problems of teachers. Even more important, the cooperative relationships among experienced teachers, college personnel, and beginners should make more vital and realistic the programme for boys and girls. Parents, teachers, administrators, members of college faculties, the children themselves—each has a unique responsibility and a special contribution to make. In our cooperative endeavors lies the hope for the schools of tomorrow.

REFERENCES

Cottrell, Donald P. (Editor). *Teacher Education for a Free People.* Oneonta, N.Y.: The American Association of Colleges for Teacher Education, 1956, Pp. xiii + 415.

Curtis, Dwight K., and Andrews, Leonard O. *Guiding Your Student Teacher*. Englewood Cliffs, N.J.: Prentice-Hall, 1954, Pp. xvi + 384.

Four Went to Teach. Thirty-fifth Yearbook of the Association for Student Teaching. Lock Haven, Pa.: The Association, 1956, Pp. xvii + 173.

Milner, Ernest, J. *You and Your Student Teacher*. New York: Bureau of Publications, Teachers College, Columbia University, 1954, Pp. v + 42.

Stratemeyer, Florence B., and Lindsey, Margaret, *Working with Student Teachers*. New York: Bureau of Publications, Teachers College, Columbia University, 1958. Pp. x + 502.

Cooperating teachers will also find helpful the professional bulletins of The Association for Student Teaching. The Association, Lock Haven, Pa.